Elizabeth Bowen
The Later Fiction

Lis Christensen

ELIZABETH BOWEN

THE LATER FICTION

Museum Tusculanum Press
University of Copenhagen
2001

Lis Christensen: *Elizabeth Bowen – The Later Fiction*
© Museum Tusculanum Press, 2001
Supervisors: Eric Jacobsen and Lars Ole Sauerberg
Cover design: Veronique van der Neut
Set in Garamond by Ole Klitgaard
Printed in Denmark by AKA Print, Aarhus
ISBN 87 7289 624 8

Front cover: Anonymous door
Doors and doorways are recurring features in the world of Elizabeth Bowen's fiction. They are part of the wartime background in *The Heat of the Day*. They may be entrances into other worlds, as they are in *A World of Love*. They may reflect social standing, as they do in 'A Day in the Dark' and *The Little Girls*. And they underscore the all-important theme of communication, for an open door is a sign of hospitality and a wish to relate to other people; such is the door of the impoverished vicar's family in *Eva Trout*, while it is a sad sign of the economic and cultural decline of the dilapidated Big House in *A World of Love* that 'the door no longer knew hospitality'.

Published with the support of
Landsdommer V. Gieses Legat
Lillian og Dan Finks Fond
Statens Humanistiske Forskningsråd
(The Danish Research Council for the Humanities)
Statsaut. el-installatør Svend Viggo Behrendt og hustrus Mindelegat
Velux Fonden af 1981

Museum Tusculanum Press
University of Copenhagen
Njalsgade 92
DK-2300 Copenhagen S
www.mtp.dk

Contents

List of illustrations 6

PREFACE 7

I PRELIMINARIES 9

    CHAPTER 1   Introduction 11
    CHAPTER 2   Works and Days 15
    CHAPTER 3   The Later Fiction 31

II GENERAL THEMES AND STRATEGIES 41

    CHAPTER 4   Identity 43
    CHAPTER 5   Communication 66
    CHAPTER 6   Word Clusters and Interlinking Images 84
    CHAPTER 7   Narrative Roles 98
    CHAPTER 8   Stages and Stage Properties 124
    CHAPTER 9   Time 149

III INDIVIDUAL STUDIES 163

    CHAPTER 10   A Latter-day Icarus (*The Heat of the Day*) 165
    CHAPTER 11   Doors and Entrances in *A World of Love* 174
    CHAPTER 12   Picnic on the Sands (*The Little Girls*) 186
    CHAPTER 13   The Gothic of *Eva Trout* 198

Appendix 210
Bibliography 220
Index 223

List of Illustrations

Angus McBean: Elizabeth Bowen 14
Bowen's Court 16
Clarence Terrace 17
Eudora Welty: Elizabeth Bowen 23
Bowen's Court (map) 31
Bleak House 60
Soldiers at Dunkirk 71
Bowen terrain in Kent (map) 126
Joan Hassall: Frontispiece for *A World of Love* 136
Barrage Balloons over London 147
Folkestone Old High Street 192
Dymchurch Beach 196

COLOUR PLATES

Fougasse: "Strictly between you & me..."
P Bruegel: The Fall of Icarus
Philippe Jullian: Dust cover for *Eva Trout*
John Millais: Ophelia

Preface

I thank friends and relations for encouragement and patient listening throughout the gestation of these studies. To three I owe a special debt of gratitude: to Lis Pihl, for sharing with me her extensive knowledge of Ireland and Irish literature, and for stimulating criticism; to my daughter Mette Sophie, who read the manuscript and offered many valuable suggestions; and to my husband Johnny, whose open-handed scholarship and critical acumen have marked the present book at all stages.

I am most grateful for the detailed and constructive criticism of Professor Eric Jacobsen and Professor Lars Ole Sauerberg. Professor Charles Lock kindly read the first proofs of the book; my sincere thanks for his comments and corrections.

I wish to extend my thanks also to the ever-helpful staff of the Museum Tusculanum Press.

I am grateful to Faber and Faber Ltd for permission to quote 'Musée des Beaux Arts' from W H Auden's *Collected Shorter Poems*.

Copenhagen, October 2001
Lis Christensen

I
PRELIMINARIES

Chapter 1

Introduction

Elizabeth Bowen entered the literary arena in the 1920s, at a time when the English novel was flourishing and the short story beginning to be recognized as a serious art form. Between 1927 and 1938 she published six full-length novels; it was largely the pressures of the Second World War that then caused eleven years to elapse before she brought out her much acclaimed novel of wartime London, *The Heat of the Day* (1949).

Though characters and plotline set it apart, in many other respects this medley of romance, spy-story, and psychological thriller anticipates the three novels Bowen went on to write in the 1950s and 1960s, which are all concerned with identity and communication and various aspects of time. In *A World of Love* (1955) the past impinges on the present in the tangible form of old love letters, and the dominance exercised by the long-dead writer of those letters is not broken before the letters themselves are destroyed; *The Little Girls* (1964) juxtaposes the lives of three women of grandmother age in the 1960s with events and relationships in their pre-1914 childhood; and *Eva Trout, or Changing Scenes* (1968) explores the uneasy result of a suspect heredity and rootless childhood combined with fabulous wealth.[1] Earlier criticism has on the whole tended to neglect these last three novels, dismissing *A World of Love* as out-moded, and frankly puzzled by *The Little Girls* and *Eva Trout*. It is only fairly recently that they have met with so much critical appreciation that they may now be seen to enhance rather than question Bowen's reputation.

In choosing to devote a whole book to Elizabeth Bowen's post-war fiction (the four novels mentioned above, plus a handful of short

---

[1] Bowen's last novel will be referred to below merely as *Eva Trout*. The historical overtones of the full title link up with the book's Gothic features that are discussed in Chapter 13.

stories), I am also pleading for greater interest in this late body of work. The ideas communicated through all her narratives are of existential dimensions; under the twists and turns of the plots and the clashes or reconciliations of the characters, perennial questions are not far to seek: how can we best live our lives to the full, how can we best relate to one another? As readers we are alerted to such questions, and encouraged to seek our own answers, by the increasingly flamboyant surface texture of Bowen's fiction and her mature narrator's deceptively carefree use of structural and stylistic devices. Though much of what I discuss will be familiar from her earlier writings, contours are arguably more sharply etched in the works of her maturity: ideas are more all-embracing, and the ways in which they are put across more emphatic. The question of identity, for instance, which runs through much of Bowen's fiction already in the 20s and 30s, reaches a climax in *Eva Trout* (1968) as the obsessive concern of the larger-than-life protagonist trying desperately 'to be'. Misunderstandings and lovers' tiffs such as those in *The Last September* (1929) and *To the North* (1932) are recognizable, magnified, in the wartime paralysing of free speech in *The Heat of the Day*. In *A World of Love* the criticism of *acedia*, the vice of not caring, goes beyond the blind eye turned to the unpleasant realities of Irish society in *The Last September*, and the guarded attitudes of that book become the eternal struggles to cope with life itself. There are homoerotic tensions in many of the early narratives, but none are as open as Dinah's question to Clare in *The Little Girls:* 'Mumbo, are you a Lesbian?'. The plush toy monkey that Henrietta carries about with her in *The House in Paris* (1935) becomes the evil-spirited familiar in *A World of Love*, and Uncle Bill's paranoiac fear of being late in the former book surfaces tellingly later in the question of the characters' relation to the time they are living in, and the notion of one time being more 'right' than another. Roman ruins, which provide an excuse for an afternoon's excursion in *To the North*, set in motion the whole plotline of *The Little Girls* and occasion concomitant reflections on time and death. In *A World of Love*, 'gay' and 'gaiety' have lost the positive connotations they had in *To the North* and *The House in Paris* and now suggest the irresponsibility of the pre-1914 world, particularly the irresponsibility of the old Anglo-Irish Ascendancy class; and the obelisk that is mentioned in passing as the now-gone appendage of a great house in *To The North* becomes a powerful sexual symbol throughout *A World of Love*. Add to examples like these the stylistic eye-catchers of the later Bowen, and her post-war writings emerge as the distinctive voice of a sensitive intelligence grappling with problems inherent in the condition of man and the historical moment at which one is called to live. A few years before her death, looking back on her experiences in the Second World War more than a quarter of a century later, Bowen wrote feelingly of the 'mythical intensity' that existence then had.[2] It is tempting to imagine that some of this 'mythical intensity' has spilled over more permanently into the works she wrote after the war.

Before embarking on my subject proper I have found it convenient to give brief presentations and plot summaries of the works I shall be dealing with in a preliminary chapter, 'Works and Days', which places them in the context of Bowen's life.

---

[2] Review of *The People's War* by Angus Calder. *Spectator*, 20 September 1969; quoted from *The Mulberry Tree*, 182.

Elizabeth Bowen. *Angus McBean Photograph, Copyright © The Harvard Theatre Collection, The Houghton Library.*

CHAPTER 2

Works and Days[1]

The 70-odd years of Bowen's life were a period of immense political and social change. She was born in Ireland in 1899 into the privileged world of the Anglo-Irish landowning class, and she lived to see the near-annihilation of that class by Irish Independence in 1921. The English world in which she moved as an adult was racked by two World Wars and the ensuing social upheavals, and it is perhaps a sign of the times that this daughter of an Irish Big House should end her days living in a little red-brick house in an English seaside resort. Without positing close parallels between her life and her work, it will be well to remember that the universe of her fiction is the world she lived in, and that its continuous undertow of conflict – rumours of war, war itself, and the aftermath of war – may go far, along with her divided Anglo-Irish heritage, to explain the tensions and sense of dislocation in her writings.[2]

Bowen spent what she called 'the most amusing years of one's childhood – 8 to 13'[3] living with her mother in rented houses on the Kent coast, which became part of her 'terrain' (her own word). She was at school in England for much of the First World War, and England was to be her permanent home from then on. But she made frequent trips to the family estate of Bowen's Court in County Cork, and when she inherited it in 1930 she made it the scene of much of her renowned hospitality. After the sale of Bowen's Court in 1959 she turned exclusively to England for the settings of her fiction. Though she regarded herself as an Irish novelist – so she said expressly in an interview in 1942

---

[1] For biographical details, this chapter is much indebted to Victoria Glendinning, *Elizabeth Bowen. Portrait of a Writer*; for bibliographical data, to J M Sellery and W O Harris, *Elizabeth Bowen. A Bibliography*.
[2] The role of war in Bowen's works is treated in Heather Bryant Jordan, *How Will the Heart Endure. Elizabeth Bowen and the Landscape of War*.
[3] Elizabeth Bowen to Charles Ritchie; quoted by Glendinning (93:222).

(Glendinning 93:165) – the extent of her Irishness has given rise to a good deal of discussion; it is not a question I shall take up here.[4]

Bowen's Court, from a photograph in the 2nd edition of Bowen's book of family history, *Bowen's Court*, which was first published in 1942. Bowen's Court was an extreme example of an Irish Big House: built in the eighteenth century, four-square, Italianate, isolated in a large demesne amid farmlands, far from any sizeable town. Houses like this fostered a recognizable kind of novel dealing with the lives lived in them, which has been dubbed the 'Big House Novel' (*A World of Love* comes immediately to mind, along with Bowen's early novel *The Last September*). Unlike many other Big Houses, Bowen's Court escaped burning in the troubled years of Ireland's struggle for independence around 1920, but by 1964, when the 2nd edition of *Bowen's Court* was published, the house had been demolished by its new owner. *From the photograph in Longmans' 1964 edition of* Bowen's Court.

The summer of 1923 saw the publication of Bowen's first work, a collection of stories entitled *Encounters*. This was followed by a steady stream of stories and novels written side by side with countless pieces of non-fiction, such as theatre and fiction reviews, magazine articles, and reflections on her own art. Much of this was bread-and-butter writing

---

[4] See e.g. chapters on Bowen in Roy Foster, *Paddy and Mr Punch*, and Declan Kiberd, *Inventing Ireland*.

which she kept up through the 50s in order to meet the crippling expenses of the Bowen's Court estate, and of her own lavish lifestyle.

In 1923 Bowen had married Alan Cameron, a war veteran who became much involved in the administrative side of education. Their childless marriage lasted until his death almost 30 years later, though Elizabeth had a number of affairs with other men (and, it has been suggested, women), most lastingly with the Canadian diplomat Charles Ritchie whom she had met in 1941, and to whom she dedicated both *The Heat of the Day* and *Eva Trout*. Alan Cameron's various appointments dictated where they lived: first briefly near Northampton, then for 10 years near Oxford. She was thus close to, though never of, that university, and her friends there included C M Bowra, Lord David Cecil, and Isaiah Berlin. In 1935, when Alan Cameron was made Secretary to

A present-day photograph of 2, Clarence Terrace, where the Camerons – Bowen and her husband – lived from 1935 to 1951. When they gave up the lease, it was taken over by a friend and countryman of Bowen's, the poet Louis MacNeice, who was working at the BBC, five minutes' walk away. Describing it to Virginia Woolf, Bowen wrote: 'It is a corner house, which I think is nice, don't you, as the windows look different ways. It has high windows and ceilings, and pale-coloured modern parquet floors' (quoted Glendinning 93:92). Lighting was important to Bowen in real life as it was in her books. *Author's photograph.*

the Central Council of School Broadcasting at the BBC, the Camerons moved to what has been called one of London's most beautiful houses, overlooking the trees and lawns and lake of Regent's Park (another part of Bowen's 'terrain'), where they lived for 17 years. Though she disclaimed any talk of belonging to a literary clique, she had a wide circle of friends and acquaintances among the greater and lesser literary lions of the time and collaborated with several of them, e.g. writing theatre criticism for Graham Greene's short-lived periodical *Night and Day* in 1937 and contributing regularly to Cyril Connolly's *Horizon* throughout the 1940s.

In the late forties Bowen could look back on her experiences in the Second World War with no regrets. She had had, she said, a good war. Certainly she had been in the thick of things. Her house in Clarence Terrace was severely bombed in the Blitz of 1940 and much damaged again in the summer of 1944, when the Camerons moved out, temporarily, after a blast had brought down the ceilings and only a mere chance saved them from being killed. Bowen was an Air Raid Warden throughout the war, and beginning in the summer of 1940 she ran the hazards of wartime travel to Ireland to report on Irish neutrality to the Ministry of Information.[5] Her experience rarely found its way directly into her fiction, but there is a notable exception in the description of the bombed house in 'The Happy Autumn Fields', which was written soon after the Clarence Terrace blast in 1944. This is one of the score of short stories Bowen published during the war years, which enhanced her reputation at the time and confirmed it for the future. She spoke of them as 'wartime', not 'war' stories: they are not 'straight' pictures of war action or the wartime scene, but, rather, studies of the wartime climate, where 'the backgrounds, and sometimes the circumstances, are only present by inference'.[6]

---

[5] Bowen's reports were published in 1999 by the Aubane Historical Society: *Notes From Eire. Espionage Reports To Winston Churchill, 1940-2, with a review of Irish neutrality.*
[6] Preface (dated October 1945) to *Ivy Gripped the Steps and Other Stories* (Knopf, 1946), which is the first US edition of *The Demon Lover and Other Stories* (Cape, 1945); quoted from *The Mulberry Tree*, 95, 98.

1945 – 1949

Immediately after the war in Europe ended in May 1945, Bowen registered the current weary and apprehensive atmosphere in London in a very brief story, hardly more than a sketch, 'I Hear You Say So', which was published in September that year.[7]

> 'I Hear You Say So' tells of the first nightingale of the year. It is heard by a girl lying with her lover on the grass in Regent's Park, a family looking down the lake from the bridge, two women friends sitting on a bench, a suspicious-looking man prowling around, an old gentleman on a balcony who hopes to be the first to write about it to *The Times*, and a young war widow in one of the houses overlooking the park. The movement of the story is the reverse of Keats' 'Ode to a Nightingale', which is recalled at the very end in the young woman's thoughts. In the Ode, it is the bird that moves: past a meadow, over a stream, up the hill-side and into the next valley. In Bowen's story the nightingale – or, rather, its song – remains in the same place, while the camera-eye of the narrator moves from one group of listeners to another.

September 1945 also saw the first publication of a long 'war story' set in late 1944, 'Ivy Gripped the Steps'.[8]

> 'Ivy Gripped the Steps' is the story of an early infatuation that has crippled the protagonist emotionally for life. A forty-ish bachelor revisits the town where he spent some weeks as a child in the house of a beautiful but callous widow, Mrs Nicholson. He adored her, but realized at the end of his stay that she had merely been using him for her own reasons: to alleviate her boredom, for the convenience of having someone to squire her about, and to lend an air of respectability to her assignations with a married man. In 1944 the young boy of 1910 has become a sexual predator habitually on the look-out for a woman to pick up; he has been strangled emotionally in the same way as ivy has strangled the once-distinguished house where Mrs Nicholson lived.

Along with 'Ivy Gripped the Steps' it will be natural to mention another late war story, 'The Dolt's Tale'.[9]

---

[7] *New Writing and Daylight* no. 6.
[8] *Horizon* 12 no. 69.
[9] 'The Dolt's Tale' was published in *A Day in the Dark and Other Stories* (Cape, 1965). Sellery and Harris give no earlier date of publication, but Bowen herself dated the story 1944 in this 1965-volume.

> This is one of Bowen's few first-person narratives. The unprepossessing, gullible narrator is flattered and duped by a group of small-time criminals and finally warned to pull out by an arty 'type', whose relationship with the flighty female character (as is obvious to the reader) is by no means as innocent as the 'dolt' believes. Apart from the double vision whereby the narrator gives a convincing portrait of both himself and his surroundings, the story is interesting for its picture of the seamier side of life; this is not found so often in Bowen's works, but it surfaces obliquely as a kidnapping racket in her last novel, *Eva Trout*.

A quite different end-of-the-war story appeared in January 1946: 'Gone Away'.[10]

> This slight sketch is a rarity among Bowen's writings: a science-fiction vision of the future. A storybook clergyman receives a visit from an old friend pointedly named Van Winkle, and takes him on a guided tour of the neighbourhood. It turns out that the vicarage and church are mere showpieces in a sham village. They stand in a fenced-in Reserve surrounded by the ghost-town of 'Brighterville', where the avenues are well laid-out, and in the cafeteria and gymnasium even the machinery keeps working. But there are no people.

Some of Bowen's wartime stories had been collected in book form in *Look at All Those Roses* (1941),[11] the majority in *The Demon Lover and Other Stories* (1945).[12] The most substantial outcome of the war years, however, her first novel since 1938, had to wait until 1949 before it was published as *The Heat of the Day*. She was not wholly satisfied with the work she had done on this major undertaking during the war years, and she decided later to rewrite the first five chapters, which in their original form had been finished by the summer of 1944 and sent out of London for safe keeping. The book was brought out simultaneously in America and England[13] and was well received: 45.000 copies were sold almost at once, and there were many impressions of the first editions both in England and America. It was also a critical success and is often mentioned along with Henry Green's *Caught* as the foremost evocation of wartime London.

---

[10] *Listener* 35 no. 886.
[11] London: Gollancz, 20 January 1941; New York: Knopf, 4 August 1941 (a different, larger selection of stories).
[12] London: Cape, October 1945. Published in USA as *Ivy Gripped the Steps and other Stories*. New York: Knopf, April 1946.
[13] New York: Knopf; London: Cape; both 21 February 1949.

The main events in *The Heat of the Day* take place in London in the autumn of 1942, with a brief flashback to the May of that year, and a coda in the last chapter covering 1943 and 1944. The plot centers on the love-affair of the gentle, hesitant Stella Rodney and the debonair traitor Robert Kelway. Robert is dogged and finally cornered by a wily, rather seedy counter-spy, Harrison, who has insinuated himself into Stella's life with thoughts of sexual blackmail. The exact nature of Robert's treason remains unexplained, and this is no traditional spy story; it is, rather, an exploration of the poisonous climate of secrecy and suspicion engendered by wartime, where people watch what they say and weigh what they hear. The story hinges on Stella's growing doubts about Robert's loyalty to his country and her qualms about confronting him with a direct question. His disaffection has been put to her by Harrison, and though at first vehemently rejecting the very thought, she cannot in the long run remain immune to Harrison's allegations. A visit to Robert's family home gives her a frightening glimpse of the stultifying English middle-class version of democracy that her lover grew up in, which is ostensibly largely responsible for his defection. Later, a visit to Ireland on behalf of her soldier son Roderick (who has inherited a property there, Mount Morris, from a distant Cousin Francis) convinces Stella of Harrison's fundamental truthfulness and strengthens her resolution to have it out with her lover. Coming at the dead centre of the novel, the Irish intermezzo is a turning point in the plotline, coinciding with the Allied victories in North Africa that proved a turning point in the war. When on her return from Ireland Stella asks Robert whether it is true that he is passing information to the enemy, he incriminates himself with evasions and blustering denials plus an untimely proposal of marriage. He finally confesses to her when it is too late, and his attempt to get away over the roof of her flat is so dangerous as to be virtually suicidal.

At the open-air concert that introduces the novel, Harrison happens to sit next to one of a pair of ill-assorted room-mates whose doings and sayings fulfil the traditional role of comic subplot: the flighty Louie, a naïve counterpart to Stella (who in fact has an undeserved reputation for being flighty), and her bossy friend Connie, a mirror-image of Robert's larger-than-life sister Ernestine (alike even to the fact that both wear uniform: Connie is an Air Raid Warden, Ernestine in the WVS, the Women's Voluntary Service). In terms of the story of events, the two friends have only a tenuous connection with the main plot, and what there is depends on coincidence. Thematically the two plots are closely linked, however. As Stella is betrayed politically by Robert, so Louie is betrayed on a less idealistic level by the men she casually takes up with, and even by Connie, who is writing to tell Louie's long-absent soldier husband that his wife is expecting a child with someone else when she is interrupted by news of his death. Fully as much as Stella, moreover, Louie is in search of guidelines in her life, which she finds in the morale-boosting propaganda of the press. In other respects, too, Louie is close to a central concern of the novel, the question of language. Her compulsive fibs that fool no-one are a low-scale counterpart of Robert's lies, and also of Stella's glib evasions in the final chapter, at the inquest after his death.

The novel ends ironically on a hackneyed note of hope for the future, with Louie holding up her baby son to see three swans flying in the direction of the west.

Alan Cameron's health, particularly his failing eyesight, forced him to give up his job at the BBC in the mid-1940s, and the Camerons planned to spend half the year at Bowen's Court. It was not a question of Bowen withdrawing from public life, however, quite the reverse. She took an active part in adult education, for example, and for three years (1948-50) she was principal of the Kent Education Committee's summer school for teachers of English at Folkestone; she also lectured at summer schools in Oxford for the Extension Lectures Committee, besides making several lecture tours abroad for the British Council. One of the most important friendships of her later life dated from soon after the war, when she met the American writer Eudora Welty, a kindred spirit with whom she shared, among other things, a total commitment to writing, a fascination with places, and a taste for the Gothic.

It is a measure of the esteem in which Bowen was now held that she was made Companion of the British Empire in 1948, and the following year appointed member of the Royal Commission on Capital Punishment. It was in 1949, too, that she was given an Honorary Litt. D. by Trinity College, Dublin.

1950 – 1959

In 1950 Longmans published some of Bowen's essays, reviews, feature articles and prefaces under the title *Collected Impressions*. These include what is probably her best known piece of literary criticism, the introduction written in 1946 for the reprint of Sheridan Le Fanu's *Uncle Silas*.[14] In 1951 there was an American reprint of her first two books of stories for which she wrote a preface;[15] there was also an Irish selection

---

[14] The Cresset Press, 1947; reprinted in *The Mulberry Tree*, 100-113.
[15] *Early Stories [Encounters & Ann Lee's]*. Knopf, 1951.

of her stories, plus a more lightweight venture: a history of Dublin's prestigious Shelbourne Hotel,[16] which she wrote with a mixture of social atmosphere and anecdote that throws into relief her more serious book about Bowen's Court from the early years of the war.[17]

This photograph of Bowen was taken in Ireland in the 1950s by the American writer Eudora Welty, who was also well known as a photographer. The two women had met shortly after the Second World War; they became firm friends, and Welty was a welcome guest at Elizabeth Bowen's house in Ireland, Bowen's Court. During one of her visits, in 1951, Bowen wrote to Blanche Knopf, her American publisher: 'Eudora Welty is staying in the house - working away at one of her great short stories in another room. This is ideal: I'm so fond of her, and her preoccupation during the day with her own work gives me a freedom unknown when one has an ordinary "social" guest' (quoted Glendinning 93:210). – In the photograph Bowen is characteristically wearing gloves, for which she had a weakness that she put to excellent comic use in 'Hand in Glove'. An inordinate importance attached to gloves is also ridiculed in *The Little Girls*, when the beautiful Edwardian widow of that novel, feeling bound to chastise her daughter for having conspired with her friends to blow up a garden shed with gelignite, comes up with: 'She must go to the Beakers' [the owners of the shed] properly, wearing gloves, after a day or two, and tell them that she is extremely sorry' (LG 80). *Eudora Welty Collection - Mississippi Department of Archives and History.*

---

[16] *The Shelbourne Hotel*. New York: Knopf, 1951. *The Shelbourne. A Centre in Dublin Life for more than a Century*. London, Toronto, Wellington, Sydney: Harrap, 1951.
[17] *Bowen's Court*, 1942.

The Camerons' plans to spend more time in Ireland were roughly broken off by Alan's death in August 1952. His wife stayed on at Bowen's Court for several years in the face of increasing financial problems, with periods of intense loneliness despite visits from old and new friends and trips abroad. October of that first lonely autumn saw the publication of one of her most light-hearted stories: 'Hand in Glove'.[18]

> 'Hand in Glove' is an extravaganza about two man-hunting sisters in Ireland around the year 1900. They keep their failing aunt under lock and key in order to break into the trunks containing her bridal finery; only her long gloves elude them. When the old lady finally dies the elder sister, not giving herself time to close her relative's eyes, steals her keys and dashes up to the attic to open the only trunk that has withstood their attacks. True enough, it does contain the coveted gloves, but when the girl opens it, one of the gloves reaches up and strangles her. There is the merest suggestion that this may have been done by her younger sister, and the supernatural is thus allowed some degree of rational explanation.

By 1953 Bowen was working hard on her next novel, which came out two years later.[19] She called it *A World of Love*, with a title taken from the *Centuries of Meditations* of Thomas Traherne (1637-1674); it is in effect a 'meditation', on love and death and the relation of the living to the dead. Apart from *The Last September* (1929) it is the only Bowen novel set entirely in Ireland, and it is by far the shortest – deliberately so, she said, because it is 'on the periphery of passion'.[20] The Traherne quotation from which the title is taken is used as the epigraph: 'There is in us a world of Love to somewhat, though we know not what in the world that should be... Do you not feel yourself drawn by the expectation and desire of some Great Thing?'

> The plot of *A World of Love* is woven round the discovery of a bundle of old love letters, which pass through several hands before finally being burnt. The action covers four days of a sweltering June and is limited to a narrow cast of related characters trying to make both ends meet in a dilapidated Big House, Montefort in County Cork: 20-year-old Jane, the beautiful golden

---

[18] *The Second Ghost Book*, ed. Cynthia Asquith. James Barrie, 1952.
[19] New York: Knopf, 17 January 1955; London: Cape, 1 March 1955.
[20] Letter from Elizabeth Bowen to the American writer May Sarton, quoted by Glendinning (93:200).

girl on the threshold of womanhood; her ill-matched parents, Lilia and Fred; her young sister Maud; and Antonia, who has inherited the estate, has some (but not much) money, and has more or less adopted Jane. Of the supporting cast, the most interesting is the nouveau-riche chatelaine of a nearby castle, Lady Latterly, who takes it into her head to invite Jane to a ghostlike dinner party of phantasmagoric dimensions.[21]

A note of sexual passion is struck on the first page of the novel by the potent symbol of the obelisk in front of the house; this crops up several times in the book, often as a backdrop to the Lawrentian figure of Fred. The erotic atmosphere is enhanced by the heat-wave and highlighted by the frequent mention of heat, fire, cigarettes, matches, lamps, candles – these latter linking up with the motif of black magic and voodoo represented by Maud, a particularly repulsive version of Bowen's many horrible little girls.

It is Jane who finds the letters in a trunk in the attic. They are from the former owner of Montefort, Guy, who was engaged to Lilia before he fell in the First World War. Whether he wrote the letters to Lilia or to his half-cousin Antonia remains a speculation for much of the story (it appears towards the end that they were written to an unknown third woman). More importantly, the letters awaken a latent sexuality in the characters – Jane especially, and also Lilia and Fred, who recover some of the passion of their early wedded life in a marriage forced on them by Antonia. The story predictably ends with Jane falling in love, when the long-awaited coming of rain coincides with the arrival of the princely young Richard Priam at Shannon Airport, a hero from afar come (as it might be) to carry her off from the *bois dormant*.

The last of Bowen's short stories to be included in her posthumous *Collected Stories* also appeared in 1955: 'A Day in the Dark'.[22]

This is a classical Bowen story about a young girl's awakening to the sexual tangles of adult life. Venturing into the neighbouring town on behalf of her farmer uncle in order to ask for the loan of a thistle-cutter, the 15-year-old Barbie is met with sarcasm and snide suggestions about the nature of her relationship with her uncle. Miss Banderry, who owns the implement in question, is an unprepossessing, unscrupulous woman who has hounded her own brother to death and now harasses Barbie's easy-going uncle (whom she sarcastically refers to as 'my lord') in a sparring-match with unmistakable sexual undertones. In the story it is Barbie who has to bear the brunt of the

---

[21] The chapter containing the dinner scene at the castle was originally published separately as 'The Dinner Party': London Magazine 1 no. 1, February 1954, and Irish Writing 27, June 1954.
[22] First published in *Botteghe Oscure* 16, Autumn 1955.

older woman's domineering, hectoring manner, and she emerges from the ordeal with a lifelong feeling of dread – so she herself says, but most readers will probably focus more on her budding, unacknowledged love for her uncle than the shadow cast on it by Miss Banderry.

Bowen spent a good deal of her creative energy in the 50s in writing features and short stories, primarily for magazines. Physically her energy was unabated, and from 1950 travelling regularly included visiting America as lecturer, fellow, or writer-in-residence, at Vassar, Princeton, Bryn Mawr, and many other universities and colleges. She was in England in the summer of 1956 to receive a doctorate from Oxford University, and she made several visits to Rome in connection with the book she was writing about that city, *A Time in Rome*, which she had started on in 1953, partly as therapy after her husband's death.

1960 – 1973

Bowen entered her sixties in a state of profound agitation. Her financial worries came to a head at the end of the 1950s, leading her to sell Bowen's Court, at great emotional cost, to the first serious bidder. The house was demolished by its new owner, who apparently had wanted the estate for the land and the timber, and not, as Bowen seems to have believed, because he intended to live there. When the door of Bowen's Court closed behind her for the last time in January 1960 she went straight to America, but she was in England again that summer. For a time she borrowed a flat in Stratford-on-Avon before finding a more permanent place to live: a first-floor flat in White Lodge at Old Headington near Oxford, within view of the house where she and her husband had lived for ten years. It was at White Lodge that she started working on her new novel, *The Little Girls*. About this time she also collected a number of earlier miscellaneous writings, to appear in America under the title *Seven Winters and Afterthoughts*,[23] in England as *Afterthought: Pieces about Writing*.[24]

---

[23] Knopf, June 1962.
[24] Longmans, November 1962. This English edition does not contain *Seven Winters*, which had already been published both in Ireland (Cuala Press, 1942) and England (Longmans, 1943, subtitled *Memories of a Dublin Childhood*).

The Little Girls was published in 1964.[25] Like much else of what Bowen wrote, the novel is in a sense a working-out of ideas that had been voiced previously in more than one of her books. This is Stella in *The Heat of the Day*:

> 'Whatever has been buried, surely, corrupts? Nothing keeps innocence innocent but daylight. A truth's just a truth, to start with, with no particular nature, good or bad – but how can any truth not *go* bad from being underground? Dug up again after years and laid on the mat, it's inconvenient, shocking – apart from anything else there's no place left in life for it any more. To dig up somebody else's truth for them would seem to me sheer malignancy; to dig up one's own, madness. I never would.' (HD 228-229)

From a technical point of view, *The Little Girls* marks a break with Bowen's earlier narrative approach: the reader is not granted direct access to her characters, and their words and actions are left to speak for themselves (aided and abetted by various moves on the part of the narrator).

> The 'Little Girls' of the title are three eleven-year-olds – Diana Piggott, Clare Burkin-Jones, and Sheila Beaker – day boarders at St. Agatha's in 'Southstone' on the south coast of England just before the First World War. Inspired by hearing of Roman remains, they bury in one of the school shrubberies a coffer containing, among other objects, one secret memento from each of them. The girls are separated abruptly by the coming of war and only meet again some 50 years later, when Diana, now calling herself Dinah and currently engaged in collecting other mementoes in a cave in her garden, remembers the treasure buried in her childhood and contacts her former classmates. They manage to unearth the coffer, only to find it empty. This has an unsettling effect on all three and brings about a nervous crisis in Dinah, who at the end of the book is recovering from a breakdown. So attempting to dig up one's own past does in fact lead to a kind of madness, and in this respect the truth of a remark made by several Bowen characters is borne out: 'Better let sleeping dogs lie'. On the other hand, digging up the past may repair some of the damage that was done then, as the renewed, apparently lesbian friendship between the adult Dinah and Clare bids fair to make good their painful parting as children; this is clearly suggested in the very open closure of the novel, which ends with a question of Dinah's to Clare.

> The grown-up Dinah of the 1960s is reminded of her childhood experience partly by a chance question about sealing up her cave, and partly by seeing, as though for the first time, a crooked swing in her garden – for at St.

---

[25] New York: Knopf, January 1964; London: Cape, February 1964.

Agatha's there had also been a swing that did not hang quite evenly. The swing introduces an unmistakable air of sexuality, and the fact that it is crooked prepares the reader for the novel's suggestions of unconventional sexual relations.

The memento Sheila puts into the coffer is the most unusual: her witch-like sixth toe, a deformity that had been removed immediately after her birth but preserved as a kind of mascot. Earlier references to *Macbeth* are thus pointed up in an image fully as macabre as the pilot's thumb that Shakespeare's witches put into their brew. In addition to these Shakespearian echoes, *The Little Girls* makes extensive use of other literary allusions, and several passages of poetry are cited prominently in the text. Lines from Wordsworth's Immortality Ode, for instance, recall the epigraph of that poem, 'The Child is father of the Man,' which might be said to sum up one of the basic themes of the novel. In the adult section of the book Clare quotes several lines lines from George Meredith's poem about the enchanted 'Woods of Westermain' – and enchantment is a prominent motif in the novel, represented notably by Dinah's mother, Mrs Piggott.

The three friends are centre-stage both as children and adults, with a few other characters hovering in the wings to supply thematic emphasis or to set the plot in motion. The cliché lower-class Mrs Coral does both. Coming to collect Dinah's overdue subscription for the Mothers' Union, she neatly punctures all talk of leaving clues for posterity with the remark, 'Should there be any posterity', and it is she who asks the operative question about sealing up the cave. Towards the end of the book, Mrs. Coral's one granddaughter and Dinah's two form a trio of little girls in a scene that constitutes a caustic comment on the antics of the older three.

In 1965 Bowen bought a small, newish red-brick house in Hythe in Kent, where she had spent much of her childhood. She called the house Carbery after an estate in Ireland that had belonged to her mother's family.

1965 was a full year for Elizabeth Bowen the writer. In June Cape brought out a collection of some of her earlier stories, *A Day in the Dark and Other Stories*; for this she had written the preface. In October appeared the American edition of a children's story, *The Good Tiger*.[26] In that year she also wrote an introduction to Le Fanu's *The House by the Churchyard*,[27] and she started on what was to be her last novel, *Eva Trout*.

---

[26] English edition: Cape, 1970.
[27] *The House by the Churchyard (by J Sheridan Le Fanu)*. London: Blond; New York: Stein and Ady; both 1968.

Eva Trout came out in America in the autumn of 1968, in England a few months later.[28] The American and English dust covers, though dissimilar, both depict a castle, transparently heralding that *Eva Trout* will be a story in the Gothic mode. For the familiar everyday ambience of Bowen's earlier works is now peopled by fantasy, larger-than-life characters, with recognizable trappings of historical Gothic fiction transposed into the 20th century: the orphaned heroine is not the scion of an ancient aristocratic family, but the daughter of a wealthy bisexual financier and a neurotic adulterer; she is at the same time a changeling whose adopted son is also an alien; her knight in shining armour is a brash, boozy garage mechanic; instead of a villainous defrocked priest, there is a sleek, worldly East End priest who seems to spend most of his time in Knightsbridge; and the isolated castle that dominates the whole story is a sham.

> Eva Trout is the story of a young woman who cannot come to terms with the norms of contemporary society. Her mother left her father for another man while Eva was still a baby, and was immediately killed in an air-crash. Eva spends her childhood being dragged round the world by her father from one expensive hotel to another, with no place she can call home and with practically no schooling, and no prolonged contact with anyone her own age, before she is almost 16.
>
> For two periods Eva knows the happiness of being with other children – first, briefly, at an experimental school housed in the crumbling mock-castle, where she forms an attachment to a little near-albino, Elsinore (Elsie-Nora); then at a girls' school, where she becomes devoted to one of her teachers, Iseult Smith. When Eva's father dies by his own hand Eva is 24 and it is arranged that she should live with the now married Iseult and her husband, Eric Arble. Eva's presence proves to be the final straw in their toppling marriage; she on her side feels emotionally betrayed by Iseult and takes flight across the country to a run-down seaside villa, Cathay, on the east coast of Kent. She is easily found by both Iseult's husband and her own guardian, a wealthy, enigmatic business man called Constantine Ormeau. But this running away sets the pace for the rest of the novel: Eva is always on the run, from one hotel to another in England and America and France, leaving no forwarding address. She is not long at Cathay, but is soon off to America, to adopt (illegally) a baby boy, Jeremy. He turns out to be deaf-mute, and when he is eight years old or so he shoots her dead on the last page of the book – accidentally, it seems, as though he were acting out a movie or TV-play.

---

[28] New York: Knopf, 14 October 1968; London: Cape, 23 January 1969.

The novel falls into two halves separated by the eight years that Eva spends in America, acquiring Jeremy and seeking help from countless ear-and-speech doctors to cure his defect. Eva's journey from England to America is rendered in the book by a letter from a hypochondriac professor which provides one of the high points of comedy in the book. Meeting her on the flight, he is apparently quite taken with her and on landing writes her a long confessional letter which, in common with some of the other missives in the book, remains forever unclaimed. It is from this letter that we realize much of the forceful impression made on people by Eva's 'lengthy and unencumbered physique', while the Biblical associations of her name are highlighted in a grotesque incident involving an apple that rolls across the aisle towards him. The absurdity of the professor effectively prefigures the absurd way Eva goes about adopting a child.

Eva's relations with her one-time teacher, Iseult Smith, later Iseult Arble, provide a good deal of the emotional conflict in the book and have attracted the attention of feminist criticism (see Chapter 4, 'Identity'). Iseult's unintellectual, rather macho husband Eric is responsible (perhaps through no fault of his own) for the misunderstandings that lead some of Eva's friends, and, for a time, perhaps even the reader, to suspect him of fathering Jeremy. A major part in the story is played by the family of the vicar, the Rev. Alaric Dancey. Eva makes friends especially with his eldest son Henry, who as a bright twelve-year-old conspires with her to sell her only possession, her car. Nothing comes of this project, but in the second part of the book Eva makes a point of visiting the Danceys on her return from America. Henry is now an elegant albeit vacillating Cambridge undergraduate, whom Eva falls in love with; she casts him as the bridegroom in her fantasy-turned-real wedding departure at Victoria Station at the end of the book.

Eva Trout was the last novel Bowen finished. After her death from lung cancer in 1973, her fragments of an autobiography were published by her own wish. Together with other pieces, among them a chapter of a novel she was working on, 'The Move In', they make up the volume entitled *Pictures and Conversations*.

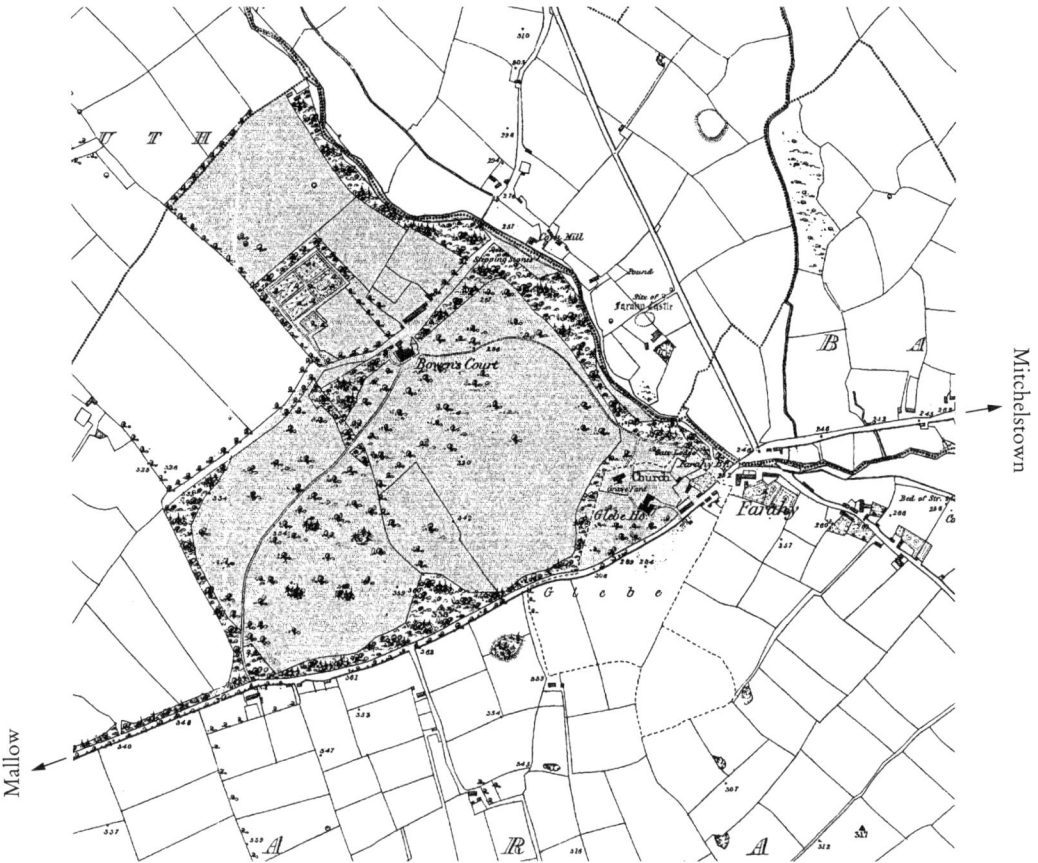

A section of the Ordnance Survey map of 1844-1845 showing Bowen's Court in County Cork on the east-west road from Mitchelstown to Mallow, some 40 kilometres north of Cork City as the crow flies. It was at Mitchelstown Castle, on August 5th 1914 – the day after Britain had declared war on Germany – that the 15-year old Elizabeth attended a windy garden party, which was to be the last great gathering of the Anglo-Irish gentry in County Cork. Mitchelstown Castle was burnt down in 1922, and when Bowen wrote her family history some 20 years later, 'the terraces [were] obliterated, and grass [grew] where the saloons were' (BC 324).

At the south-east corner of the Bowen's Court demesne can be seen the tiny, now disused Protestant church of Farahy and its churchyard, where Elizabeth Bowen is buried.

Photograph: Royal Library, Copenhagen, Dept. of Maps, Prints and Photographs.

Chapter 3

The Later Fiction

Elizabeth Bowen's last novel, *Eva Trout*, is to all intents and purposes a mock-Gothic story. There is a certain aptness in this, for the extravagances of the Gothic mode are increasingly well matched by her approach to writing, even within the confines of polite mid-century fiction. Plotline episodes are often grotesque: three elderly women armed with spades digging around in somebody else's garden after nightfall, for instance, as in *The Little Girls*; or a millionaire heiress dining alone on milk and a Swiss roll in a dilapidated seaside villa, as in *Eva Trout*. The texture of all the works dealt with in these studies is nothing if not extravagant, and it is hardly surprising that charges of overwriting and mannerism have been levelled against Bowen over the years. The stylistic devices she employs are laboured and repetitive to the point of parody;[1] her use of dress, hairstyle and jewelry as characterisers is over-the-top, her irony often heavy-handed; time-markers appear with predictable regularity; sexual connotations of landscape and weather are commonplace, intertextual references at times almost condescendingly explicit; and altogether pointers are too thick on the ground for comfort, certainly too many for any complacency or self-congratulation on the part of the reader. In *Eva Trout*, for instance, any satisfaction we may feel at recognizing an allusion to the painter Sir John Millais in the text's 'Millais wild roses' is deflated a few lines further on when we read that the flowers stand out 'as though painted' (ET 233).

As against this, Bowen's device-laden style, which detractors have found such an easy target for ridicule and which may at times try the patience

---

[1] In a welcome defence against the general run of reserved or hostile reactions to Bowen's style, William McCormack points out that James Joyce's 'manipulations of grammar, syntax, spelling and punctuation' far exceed Bowen's 'gentilities'. *Dissolute Characters*, 218.

even of her admirers, can also be seen as a source of her strength, in that it provokes readers to seek behind the elaborate expressions of the narrative persona to form their own version of the story, perhaps even its 'poetic truth', to quote a favourite term of Bowen's. Foregrounding the textual surface as she does may well have the effect of drawing attention to all that is *not* said in her fiction, or not said immediately, or not said in so many words; and the suppression of information by the narrator readily brings our imagination into play – to fill in gaps in the storyline, for instance, or constantly to re-assess our understanding of character and theme. As Hermione Lee has pointed out (81:237), Graham Greene praised Bowen's use of gaps in tracing the passage of time as early as 1935: 'She has made of her omissions a completely individual method,' he wrote apropos of *The House in Paris*, '... she has made capital out of the gap in the records; how can we doubt the existence of a past which these characters can so easily convey to each other?'[2] One case among many in the later fiction is that of a young man from America who is expected at the local castle in *A World of Love*. We have been led to think of him, partly by the self-dramatization of the chatelaine, as a cast-off lover of her own, but it seems equally likely that he is in fact a dutiful son coming expressly to visit his mother – he had apparently been at the castle with her on a previous occasion and had only 'stuck it out' because of the fishing. Our source for this information is another of the characters, however, the castle chauffeur, and there is no knowing how reliable he is. So we must ultimately fall back on our own judgment and our own imagination; Bowen's fiction does not invite passive reading. On a structural level, we may extend Greene's remarks to include also the way the novels make a virtue of necessity by deliberately exaggerating the effect of missing links or gaps between one chapter and the next, e.g. by starting a new chapter abruptly in the middle of a piece of dialogue. In *The Heat of the Day* such jolts underscore the dislocations of the book's wartime ambience; in *Eva Trout* similar violent transitions are part of the very fabric of a novel suggestively subtitled 'Changing Scenes'.

Not unlike the contrast between surface texture and content, there is a contrast between the wealth of realistic details in Bowen's fiction in

---

[2] Graham Greene, 'The Dark Backward: A Footnote', 1935. *Collected Essays*, 72.

general and the absurdities of her later plots. *Eva Trout* is an extreme example, where the bizarre action and bizarre characters are markedly at odds with normal everyday details – food and dress, for instance: a bag of macaroons, a punnet of strawberries; belted overcoats and Fair Isle gloves, scarlet stockings and lambskin bootees. This kind of surface realism may well be partly responsible for Bowen's former reputation as a traditionalist writer not given to experiment, but her 'realism', such as it is, is increasingly being seen as a thin veil over themes that touch the depths of human experience. In the words of Andrew Bennett and Nicholas Royle, 'Bowen's texts present us – often comically – with issues of life and death in provocatively secular terms' (xviii).

Bowen had made a name for herself as a writer of short stories as well as novels, and during the war 1939-1945 she wrote over a dozen short stories that more than confirmed her reputation. Among them were such classics of the genre as 'The Demon Lover', which captures the psychological terror of wartime in the story of a dead soldier who returns to claim his long-married fiancée, and 'Mysterious Kôr', where the unearthly city of Rider Haggard's *She* is superimposed on the eerie moonlit townscape of a raid-free night in London. Apart from practical reasons that dictated this emphasis on shorter fiction during the war years – paper shortage, for one, and the impossibility of settling down to any uninterrupted period of work – Bowen also seems to have been quite happy with what she called the short story's 'kinship to poetry':

> The short story is at an advantage over the novel, and can claim its nearer kinship to poetry, because it can be more concentrated, can be more visionary, and is not weighed down (as the novel is bound to be) by facts, explanation, or analysis.[3]

This was written in 1959. In point of fact, the novels that Bowen went on to write in the 1960s can hardly be said to be 'weighed down ... by facts, explanation, or analysis'. The comparison of the short story to poetry still holds good, however, provided that one takes 'poetry' to mean lyrical poetry in general or the short lyric in particular. The adjectives 'lyric' and 'poetic', or 'lyrical' and 'poetical', are often bandied about in descriptions of Bowen's fiction, and not only by

---

[3] Preface to Vintage Books edition of *Stories by Elizabeth Bowen* (1959); quoted from *The Mulberry Tree*, 128.

blurb-writers, seemingly with reference to her sensitive evocation of atmosphere and subtle registration of emotion. For the purpose of the present studies it will be more useful to think of Bowen's fiction as 'poetic' in another sense, however, taking it to mean that it employs a wide range of stylistic devices more commonly met with, or more commonly drawn attention to, in verse composition. Prominent among these is verbal repetition (see Chapter 6, 'Word Clusters and Interlinking Images').

In almost 30 years of writing after the Second World War, Bowen published, along with four novels, more than a dozen stories. None of these is later than 1959, however, and a mere four were included in the last selection of her stories that she made in her lifetime, *A Day in the Dark and Other Stories* (1965): 'I Hear You Say So' (1945), 'Gone Away' (1946), 'Hand in Glove' (1952) and 'A Day in the Dark' (1955).[4] Apart from the economic consideration that after 1960 she no longer needed vast sums of ready money for the expenses of keeping on Bowen's Court (sums that short stories supplied more readily than novels), and that the sale of the house removed her anxieties about its upkeep that 'slowed down [her] power to write', as she said herself,[5] it is tempting to explain the predominance of longer narratives at the end of her life largely by a new-found appreciation of the novel and its possibilities, or at least by a desire to explore such possibilities.

The novels Bowen wrote in the 1960s were marked by overwhelming changes of subject-matter and narrative approach. They still recognizably conform to a traditional pattern, with a storyline that is wound up at the end and a handful of characters that are traced through crisis or development. But of the earlier love interest there is hardly a trace in *The Little Girls*, while in *Eva Trout* honeymoon and marriage are merely the stuff of mockery. The courtship plot is sinking fast already

---

[4] These are the four 'post-war' stories in the posthumous *Collected Stories of Elizabeth Bowen* (1980). Going by date of publication rather than subject-matter one may add 'Ivy Gripped the Steps', which was not published until September 1945 though it is in setting a 'wartime' story; and also 'The Dolt's Tale', which is dated by Bowen to 1944 in *A Day in the Dark and Other Stories* but not recorded by Sellery and Harris in their bibliography of Bowen as being published before it appeared in that volume in 1965. *The Heat of the Day* is in subject-matter also a war story; the novel was conceived and begun during the war, though it did not appear until 1949.
[5] Revised 'Afterword' to second US edition of *Bowen's Court* (Knopf, 1964); quoted from Heather Bryant Jordan, *How Will the Heart Endure*, 181.

in *The Heat of the Day*: the lover dies well before the end of the book and the female protagonist is faded out in the last chapter, confirming the reader's suspicion that love is not the only issue in the book, perhaps not even the most important. And if there is any pretence at a traditional love story in *A World of Love*, it is undercut by the fact that the golden-girl heroine is in love with a dead man and does not meet her own flesh-and-blood Prince Charming until the very last page of the book; the final lines, with their quotation from *As You Like It:* 'They no sooner looked but they loved' (V ii 37), may be said to ring down the curtain on the courtship-and-romance plot in Bowen's fiction. Courtship is emphatically absent in *The Little Girls*, which simply skips the married or marriageable years of its three women and focuses our attention instead on their girlhood friendship and its revival in their late adult life. The 'courtship' of *Eva Trout* is almost equally non-existent; it is in line with the Gothic mood of the book that Eva's first passions should be for members of her own sex and her final wedding departure a self-staged happening.

The qualities that make *The Little Girls* so different from Bowen's earlier works include a new narrative stance on the part of the author. Instead of analysing the minds of her characters as she had done hitherto, Bowen had now decided to present them from the outside, and 'never to tell the reader what her characters were thinking or feeling', as she said to her literary adviser Spencer Curtis Brown.[6] This puts the onus of explication on the words of the characters themselves and on the way these words are represented in the text, plus of course on the skill with which the writer organizes her story so as to let one part illuminate another, and on her choice of e.g. imagery and intertextual references; and it would seem to contradict Bowen's 1959 statement quoted above about the novel being bound to be 'weighed down ... by facts, explanation, or analysis'. Her new approach is in fact not unlike that of Flaubert, which she had pointed to in 1941, in a laudatory review of the English translation of *L'Education sentimentale* (one of the books she most admired). Flaubert's method, she says there, is 'visual; thought is not analysed, and no consciousness is examined from the inside'.[7]

---

[6] Foreword by Spencer Curtis Brown to *Pictures and Conversations*, xxxviii. Bowen had written already in 1945 that 'dialogue *should* ideally be so effective as to make analysis or explanation of the relationships between the characters unnecessary'. 'Notes on Writing a Novel', *Orion* 2; quoted from *The Mulberry Tree*, 41.

[7] *Spectator*, 15 August 1941; quoted from *The Mulberry Tree*, 157.

In another respect, too, Bowen's last two novels stand out: in the comedy which is such a notable feature of her fiction. Hitherto, scenes of burlesque or high comedy have generally been reserved for minor characters or subplot – the funeral reception in *The Heat of the Day*, for example, or the village hairdresser in *A World of Love*. The heroines of those books are never placed in the hilarious situations where we find the central female characters of the 60s novels – a slim overdressed woman in a hat of pink roses and a stout dark-suited one in a black turban sharing a good gossip and minuscule cress sandwiches in the tearoom of a Knightsbridge department store, for instance, as in *The Little Girls*; or, in *Eva Trout*, the outsize heroine struggling into a Chicago coffee shop with an outsize Christmas parcel, or niggardly buying groceries and floral bed linen (one set), or to all appearances falling asleep with her mouth open in public. Comedy permeates these last novels at all levels.

* * *

While taking into account these new narrative approaches in Bowen's last two novels, the following studies will be concerned primarily to examine aspects that are common to all her post-war fiction. I discuss first and foremost the works separately as they stand on their own merit, and my immediate purpose is not to trace any development between them; likewise, I only touch briefly on the numerous parallels that patently exist between Bowen's later writing and the work she published before 1945. My emphasis will be on the novels, with occasional glances at the shorter fiction written after, or at the end of, the Second World War.

With these considerations in mind I shall discuss first what I consider to be Bowen's major themes, Identity and Communication, which ultimately link up with the values of rootedness and openness underlying much of her writing: identity as a fixed anchorage amid the ebb and flow of life, communication as a fundamental human good that implies frankness and hospitality. In Chapter 4, 'Identity', Stella in *The Heat of the Day* and the eponymous heroine of *Eva Trout* will be treated as examples of characters searching for identity; this chapter also looks at sexual identity, including the woman-to-woman relationship that figures conspicuously in *The Little Girls* and *Eva Trout*. In Chapter 5, 'Communication', *The Heat of the Day* and *Eva Trout* exemplify a major preoccupation of Bowen's: *The Heat of the Day* shows that one of the greatest evils of war is that it deprives us of the supreme human good of free speech, the give-and-take of conversation; and *Eva Trout* illustrates in no uncertain way the sad linguistic poverty stemming from a careless upbringing, and the questionable results of non-verbal communication.

I then turn from Bowen's themes to some of the strategies she employs. Chapter 6, 'Word Clusters and Interlinking Images', examines the part played in the overall pattern by the recurrence of linguistic and non-linguistic entities. The word clusters I have chosen to discuss are those dealing with spy-hunting in *The Heat of the Day*, fire and burning in *A World of Love*, death and enchantment in *The Little Girls*, and imprisonment and the underworld in *Eva Trout*. These examples are of necessity selective, but the principle of repetition involved in fact embraces large areas of Bowen's discourse. In Chapter 7, 'Narrative Roles', I distinguish between several different accents adopted by her narrator, from empathetic or distancing comments on her own fictive characters to an almost schoolboyish punning.

I have devoted a chapter each to Place and Time, which Bowen herself called 'actors' rather than 'elements' in her work (Chapters 8 and 9).[8] Landscapes and townscapes, the houses in them, the rooms in the houses, and the furniture and fireplaces and knicknacks in those rooms – these are as important in her fiction as a well-set stage is in the theatre, and are discussed in the chapter I have called 'Stages and Stage Properties'. They play a crucial part in conveying character and atmosphere and theme, from the sunless terrace-house of Miss Banderry in 'A Day in the Dark' to the mock castle that dominates *Eva Trout*. Similarly, the prominent treatment of time is responsible for much of the thematic import of the books, e.g. the active roles of past and future; and attention is repeatedly drawn to the actual passing of time by countless watches and clocks relentlessly ticking away in the texts. The presentation of time rarely describes a steadily progressive chronological

---

[8] 'I am, and am bound to be, a writer involved closely with place and time; for me these are more than elements, they are actors.' Preface to *The Last September*, second US edition (1952); quoted from *The Mulberry Tree*, 123.

line, and flashbacks in the minds of the characters are placed strategically for emphasis of theme or character; this also applies to long descriptions and scenes of earlier events given largely in the normal narrative tense, such as Chapter Four in *The Heat of the Day*, that describing the funeral of Cousin Francis Morris, which demonstrates the diffidence of the heroine and her outsider status (postponed until we have actually met her together with the counter-spy Harrison and then with her son in the preceding two chapters, but not yet together with her lover). Charts and surveys are included in an Appendix in order to illustrate something of these frequently disjointed or convoluted time structures, and the time gaps that are so remarkable in *The Little Girls* and *Eva Trout*.

After these six general chapters I append short studies of salient features in the four novels under consideration: *The Heat of the Day* is seen as a retelling of the myth of Icarus, and *A World of Love* as a story concerned with the crossing of thresholds; undertones of war are traced in *The Little Girls*; and *Eva Trout* is interpreted as a modern version of a Gothic novel.

II
GENERAL THEMES AND STRATEGIES

CHAPTER 4

Identity

'What a slippery fish is identity,' reflects Eva Trout; 'and what *is* it besides a slippery fish?' (ET 193). Bowen's texts give no answer; but they do refer, in many different words and phrases, to those features that characterize or define a person as being different from anyone else: *persona, personality, being oneself, deeper nature,* etc., plus the word *identity* itself.

The 'slippery fish' assumes diverse shapes. *National identity*, for instance, is prominent in the wartime ambience of *The Heat of the Day*, where Robert Kelway's attraction to the group identity of a totalitarian political regime makes him a traitor to his country. On the opposite side there is the obstinate Irish landowner Francis Morris, to whom Ireland's abstention from the Second World War is a severe blow, while strident nationalism is reserved for the press propaganda that the subplot's Louie accepts unquestioningly. The identity stemming from one's *profession* or *place of work* may be exemplified by Clare in *The Little Girls*; this self-made woman identifies herself with her chain of gift-shops so much that she proudly announces that she *is* 'Mopsie Pye', as she calls her shops (with scant feeling for the nursery-size Beatrix Potter associations of the name – Clare, the text makes clear, is a very large woman). *Homes* are likewise indications of their owner's personality, and characteristically the identity-seeking Stella in *The Heat of the Day* and Eva Trout have no permanent home of their own: Stella's furnished flats and Eva's hotels are poor substitutes, and Eva's acquisition of somebody else's cast-off seaside villa is one big mistake. The question of *woman's identity in marriage* comes into *The Heat of the Day* in the earlier ladies of the house that the diffident Stella feels herself akin to, and in the character of Cousin Nettie, the former mistress of Mount Morris, who has of her own free will spent years in a mental home because she felt that, childless as she was, she could not live up to what was expected of her as a wife; and Mrs Dancey in *Eva Trout* has so little identity apart from her husband and children that she is not even given a Christian name. *Sexual identity* looms large in Bowen's last two novels, which are shot through with open or barely-veiled homoeroticism. I return to this aspect of identity later.

'Identity' may signify merely 'identification'. In this sense it enters briefly into *The Heat of the Day* in the silent watcher outside Stella's flat, who turns out to be the counter-spy Harrison on one occasion, but whose identity on the fatal night of Robert's death is not made clear. It is fundamental to the plot of *A World of Love*, where the actual identity of the woman to whom the all-important letters are addressed remains a mystery throughout. A typographical ploy on the part of the author suggests that there is more to this concern with identification than mere suspense: the frequent italicizing of 'you'. In one of Guy's love-letters it is both italicized and capitalized: '"*I thought*," he wrote, "*if only YOU had been here!*"' (WL 48). Immediately, a page later, 'you' is italicized again when Maud says to Jane: '"Just wondered what *you* were making up"' (WL 49). Lilia and Antonia are also addressed in this emphatic way. This would seem to indicate that all three women who have been under Guy's spell – Antonia, Lilia, Jane – partake of the identity of the unknown beloved; we are therefore hardly surprised that the actual name of the stranger should not be revealed. At the end of the book, Jane is explaining why it was she herself and not Kathie, the superstitious little maid, who burnt the letters:

> 'Kathie got frightened. She found a name in them.'
> 'Oh?' said Antonia.
> Jane gave the unknown name, naturally adding: 'So who was she?'
> 'I don't believe I remember,' said Antonia. (WL 139)

The illegitimate Fred, whose married life has been lived in the shadow of his high-powered cousin, is also at one point a '*you*'; this also goes for the sinister Latterly chauffeur and the freak daughter of the house, Maud, who bring in an element of the supernatural, suggesting that there is a further mystical dimension to this form of address. There is also a hint of the supernatural when Antonia calls at Latterly Castle to fetch Jane (WL 71); she has apparently introduced herself to the butler as 'Jane's cousin', but she will not come in, and for a brief moment, when Lady Latterly asks who the young lady's cousin is, we are not quite sure that it is not Guy who is waiting outside for the young girl. (This is taken up later in Chapter 10, 'Doors and Entrances in *A World of Love*').

The question of identity in a wider sense is not easily solved, and *Eva Trout* may well be read as Bowen's most notable contribution to this popular, if loosely defined, literary theme. Seen in this light it is the story of a sexually and socially unformed girl whose only 'identity' is her enormous wealth; as Henry Dancey puts it: 'When you came cracking into the vicarage you'd already been pointed out as A Very Rich Girl. We had none of us ever seen one – it was like knowing a violinist, or something' (ET 236). Eva's adult life is spent searching for another identity, which may partly explain her adoption of a baby son who was to be everything that she herself would not be. In the last part of the story Eva is still a Very Rich Girl, but with a difference: her early same-sex loves have forcibly come to an end, and she seems to find some degree of compensation in motherhood until the growing need for independence of her adopted son Jeremy is resolved by her death. Jeremy is arguably Bowen's supreme example of that 'slippery fish', identity, and his sleek, slippery nature is highlighted by both sense and sound in many of the words associated with him: when he gets down from the vicarage tea-table, he *slides* off his cushion (ET 160), when he goes to look at the garden in the square he *slants* across the roadway (ET 169), one of his puzzles *slithers* about on the car seat where he has been sitting (ET 202), his smiles are *sliding* (ET 205), and when he gives up reading his *Asterix* he *shelves* it (ET 256). The boy's angelic behaviour proves to be only skin deep, and at the end of the book we are left wondering whether his outbursts of violence go back to his unknown heredity or whether they result from the psychological shock of being transplanted into a world that is strange to him but familiar to Eva – the concepts of Predestination and Environmentalism having been helpfully pointed out for us by the French doctor to whom Eva has entrusted her son.

Names
Before looking more closely at Eva, it will be convenient to consider an aspect of identity that carries a good deal of meaning in the novels: the naming of the characters. The importance of a person's name appears

perhaps most clearly in *The Little Girls,* where Clare distances herself from her failed marriage by reverting to her unmarried surname (LG 32), and Diana deliberately changes her name to Dinah rather than be called after 'that bristly goddess' (LG 52). In the climactic scene after their coffer has been found empty, the confusion in the minds of the women is reflected in the suppression of their names: though they are still occasionally 'Dinah', 'Clare', and 'Sheila', at times these names give way to general nouns (which are in fact used liberally throughout the novel): Sheila is now e.g. 'the hostess' (LG 161, 162, 168), 'the settee's owner' (LG 162), 'the speaker' (LG 163), 'the owner' of a large watercolour of the Old High Street in Southstone (LG 166); Dinah 'the late-comer' and 'the third of them' (LG 162), 'the culprit' (LG 164), 'the guest' (LG 169); Clare 'the magazine-addict' (LG 161) and 'the occupant of the settee' (LG 162). In thus being nameless, the women have now lost one of the foremost signs of their identity, just as they have lost their past because the coffer they buried as children is now empty. That we are meant to notice this non-naming is suggested by the mention of the names over the shops in the picture of the Old High Street, where one can 'read the right names over the right shops', as Dinah says (LG 166).

As 'little girls' the main characters use nicknames for each other: Dicey (Dinah), Mumbo (Clare), Sheikie (Sheila) – fitting names for them as adults, too; for Dinah is not always reliable or predictable, Clare is clumsy and has grown to almost elephantine proportions, and Sheila has much of the romance and secretiveness many like to associate with an eastern prince. It is notably Dinah and Clare who keep up this intimate naming habit as grown-ups – until, in the very last line of the book, Dinah finally faces the fact that they are no longer children and calls her friend 'Clare'. As a general rule I have used the nicknames when referring to the childhood scenes.

Naming often displays a considerable degree of irony. In *The Heat of the Day,* for instance, Stella's less than victorious husband, who dies just after their divorce, is called Victor. For a parallel example from a short story, one could instance the 'amorist' protagonist of 'Ivy Gripped the Steps', Gavin Doddington. Gavin or Gawain is the title figure of the 14th century poem *Sir Gawain and the Green Knight*, whose courtly mediaeval ambience is recalled in the text of Bowen's story by a remark from Gavin's mother: 'Why, Lilian has made quite a little page of you!' (CS 697); Gawain was the most perfect of King Arthur's knights and the very opposite of 'amorist'. Similarly, Constantine Ormeau in *Eva Trout* is hardly the most constant of men, nor is Professor Portman C Holman the most manly; and conversely, the most incorruptible figure and stern moral touchstone of the book, the Rev. Alaric Dancey, bears the name of the Goth leader who sacked Rome. Vesta Latterly in *A World of Love* has the name of the Roman goddess of hearth and home though she is the very opposite of a home-maker – she cannot keep her friends or her servants, she does not bother to introduce her guests, and she has in fact forgotten to invite a guest she is expecting; and the chaste Roman vestal virgins conjured up by this first name clash grotesquely with a surname that recalls D H Lawrence's *Lady Chatterly's Lover*, besides indicating that she has only lately become rich: 'She was *nouveau riche;* but, as Antonia said, better late than never' (WL 57). Some names are almost Dickensian in their inventiveness: the mercenary Sheila in *The Little Girls*, for instance, who judges pictures by their price, is Mrs Artworth; the sharp-witted cleaning lady in *Eva Trout,* who adapts her words to her surroundings just as a stoat changes colour winter and summer, is Mrs Stote; and it is a Mrs Caliber who brings Jeremy to Victoria Station in the same book and makes the grisly remark that 'a child likes to play gunman, it's only human nature' (ET 265). Some names are only mildly ironical, as that of the uxorious estate agent, Mr Denge, also in *Eva Trout,* who is inordinately proud of his town and is appropriately named from a Kentish locality, Denge Marsh; or that epitome of small-town respectablity and limited horizon, Mrs Tringsby in *The Heat of the Day*, whose name brings to mind the quiet Hertfordshire town of Tring.

There is a good deal of recycling in the names Bowen gave her characters. It seems worth noting that the counter-spy Harrison in *The Heat of the Day* and Harris, the chauffeur in *A World of Love* who wears 'Martian gauntlets' (WL 53), bear surnames reminiscent of a well-known nickname for the Devil, 'Old Harry': they are both, in a sense, emissaries from the Underworld. But from one novel or short story to another it is often difficult to see any connection between characters bearing the same name – between Roderick's guru-like friend Fred in *The Heat of the Day* and the down-to-earth Fred of *A World of Love*, for instance. Within the individual texts it is another matter: in *The*

Little Girls there is a significant contrast between Dinah's obnoxious house-boy Francis and her doleful neighbour Frank Wilkins, whose given name would presumably have been 'Francis'; in *The Heat of the Day*, it can be no coincidence that the idiosyncratic Irish landowner is called Francis Morris, for the familiar form of his name links up with the idea of being 'frank' that is central to that novel. There is an obvious pointer, too, in the fact that spy and counter-spy in *The Heat of the Day* are both called Robert, a name that associates phonetically with the name of Stella's son Roderick and their surname, Rodney.

Naming is closely linked to theme and subject-matter in Bowen's last novels in the case of Dinah's and Eva's family names, Piggott and Trout. Stuart Piggott was a well-known archaeologist some dozen years younger than Bowen; he was the author of several works on early civilizations,[1] and in *The Little Girls* the surname forms a running accompaniment to the plotline motif of digging up relics of the past. Eva Trout's surname chimes in with the many occurrences of the word 'fish' in *Eva Trout* to underline the theme of that 'slippery fish', identity. In *The Heat of the Day* Stella's surname, Rodney, is also interesting. Admiral Lord George Rodney (1718-1792) was next to Nelson England's most illustrious naval hero, whose name was much in people's minds in the Second World War on account of the battleship named after him.[2] Rodney is reputedly a 'nice rich English name', as a character in Virginia Woolf's *Night and Day* (1919) has it, and it is a subtle reminder of Stella's love for her country[3] that goes some way towards explaining her violent reaction to her lover's treason.

A character's role-playing is frequently signalled by a change of designation in the narrative voice; thus Sheila is regularly 'Mrs Artworth' when she is putting on airs and enacting her public persona, just as she was 'Miss Beaker' when she remembered to stand on her dignity as a child (LG 97, 102). Texts often veer between Christian names, full names, and titles plus surnames to reflect the presence or absence of narrative empathy, and to mirror both character relationships and the niceties of social behaviour. We are only a few pages into *The*

---

[1] E.g. *Neolithic Cultures of the British Isles* (1954).
[2] HMS Rodney played an active part in WWII, e. g. at the Sicilian and Normandy landings.
[3] I differ here from those critics who assume that Stella's family background is Anglo-Irish; I have found no indication that such connections are not solely her husband's.

Little Girls, for instance, when we are brought up sharp on hearing Dinah introduce her friend and neighbour – whom we by now already know as 'Frank' – as 'Major Wilkins': a subtle exercise of narrative control that without further comment confirms our initial point of view as being identical with Dinah's. In Bowen's last novel, a scene at the girls' school between Eva Trout and her teacher likewise needs no analysis by the narrative voice, for the fluctuations in their degree of intimacy are fully reflected in the alternating names: Miss Smith, Iseult, Iseult Smith. Roles are also reflected in the frequent use of personal nouns rather than names, which may not always be put down to a desire for 'elegant variation' or to a suggestion of loss of identity, as in the climactic scene in *The Little Girls* referred to above; in the parting scene between Mrs Piggott and Major Burkin-Jones in the same book, to take another example, Dicey is ostensibly outside the adults' conversation and is often referred to in the text as 'the child'.

Dress and Hair-style

In a lighter vein, 'being oneself' is a recurring phrase. In many contexts it often entails little more than a change of dress, sometimes carrying a load of irony – as when Stella says that her son is looking more like himself once he is out of uniform, though when she says it he is in fact wearing her lover's dressing-gown (HD 47). The way a person dresses is never unimportant; as one of Bowen's early characters puts it: 'One's clothes are part of what one has got to say'.[4] Accessories and jewelry are similar personality-markers; and even if we did not suspect that Cousin Nettie was probably in some sense the wisest and most level-headed of all the characters in *The Heat of the Day*, the fact that she wears an opal ring (HD 207) not only tells us of the bad luck that has dogged her life, but also confirms her role as clairvoyante and, we assume, a reliable source of family history.

Texts often remark on the suitability of what a person is wearing. Thus in *The Heat of the Day* we hear of Stella that 'her clothes fitted her body, her body her self, with a general air of attractiveness and ease' (HD 25). Frank Wilkins, too, in *The Little Girls,* suits his clothes, and his clothes suit him: 'this fortunate man not only liked his clothes but was liked by them' (LG 190). The minute attention to dress in this book

---

[4] Mrs Roche in 'Sunday Evening'. *Encounters*, 1923; CS 90.

means tailor-mades for the formidable business woman Clare and soft colours and soft fabrics for the mermaid-like Sheila, while the countrified lady-of-the-manor Dinah rarely wears anything more formal than slacks and a sweater. The novel carries identification by dress to comic lengths in its introduction of Clare and Sheila, who are referred to by the hats they are wearing:

> A big woman wearing a tight black turban, and on the lapel of her dark suit a striking brooch, sat down, with all but no hesitation, opposite a woman already there at the table ... Her hat was composed of pink roses.
> ... Black Turban, settling into her chair, bumped a leg of the table with her knee, whereat Pink Roses tittered. (LG 30)

At the opposite extreme, the message conveyed by the clothes worn by the chauffeur in *A World of Love* (including the 'Martian gauntlets' already mentioned) is positively sinister. On his first appearance he is in a 'disaster-dark' uniform (WL 53); the second time we see him he is wearing a 'sort of a compromise get-up, dark coat, groom's breeches' (WL 138) reminiscent of the dark green tunics and khaki trousers of the notorious Black and Tans that terrorised the country during Ireland's War of Independence 1919-1921.

Change of style in dress is a useful indication of character development. In the beginning of *Eva Trout*, Eva with supreme lack of taste sports a Robin Hood hat and an ocelot coat, and bright scarlet stockings (ET 29, 74); her transformation in the second half of the book is suggested immediately by her elegant grey flannnel suit. Anticipated in complimentary remarks by other characters, the going-away scene at Victoria shows a total metamorphosis from the ugly duckling of the first chapters:

> There stood Eva.
> Not far off, in one of those chance islands of space, she stood tall as a candle,[5] some accident of the light rendering her luminous from top to toe – in a pale suit, elongated by the elegance of its narrowness, and turned-back little hat of the same no-colour; no flowers, but on the lapel of the jacket a spraying-out subcontinent of diamonds: a great brooch. A soft further glow

---

[5] It is tempting to see in this image an echo of W B Yeats' Cathleen ni Houlihan in 'Red Hanrahan's Song about Ireland' (1894): 'But purer than a tall candle before the Holy Rood / Is Cathleen, the daughter of Houlihan'. *Collected Poems*, 90.

had been tinted on to her face; her eyes were increased by the now mothy dusk of their lashes. (ET 261-262)

As with Eva, a change of dress often means a change of personal or sexual identity; in *A World of Love*, for instance, the adolescent Jane comes to womanhood on the day she puts on a new striped blazer. Iseult's transformation into a Bohemian in *Eva Trout* is also reflected in her dress. As a teacher, in the first chapters of the book, she wears a dark nun-like suit (ET 58); later, meeting Eva in Dickens' house in Broadstairs, her new dress is provocatively feminine: 'pinkish, diaphanous as the day demanded, becoming to the young woman she still was.... The garb of a votaress, with a touch of the ball gown' (ET 113). Her later Bohemian disguise includes a new hairstyle (for one's hair is also part of what one has to say, to misquote Bowen): when she makes off with Jeremy she has a deep fringe and looks like a Zola harlot; at the end of the book she is ostensibly the respectable Mrs Arble again and wears her hair off the forehead with a little-girlish Alice band – ironically, in view of her blatant lack of innocence.

On a different level, having one's hair cut takes on ritual significance in *A World of Love* when Lilia's shorter hair signals that she has finally broken with the past and is free to accept her husband without the image of her dead fiancé coming between them. Lilia's decision to have her hair cut becomes particularly significant from having been taken in the pivotal night when Jane comes home late from the castle dinner and Antonia communes with the spirit of Guy in the landscape. Her visit to the hairdresser's gets a good deal of emphasis by occasioning an outing to the village of Clonmore that takes up nearly a whole chapter, and incidentally includes a good deal of social comedy.

In Search of Identity
In *The Heat of the Day* Stella sees, on the table at Mount Morris, her gloves 'shaped by her hands', and her handbag 'containing every damning proof of her identity' (HD 164). What 'proof of her identity' can the bag hold? Name and address, place of work, passport, tickets, keys, identity card; enough to identify her in case of accidents, yes. Powder compact, lipstick, handkerchief, loose change, cheque-book perhaps – together with the bag itself and her gloves, enough to suggest her femininity, her elegance, her expensive taste, her economic standing. But will there be anything to show what kind of woman she is, how

gentle, how hesitant, how unwilling to ask too many questions? Or that her divorced husband is dead, her son in the Army, the flat she lives in full of somebody else's furniture, her lover suspected of treason? Of this kind of identity a handbag can surely say very little.

When Stella takes a lamp in the darkened drawing room to study in a mirror 'the romantic face that was still hers' she becomes for a moment 'the lady of the house, with a smile moulded against the drapery of darkness. She wore the look of everything she had lost the secret of being' (HD 173-174). This would seem to mean that she has lost all power of decision and authority normally associated with a 'lady of the house'; and that she is groping for her identity, as the text has it two or three pages later, is palpably one way of saying that she is seeking the resolution to confront her lover with Harrison's allegations.[6] The Irish intermezzo serves largely to give substance to those allegations, confirming them for her in confirming that Harrison has in fact been to Mount Morris and that he is, in all probability, what he makes a show of being.

Stella's uncertainties are echoed in the subplot in the character of the working-class Louie, who gratefully and uncritically accepts the variety of identities offered by the popular press; as an illustration of the confusion attaching to the notion of 'identity', this can hardly be bettered (it is also a good example of that fondness for agent nouns which is apparent even in Bowen's last novel):

> Was she not a worker, a soldier's lonely wife, a war orphan, a pedestrian, a Londoner, a home- and animal-lover, a thinking democrat, a movie-goer, a woman of Britain, a letter writer, a fuel-saver, and a housewife? She was only not a mother, a knitter, a gardener, a foot-sufferer or a sweetheart – at least not rightly. (HD 152)

In *Eva Trout*, it is, at least in Eva's own view, the frustration of her attempt to form a personal identity for herself that is behind her deep disappointment at her teacher's defection. We owe some of this understanding to the Inquisitor-like but less than percipient Father Clavering-Haight, who extracts the following confession from Eva:

---

[6] At Mount Morris Stella wakes in the morning not knowing where she is, or what time it is: 'Her watch told her the hour, but then so did instinct – what she was forced to grope for, as though for her identity, was the day of the week, the month of the year, the year' (HD 176).

'What *did* she do?'

'She desisted from teaching me. She abandoned my mind. She betrayed my hopes, having led them on. She pretended love, to make me show myself to her – then, thinking she saw all, turned away. She –'

' – Wait a minute: what were your hopes?'

'To learn,' said Eva. A long-ago tremble shook her. 'To be, to become – I had never been.' She added: 'I was *beginning* to be.'

He remarked, with enthusiasm: 'A gifted teacher.'

'Yes. Then she sent me back.'

'Sent you away?'

'No; sent me back again – to be nothing.' (ET 184-185)

Some pages later, speculating whether it really is her former teacher who suddenly has rung her up after eight years (here is the question of identity as identification), Eva plunges into the reflections referred to above about that 'slippery fish', identity, and makes an excursion to the National Portrait Gallery to try to find an answer. She is disappointed by the faces she sees, but the visit does at least set her mind at rest on one point: 'there is no hope of keeping a check on people; you cannot know what they do, or why they do it'.

> No, no getting through to them. They were on show only. Lordlily suffering themselves to be portrayed, they'd presented a cool core of resistance even to the most penetrating artist. The most martial extroverts, even, nursed their mysteries. Each was his own affair, and he let you know it. Nothing was to be learned from them.... In so far as they had an effect on the would-be student, it was a malign one: every soul Eva knew became no longer anything but a Portrait. There was no 'real life'; no life was more real than this. This she had long suspected. She now was certain. (ET 195-196)

These reflections would seem to be in line with the fact that Eva's own features are not described, and in the Chicago coffee-shop it is not her face but her hand lying on the table, as it lay on Elsinore's bed in their childhood, that makes Eva recognizable to her early room-mate. It is generally the male characters who come in for detailed facial description: Eric Arble, Constantine Ormeau, Clavering-Haight, Jeremy, and Mr Anapoupolis in Chicago; Constantine's inscrutable 'shadowless face' in particular claims a good deal of attention, here in a striking tour de force:

> The blond, massaged-looking flesh of Constantine's face seemed, like alabaster or indeed plastic, not quite opaque, having a pinkish underglow....

> Now and then some few creases came into being, to supply their owner with such degree of expression as at that particular moment he chose to grant himself – or occasionally (though this was rarer) there was a calculated levitation of the eyebrows. Anything of that sort was, though, almost instantly wiped away.
>   Colour entered the picture, though used sparingly. Lips, for instance, were the naive fawn-pink of lips in a tinted drawing. Less perceptibly pencilled-in were the eyebrows, lashes, the exhausted pencil employed being gold-red. And the same tone reappeared in the hair; well-nourished, though back from the forehead. And the eyes? These too were in the convention: a water-colourist's grey-blue. If they glinted beneath their lids, this appeared phenomenal. They were to see with, chiefly. (ET 36)

In contrast to the mocking tone of these last lines, eyes are used in *The Heat of the Day* seemingly without irony as character markers. Thus the fact that Robert Kelway's would-be dominant father insisted so much on his son seeing him in the eye is responsible, Robert himself explains, for the fact that he himself seldom looks into Stella's eyes (as ever, he has a neat explanation for his own deviousness). In the same book, the uneven set of Harrison's eyes and his way of 'using both eyes at the same time', in Stella's words (HD 101), mark him out clearly as a spy (Bowen gives a hilarious take-off on this character of hers in the secret agent *manqué* Francis in *The Little Girls*, who has not a squint but a cast, 'one eye stay[ing] riveted to his profile, leaving the other to dart where it would' [LG 24]). It goes for many of the characters, however, that their stance and movements are more revealing than their faces. In *Eva Trout*, Eva herself is first pictured ungracefully straddling with her hands behind her back; as the book progresses attention is more often drawn to her upright carriage: she stands 'like a ramrod' (ET 148), 'tall as a candle' (ET 261-262), which we may see as an indication of her fundamentally upright nature. Conversely, Henry's uncertain attitude to life in general and love in particular is captured in his habit of balancing on one foot, and he characteristically weaves his way through the crowds at Victoria Station rather like a dancer (ET 259; cf. his surname, Dancey).

Sexual Identity
Woman-to-woman relationship as an early motif in Bowen's fiction was pointed out already in 1975 by Jane Rule, who remarked that 'it was not until late in her career, after the death of her husband, that Elizabeth Bowen returned to a concern for relationships between women' (115).

This statement has been modified and elaborated by more recent feminist criticism: Patricia Coughlan has pointed out, for example, that in *The Heat of the Day* Louie's admiration for Stella certainly has sexual overtones (121). And there can be little doubt that sexuality colours the friendship between Louie and Connie, who are both promiscuously fond of men yet share a bed (though Connie has her doubts about this being 'healthy' [HD 242]), and who have met one another in that sexually suggestive location, a staircase – in a cascade of tumbling vegetables, no less. Male homosexuality runs through the novel in numerous instances of the adjective 'queer', which is frequently used by one character about another, along with 'funny', in a naïvely non-sexual sense that leaves the reader with a strong suspicion that the narrator is speaking with her tongue in her cheek. In *A World of Love* there is an undertone of sexual attraction between Jane and Antonia that lasts until the end of the book, when Jane simultaneously frees herself from the domination of the long-dead Guy and that of his living counterpart, Antonia. Nevertheless, it is not until Bowen's last two novels that unconventional feminine sexuality comes into the open as a central issue. 'Mumbo, are you a Lesbian?' asks Dinah in *The Little Girls* (LG 197), and Eva Trout is asked whether she is a hermaphrodite (ET 51); characteristically, Clare does not answer the question, and Eva does not know, or perhaps does not understand the word.

The Little Girls
Of course Clare does not answer Dinah; she is accustomed to hiding her feelings, and also to actually hiding away. We recall that even as a child she lies on the ground 'in what felt like hiding' when she is making up the secret language for their coffer (LG 112), and she sits in the dark attic box-room rather than go down for a candle, for 'downstairs was all party voices and, worse, laughter' (LG 115). She dresses unobtrusively and finds the striking brooch she has put on to meet Sheila not really her style – 'too much of an eye-catcher' (LG 30). Towards the end of the book, her words and actions leave little doubt about her unarticulated same-sex leanings: it is after Dinah has asked her openly whether she is a lesbian that Clare, having scolded Dinah for always running for cover, herself 'runs away' by declining to spend the night at her house. This behaviour is noted by Patricia Juliana Smith as a narrative manifestation of lesbian panic. Clare's action precipitates Dinah's breakdown: a few hours after Clare has left, Dinah is found

unconscious with a bruise on her forehead, perhaps, as Smith suggests, 'the result of striking her head against the wall in her frustration and shame' (2).

Clare apparently regrets her angry departure very soon, for she telephones the house in the early hours of the morning and sends for Sheila to nurse their friend. Later she herself slips into the room where Dinah is sleeping; she looks at the china she used to love that belonged to Dinah's mother, whom she adored as a child, and love thus receives our full attention on this final page:

> Clare turned round and, facing the chimneypiece, dared again to look into the world of china. Shepherds and shepherdesses branched towards one another their mended arms; beautiful bowls stayed cradled within their network of cracks; stitches held obstinately together what had been broken; handles maintained their hold on cups by grasping with tiny alloy claws. She was looking into a fragile representation of a world of honour, which was to say unfailingness.
> ... She looked with longing at the everlasting seashores, mountain peaks, bays and lakes, even at the castles, on the frail rounded sides of the cups and bowls. Never had she found them anywhere else. She had loved them because they were not for her. (LG 236)

Deciding to leave, Clare thinks of the goodbye she never said to Dinah as a child after the birthday picnic on the beach all those years earlier:

> Turning to go, she thought of her last sight of the sands, from the seawall: the wide sands and the running figure.
> 'Good-bye, Dicey,' she said – for now and for then.
> The sleeper stirred. She sighed. She raised herself on an elbow, saying: 'Who's there?'
> 'Mumbo.'
> 'Not Mumbo. Clare. Clare, where have you been?' (LG 236-237)

Looking back on the whole novel from the vantage point of this closing scene, the theme of love between women appears as a constant undercurrent under the light-hearted comedy of the plot. Dinah's question in the very last words of the novel, 'Clare, where have you been?', gives the book an emphatically open closure. This last exchange between Dinah and Clare has been interpreted by Jane Rule as suggesting that they will now 'deal with the relationship the one has longed for, the other longed for but dreaded' (121). In Patricia Juliana

Smith's reading, Clare, by calling herself 'Mumbo', harks back to their childhood friendship and abrupt parting; Dinah on the other hand uses her real name to invite that friendship to continue:

> Dinah's repudiation of the childish nickname and her enunciation of the adult name indicate an acceptance of Clare's unspoken apology and a forgiveness for the offenses of the both distant and recent past, just as the final question invites the presence of one long absent. (112-113)

It bears noting, too, that earlier that day Dinah goes to take a bath and thus prepares herself to enter a new life, 'garbing herself' in her yellow dressing-gown (the wording suggesting the formality of a ritual; LG 208).

Eva Trout

The sexuality of the heroine receives a good deal of limelight in Bowen's last novel. When the book opens Eva is 24 and sexually still ambivalent. Before this, at her two schools, she has certainly felt love for members of her own sex. At the castle school she rooms with the neurotic Elsinore, who has tried to drown herself in the lake because she has been parted from the Japanese butler's son, and since gone into a coma; Eva is never happier than when they are alone together in their turret room:

> What made Eva visualize this as a marriage chamber? As its climate intensified, all grew tender. To repose a hand on the blanket covering Elsinore was to know in the palm of the hand a primitive tremor – imagining the beating of that other heart, she had a passionately solicitous sense of this other presence. Nothing forbad love. This deathly yet living stillness, together, of two beings, this unapartness, came to be the requital of all longing. An endless feeling of destiny filled the room. (ET 56)

She recalls this situation when she meets Elsinore again several years later:

> *The tower room in the castle, the piteous breathing. The blinded window, the banished lake. The dayless and nightless watches, the tent of cobwebs. The hand on the blanket, the beseeching answering beating heart. The dark: the unseen distance, the known nearness. Love: the here and the now and the nothing-but. The step on the stairs. Don't take her away, DON'T take her away. She is all I am. We are all there is.* (ET 133; original italics and emphasis)[7]

---

[7] Coughlan points to the phrase 'She is all I am' as a 'striking expression of Lesbian love as identification' (126).

After the castle school has folded and Eva is allowed to go to an ordinary girls' school, she becomes devoted to one of her mistresses, Iseult Smith, who takes an interest in her and wants to improve the way she speaks. Nothing comes of this project, but the girl is dazed by gratitude that someone has actually shown her 'an attention which could seem to be love' (ET 17). The natural world is used with unequivocally erotic overtones to render Eva's awakening sexuality:

> She saw (she thought) the aurora borealis. Love like a great moth circled her bed, then settled. Air came to her from hayfields where, not alone, she had walked in a trance, or the smell of the rushy and minty and earthy wetness of moments at the fringe of the stream returned. The silence of buildings and of the garden was now and then disturbed by a sigh. (ET 63)

Looking back many years later, Eva sees things in a less romantic light, and it is clear to the reader, at this point if not before, that she is justified in feeling 'betrayed'. Thinking back to Chapter I, 5, 'Two Schools', we can see how the emotionally deprived Eva has been overwhelmed by the interest her teacher has taken in her, and we note that the narcissistic Iseult Smith was not unaware of what was going on. Two scenes at the school stand out. The first is suggestively in a showery late spring: Eva meets Iseult Smith coming across the lawn and sees her against the sun, like a vision in her yellow oilskin; in what is difficult to see as other than an invitation to intimacy, the teacher asks her pupil to help her out of the suffocating oilskin. In the library Iseult Smith encourages Eva to start reading:

> The girl took out a lovely morocco volume and nursed it, looking upon it sorrowfully. She said nothing.
> 'If you were read aloud to? Stories, at the beginning? Poetry? Shall we see what happens?'
> 'Miss Smith ...?'
> 'I think we should try, don't you?'
> 'Miss Smith ... how can you be so good to me?'
> Then a girl came in. This first manifestation took place at five ten in the evening, by the library clock. (ET 61; original ellipses)

Having withheld her sympathy by the use of the word 'manifestation' proper to spiritualist jargon and the pseudo-scientifically precise noting of time, the narrator elaborates on the scene, explaining Iseult Smith as a young teacher in a 'state of grace' who realizes her powers and is not yet aware how dangerous they can be:

About Iseult Smith, up to the time she encountered Eva and, though discontinuously, for some time after, there was something of Nature before the Fall. There was not yet harm in Iseult Smith – what first implanted it? Of Eva she was to ponder, later: 'She did not know what I was doing; but did I?' (ET 61)

The second climactic scene takes place in Iseult Smith's room a couple of months later. It is an embarrassing confrontation, where Eva asks her teacher why she cares for her and tries to extract from her a promise that her happiness will last, having poured out her subconscious love by reciting some Metaphysical verses she has learnt by heart.[8] The intimacy of the situation is reflected in the narrator's 'Miss Smith' becoming briefly 'Iseult', only to revert again to 'Miss Smith' after Eva's recitation when the teacher is aware that she has gone too far, and ending with the non-committal 'Iseult Smith' (ET 64-67). The chestnut trees outside the window are no longer in flower when her pupil leaves the room, and only the vulnerable Eva cannot see that this interlude of heightened emotion will not last.

It will be natural to bring in here a later scene between Eva and her teacher – later in plotline, for it takes place not long after Eva has turned 25, and later also vis-à-vis the reader, for it occurs almost half-way through the book, as the chapter called 'A Summer's Day'. Eva and Iseult are meeting for the first time since she has left the Arbles' home. The venue has been chosen by Iseult, with her characteristic sense of the theatre: Charles Dickens' house in Broadstairs, 'Bleak House', perched high over the town with a view over the sea. Looking her best (and knowing it), Iseult seems all set for conquest in a seductive, 'diaphanous' pinkish dress (ET 113). She is profuse in her thanks for the money gift Eva has sent her; but she is too eager to probe into the motives behind the generosity of her former pupil, who remains stolidly impervious to her teacher's blandishments. Eva has the upper hand throughout the chapter, most emphatically when the scene has changed to her own house further along the coast and she as good as tells Iseult, in a supremely ambiguous curtain-line, that her husband Eric has fathered the child she herself is going to have:

---

[8] The verses in question are from 'Euen-song' by George Herbert (1593-1633). *The Works of George Herbert*, 203.

A present-day information leaflet from the Bleak House Museum in Broadstairs shows Dickens' house standing high above the roofs of the town. The crenellations and west (left-hand) extension were added after Dickens' day, but they were there when Eva Trout met up with her former teacher Iseult Smith at the house in *Eva Trout*. In the text much is made of Iseult's commonplace, not to say kitschy, musings in the room called 'the study' with its 'lantern window' which, 'seemingly large out of all proportion, hung out into the air, straight over the sea but for a tiny apron of garden, and was filled inside by a platform on which table and chair stood – an arrangement, surely, very precarious, should the man, excited, suddenly shove his chair back?' (ET 110-111). A rope is tied across the chair, but Eva makes no secret of having sat in it; she was never one to respect petty regulations.

Reproduced by kind permission of the Bleak House Museum.

'Couldn't you possibly come to us for Christmas? ... even Christmas seems very far ahead, far too far ahead for Eric. Why, if you do come then, it will have been seven – no, eight, nine? – months since he's seen you. A long time.'
  'Nine,' said Eva, looking up at the evergreen.
  'Then at least, Christmas?'
  'Christmas is in December?'
  'It is usually. – Why? Is there anything else you think of doing?'
  'In December I shall be having a little child.' (ET 121)

Moving on to the end of the story, we note that it is Iseult who provides the weapon that is used to kill Eva. She has already bought a toy gun for Jeremy, and she significantly fails to get the real gun from him when he appears at Victoria Station flourishing it. 'Eva Trout ... inspires many forms of panic in others,' comments Patricia Juliana Smith; 'in her former teacher, later the unhappily married Mrs Arble, she evokes a particularly lethal manifestation of lesbian panic' (114).

We are given an outsider's view of Eva's rather overwhelming presence as a young adult when she flies to America, in a letter from one of her fellow-passengers, the voluble, apparently besotted professor Portman C Holman. Eva is characteristically silent, even secretive, about her personal life, and the good professor is thrown back on his own (wildly imaginative) resources when it comes to picturing her parents and supposed husband. The question of identification bothers him – who *is* this woman so obviously unimpressed by air travel but unaccustomed to flying Economy class? – and his speculations form a salutary corrective to any tendency to judge by appearances and first impressions. We who have seen the neglected state of the house Eva has leased on North Foreland will know how to interpret the professor's transports:

> Your home by the sea. It seemed to me I visited its calm great rooms with their elemental outlook, 'opening on the foam of perilous seas –'. Other though my subject is, my resort and irrational sustenance has been poetry; under its influence I perceived your echoing oaken gallery, your traditional kitchen, your garden leafy and green through every season.... I identified with your cycling trips, your work on your shell museum (do you project a catalogue?), your marketing in that ancient seaport. (ET 126)

This letter says quite a lot about the immediate impression Eva creates. In the present context it is interesting not least for the light it throws on her sexuality, for it tells us that she is wearing a signet ring, 'I should say a male one', hazards Professor Holman (ET 127).

Of the mature Eva's love for Henry Dancey the reader is never in doubt. The 'fervour' she seems to reserve for him already as a child (ET 14) is picked up in the second half of the book, e.g. in the way she looks 'with fervour, with passion almost' at a mobile in Henry's room rather than admit to him then that she is in love with him (ET 180). The large part he and his letters play in the last section of the book reflects the large part he plays in Eva's thoughts. During their trip to the castle she lays bare her feelings for him and in effect proposes marriage, and it is when he refuses that she suggests the mock wedding departure that ends the book (in the event Henry admits his love for her by declaring that he does not intend to get off their train again after all). The scene at the castle is in many ways idyllic and might have prefigured some kind of harmony for their future relationship, were it not for the 'Millais wild roses' at the edge of the larch plantation, which I have referred to earlier. The name of the painter Millais alone brings an air of art or artifice into the scene – the roses even stand out 'as though painted' (ET 233) – and to those who are familiar with his painting of the drowning Ophelia, the roses in Bowen's text introduce a positive air of doom: for there is a bush of wild roses at the river's edge in Millais' picture, and we may thus link the Millais-rose reference to Eva's ill-fated schoolmate Elsinore, who tried to drown herself and was in fact called 'Ophelia's illegit' by one of her fellow pupils.

The full-blooded Eric Arble is something of an anomaly in *Eva Trout*, where so many characters are either homosexual (Constantine Ormeau, his friend Kenneth 'of the unclouded brow and Parthenon torso' [ET 48], Father Clavering-Haight) or bisexual (Willy Trout) or ambivalent (Henry). Coughlan finds the homosexual characters treated 'with a conspicuous hostility' in *Eva Trout*, and holds that Bowen presents them as either either 'parasitic' or 'deluded' (113). Though it is difficult to disagree entirely with this latter judgement, surely the failed marriages in the book show heterosexual love as no desirable alternative: Eva's parents, Elsinore's parents, the Arbles – they all split up; the marriages we glimpse in the Chicago scenes are mere shells, and Eva's own wedding departure is in intention not much better than her early fantasy honeymoon. And if Constantine and Clavering-Haight and Trout senior are negative portraits, what are we to say of the aggressively heterosexual Eric Arble? Setting aside the marriage of the hen-pecked estate agent Mr Denge, which we can only guess at, and the childless marriage-partnership of the French Doctor Bonnard and his wife, the most stable union in the book is that of Henry's parents; we never see them together, however, and though Mr Dancey seems devoted to 'my wife' (ET 154, 160) we hear no details of their relationship beyond the fact that they have four children; given the general fogginess of Mrs Dancey's thoughts, it is difficult to see this as a marriage of true minds.

Double or doubtful sexuality is in the air throughout the novel, from the unisex berets and overcoats the children wear in the beginning to what Henry calls a 'bi-sexual' cricket match towards the end – 'Mixed', his sister corrects him, 'sex does not enter into cricket' (ET 246-247).

There is also Henry's Cambridge friendship with the androgynously named Jocelyn who leaves 'gracefully' after tea (ET 179); and, not least, there is the recurrent word-play on Eva's surname: fish, fishy, kettle of fish, fish-kettle, kingfisher, etc., which emphasizes the central image of that 'slippery fish', identity, and recalls a popular belief generalizing an observation of Aristotle's, that some fish were bi-sexual.[9]

I have already pointed to an erotically evocative landscape in *Eva Trout* and mentioned the sexual implications of the staircase on which Louie and Connie meet in *The Heat of the Day*. To this last example it will be relevant to add the curious structure of the vicarage in *Eva Trout*, whose 'ill-lit staircase climbed up a shaft in the middle' (ET 27). According to the narrative voice, it is to get away from his noisy home life that Mr Dancey has his study at the top of these stairs (ET 27); his association with stairs is repeated on a later occasion (ET 154).

Sex by Default

Though sexual attraction is an important element in all the four novels I am looking at (and in the short stories 'Ivy Gripped the Steps' and 'A Day in the Dark'), actual descriptions of the sexual act are conspicuously absent. This is perhaps not surprising, considering the general reticence on such matters at the time of writing, and considering also that Bowen found life 'with the lid on' quite as interesting as life 'with the lid off'.[10] On this urbane background, other kinds of intimate physical detail stand out with unusual force, e.g. Roderick in *The Heat of the Day* examining his bare foot – 'I say!' he shouts 'I've got a corn!' (HD 52) – and Connie scratching her armpit (HD 247). In *A World of Love* there is Lilia cutting her toenails (WL 124) and Antonia digging wax out of an ear (WL 106) or dislodging a gooseberry pip from her lower teeth with a thumb-nail (WL 42), in *The Little Girls* Clare splitting a nail to below the quick in trying to untie the knot of Dinah's cave (LG 219). The convulsive yawns of some of the characters also belong here: Eric Arble in *Eva Trout*, for instance, is 'rent by a cavernous groaning yawn, which finished its way through him in a string of shudders' (ET 97), and

---

[9] Aristotle in *Historia Animalium* IV. xi. 538a.
[10] Bowen used this expression about Jane Austen: 'The constraints of polite behaviour serve only to store up her characters' energies; she dispels, except for the very stupid, the fallacy that life with the lid off – in thieves' kitchens, prisons, taverns and brothels – is necessarily more interesting than life with the lid on.' 'English Novelists' in *Impressions of English Literature*, 246.

after he and Constantine have left Cathay Eva herself yawns 'so dismissive a yawn that it distended her ribcage to cracking-point, just not dislocating her jaw by the grace of heaven' (ET 109). These examples may simply be reminders of the vulnerability of the flesh – which they are, of course, but one may also see them as a kind of sublimation of the sexual instinct; or perhaps one should say, rather, that the reader's attention is directed to sex by default, much as the sexual pointer would seem unmistakable in the insistence on re-used handkerchiefs and re-wadded Kleenexes in *Eva Trout*. It can be no coincidence that it is the father of four, Mr Dancey, who is afflicted with hay-fever and common colds, and thus associated with bodily secretions; and the used paper handkerchiefs stuffed unceremoniously down the couch in the vicarage form a marked contrast to the snowy handkerchief – monogrammed, like Constantine Ormeau's – that the effete, homosexual Father Clavering-Haight uses to wipe his fingers.

* * *

Bowen's interest in identity, especially women's identity, is apparent throughout her writing, and in the novels under consideration all the female protagonists pass, or have passed, through some crisis revolving on their personal identity: Stella faced with her lover's defection (*The Heat of the Day*); Jane breaking away from the dominance of Antonia along with that of Guy (*A World of Love*); Sheila disappointed in her dreams of becoming a dancer, Clare carving out an independent life of her own, Dinah losing her sense of security when she sees the empty coffer as a sign that her past life has 'run away' (*The Little Girls*); and the heart-broken Eva Trout, who feels that her teacher has betrayed her by sending her back 'to be nothing' (ET 185). Male characters do not in fact come off much better: Robert Kelway submerges himself in an alien cause that gives him the confidence his father bred out of him, while the colourless Harrison's only identity is that of a spy (*The Heat of the Day*); Frank Wilkins' mournful identity amounts to little more than a military title, vegetable gardening, a fondness for playing old gramophone records, and an obsessive fear of the future (*The Little Girls*); Eric Arble becomes not the authoritative Army officer he might have been, or even a successful independent fruit farmer, but an employed garage mechanic; and what the shilly-shallying Henry Dancey is destined to become is anyone's guess (*Eva Trout*).

In all Bowen's post-war writings the existential question of what kind of life to make for oneself seems at first glance to be solved most convincingly by Stella's son, the 'tranquil' Roderick. His relationship with his mother and his role in the novel are both bound up with the notion of identity. On leave from the Army, for instance, we hear from the narrator that he gradually sheds his soldierly bearing and lack of spontaneity by watching Stella 'until, by an imitation of her attitudes he supplied himself with some way to behave, look, stand – even, you might say, *be*.... He searched in Stella for some identity left by him in her keeping' (HD 48). Later remarks of his own may be read along similarly existential lines: feeling that something should be said about her lover's death, he asks his mother: 'But by me? Why me? After all, who am I?'(HD 299), and he seems almost unduly pleased to be taken seriously: 'You do really think I am a person?' (HD 300). Yet the confidence with which Roderick makes plans for fulfilling his future identity as landowner on the Irish estate he inherits is without any suggestion of the ambivalence and precariousness inherent in such a position, aspects that Bowen had brought into *The Last September* (1929) and was to treat again in *A World of Love* (1955). The Irish scenes in *The Heat of the Day*, notably the happy feudal relationship between the Rodneys (Stella and Roderick) and the domestic servants at Mount Morris (the cliché old family retainer and his submissive daughters), put such a gloss on historical realities that they leave the reader with serious doubts about the authenticity of such an identity. We may be more confident, I think, in the future of the unglamorous, illegitimate Fred Danby. His life has been blighted for nearly twenty years by his wife's memory of her dead fiancé, for which he has compensated by throwing himself into physically strenuous work, but at the end of *A World of Love* he comes into his own as husband as well as father and master.

CHAPTER 5

Communication

In looking at how Bowen lets her characters convey their meaning to one another, I use 'communication' to embrace all exchanges that may establish or reflect a relationship between people, ranging from the serious interchange of ideas to the most casual snippets of conversation, and including also the deliberate absence of verbal expression: the eloquence of silent response.

The limitations of speech were a recurrent concern of Bowen's, culminating in her last novel with Eva Trout's obsession with communication devices and her adoption of the deaf-mute child who shoots her dead on the last page of the book. Other forms of communication besides speech also figure prominently in her fiction – letters and telegrams, for instance. Letters are of course supreme examples of imperfect communication when they do not reach their destination, as happens in *Eva Trout* to Professor Holman's long effusion (ET 129), and to a letter from Henry to Eva which she never gets because she has moved on, leaving no forwarding address: 'In the rack of the cross-eyed Paris [hotel], therefore, the letter probably is still, more flyblown with each day' (ET 214). Communication by letter receives an added twist in *A World of Love*, which centers on an old packet of love letters to an unknown woman that has repercussions on the lives of all the main characters. A quite different kind of communication is at the root of *The Little Girls*, where objects are buried in order to say something about their owners to future generations. In *Eva Trout* the way Eva communicates with her deaf-mute son is another thing altogether: 'extrasensory' (ET 158; see pp. 77-78 below).

That the one-way communication of writing is by nature imperfect and open to interpretation may be illustrated by the following seemingly pointless piece of dialogue in *The Heat of the Day*; reading the will whereby his distant cousin Francis Morris has left him his estate, Stella's son, Roderick, uses 'mean'/'meant' seven times in half a page:

> 'Which *did* Cousin Francis mean?'
>   'Which what, darling?'
>   'Did he mean, care in my own way, or, carry on the old tradition in my own way?'
>   Uncomprehending, Stella returned her eyes to the cropped top of Roderick's downbent head. 'In the end, I suppose,' she hazarded, 'it would come to the same thing?'
>   'I'm not asking what it would come to; I want to know what he meant.'
>   'I know. But the first thing is that you'll really have to decide –'
>   'What should I decide? He's decided. It's become mine.'
>   'We must think what you're going to do.'
>   'But I want to know which he meant. Does he mean, that I'm free to care in any way I like, so long as it's *the* tradition I carry on; or, that so long as I care in the same way he did, I'm free to mean by "tradition" anything I like?'
>   'There was another cousin of yours, Roderick, a Colonel Pole, at the funeral, who said –'
>   'Yes, mother, yes; but never mind Colonel Pole. What we must make out is, what Cousin Francis meant.' (HD 87-88)

That 'mean' should attract so much attention in *The Heat of the Day* is consistent with the novel's preoccupation with the corrosive influence of wartime propaganda and the restrictions on free speech. But faulty understanding dogs much communication in all the novels, and 'mean' does heavy duty in numerous spoken exchanges between characters who fail to understand one another, often in quite banal contexts: 'What do you mean?' – 'I mean to say' – 'What I mean, though' – 'You mean ...?' – 'I do wish I had said nothing ... From now on I shall. I mean I shall not.' The failure of the speakers to convey their meaning is usually resolved on the spot, in the course of conversation. Some misunderstandings have the air of serving merely to introduce a note of humour into the text, but the explanation involved may also serve the purpose of drawing attention to the subject; this happens e.g. in *A World of Love* when Lilia is explaining to Fred that she had not expected it to be him she saw in the garden:

> 'You know *I* was never one to imagine; and who was I to imagine it could be you? As we now are, anything seemed more likely. Guy seemed more

likely, dead as he is.'
'What d'you mean,' he said, '"as we now are"?'
'You know you know. What's the use of asking?'
He gave a frown.
She put her hands to her face and added: 'As we have come to be.'
(WL 102)

In the two-way intercourse of conversation, listening is of course as important as speaking, and several of Bowen's characters complain, like Louie in *The Heat of the Day*, 'Oh, you never listen to what I say' (HD 322). Yet in spite of possible inattention and misunderstandings, face-to-face conversation would still seem to be the best means of communication between people (and there are many passages of dialogue in Bowen's fiction). In *The Heat of the Day* the importance of conversation is pointed up, again by some clowning on the part of young Roderick, when he finds what Stella dismisses as 'notes on some conversation' in the pocket of her lover's dressing-gown, and this triggers off the following outburst from her son:

'Really, Mother ... conversations are the leading things in this war! Even I know that. Everything you and I have to do is the result of something that's been said. How far do you think we'd get without conversations? And can you really suppose that someone where Robert is doesn't have conversations *about* conversations, even if he doesn't have conversations himself?' (HD 63)

We may note in passing a wry comment on what counts as conversation between the sub-plot's Louie and Connie, by way of a comparison with the presumably more lofty exchanges in government circles at 10, Downing Street; the girls live at 10, Chilcombe Street, and their bickerings are called 'conversations at No. 10' (HD 153).

Telephones as Metaphors of Non-Communication
One of Bowen's most common metaphors of imperfect communication is the telephone; an obvious choice, perhaps, since one cannot see the person one is talking to. (There are of course no telephones in the Irish Big Houses, Mount Morris in *The Heat of the Day* and Montefort in *A World of Love,* where people communicate with one another more ideally, face to face).

In the novels I am considering there are not so very many full telephone conversations where we can hear both voices speaking. Exceptions include Eva's more than shady contact concerning the illegal adoption of her child in *Eva Trout*. In the same book there is also a revealing telephone conversation between her and Mme Bonnard; it is good to have this conversation in full, for it says not a little about the now chilly relations between the two women. Most telephone calls are one-sided, however. *The Little Girls* has a full-page take-off on a telephone conversation which should rightly be between three people (wishful thinking at the time the novel was written); the speaker's words to the character who cannot hear the other end of the line are given in parentheses:

> Oh, *Sheikie*, hullo! ... Why yes, of course I am me! (She knew my voice) ... I was just telling Mumbo, you knew my voice ... Yes, of course she is here. Or rather, I am with her ... In a Mopsie Pye shop ... A garden of all delights. (She wants to know what your shop's like.) ... I was telling Mumbo you want to know what her shop's like ... (LG 149; original punctuation)

Characters often complain of the impossibility of talking properly on the phone, and telephone conversations are rarely perfect, even as such conversations go. In *The Heat of the Day*, for instance, Stella sometimes speaks in her 'company voice', or lowers her voice and 'can't talk now' because Harrison is in the next room; or she cannot hear properly because Roderick is calling her from a public telephone in a station while a train is pulling in. In what is perhaps the most remarkable instance of non-communication in the book, the characters simply do not answer the 'demoniac' ringing of the telephone at Holme Dene, Robert's family home, where his mother and sister have called him down to decide whether to accept an offer for their ugly Victorian house. Well aware that the counter-spy is on his trail, Robert starts violently when the telephone rings; and the reader, too, will surely be interested in what the call might be about – much more so than the rest of the family, who spend so long debating who it might be and who is to answer it that the telephone ominously stops ringing 'of its own accord' (HD 265).

The Heat of the Day
The question of open and honest communication is a very real issue in *The Heat of the Day*. The habit of watching what one says is an integral part of the wartime atmosphere of the book, reflecting the 'Careless Talk Costs Lives' slogan launched by the Ministry of Information and

popularised in a series of striking posters by Fougasse. Stella herself moves 'at the edge of a clique of war, knowing who should know what, commanding a sort of language in which nothing need be ever exactly said' (HD 172), and Harrison complains of everyone being 'cagey' (HD 42). He himself characteristically finds it difficult to express himself ('I hardly know how to put it' [HD 29]) and speaks in clipped, jerky sentences:

> Harrison turned back to close the door behind him, but paused to ask: 'Not expecting anyone else?'
> 'No.'
> 'Good. By the way, I found your downstairs door on the latch. That in order?'
> 'Quite. I left it open for you.'
> 'Thanks,' he said, as though touched. 'So I shut it – that was in order, too?' (HD 26)

That Harrison's hesitant speech may be a sign of the universal problem of finding adequate and socially acceptable words to convey one's meaning is suggested by the fact that Stella's exemplary son Roderick uses the same expression as Harrison, 'to put it', when he is explaining to his mother why he did not apply for compassionate leave when he heard of Robert's death:

> 'I know how I could have put it; in fact I was going to put it that way if it came to the point – I should have put it that you and Robert were engaged' (HD 295).

The otherwise talkative Robert Kelway is the prime example of not 'talking' in the police jargon sense of the word. 'This is the first time I've ever talked,' he says to Stella in their last scene (HD 282), and his lack of frankness is at the heart of the love-espionage plot, culminating in Stella's heart-broken words when he has finally confessed to her: 'Still, tell me. If you had told me more – !' (HD 270). In so far as Robert's treason is explained in the text, he gives part of the explanation by referring to himself as a Dunkirk wounded man,[1] and as we know him in 1942 he still limps from his Dunkirk wound (though we note that his limp is most pronounced when he is acting The Wounded Soldier). In

---

[1] Robert was apparently a member of the British Expeditionary Force, which was evacuated from the beaches of the Northern French port of Dunkirk (Dunkerque) at the end of May 1940. See illustration opposite.

the present context it will be natural to mention another of Robert's self-justifications: the meaninglessness he finds in certain words. For him there are no countries left, only names, and words like 'betrayal' are part of a dead language that he feels he has had to steel himself against, as he tells Stella in their last scene:

> 'What is repulsing you is the idea of "betrayal", I suppose, isn't it? In you the hangover from the word? Don't you understand that all that language is dead currency? How they keep on playing shop with it all the same: even you do. Words, words like that, yes – what a terrific dust they still can raise in a mind, yours even: I see that. Myself, even, I have needed to immunize myself against them; I tell you I have only at last done that by saying them to myself over and over again till it became absolutely certain they mean nothing. What they once meant is gone.' (HD 268)

Soldiers of the British Expeditionary Force queuing up to be taken off the beaches at Dunkirk in 1940. The traitor Robert Kelway in *The Heat of the Day* is a 'Dunkirk wounded man', and one of his excuses for his defection is that he cannot get over the humiliation of having to be taken off from France by 'pleasure boats' (HD 272). Though in point of fact most of the soldiers were evacuated by ships from the Navy and the Southern Railway, many private craft crewed largely by civilians did take part – a much publicized part – in the rescue operation; they were popularly known as the 'little ships', and sometimes referred to as a 'cockleshell armada'.
Nordfoto, Copenhagen.

In the book, Robert's father is dead and the Kelway home dominated by the stifling presence of his widow, whose failings include a total insensitivity to language. When Stella is on a visit with Robert, Mrs Kelway shows no interest whatsoever in her guest and quashes any attempt on her part to make conversation; on Stella's volunteering the information that her son, like Mrs Kelway's grandson, is in the Army, she is merely met with an 'Oh' by her hostess. 'For, why *should* she speak?' comments the narrator, ' – she had all she needed: the self-contained mystery of herself. Her lack of wish for communication showed in her contemptuous use of words' (HD 109-110). Robert's grotesque sister Ernestine is always laughing wildly and barking out orders rather than speaking, in a parody of the empty language that passes for conversation in this arid atmosphere; for even with no strangers present, the Kelways 'communicated with one another with difficulty, in the dead language' (HD 252). Their contemptuous use of language also appears in the repressive upbringing that Robert's seven- and nine-year-old niece and nephew are given; crowning the amazing list of do's and don't's is the insensitive baby-talk with which Mrs Kelway addresses her granddaughter, referring to herself in the third person: 'If it's not too much trouble, Grannie would like some bread' (HD 112). With an upbringing in this language-inimical house, it is perhaps not surprising that Robert Kelway should have a warped attitude to words.

The question of language also informs the sub-plot revolving on the two working-class girls, Louie and Connie. Louie is in many ways close to this central concern of the novel. Her compulsive fibs that fool no one are a low-scale counterpart to Robert's deceitfulness, and also to Stella's glib performance in the final chapter, at the inquest after Robert's death. It is this simple-minded factory-girl, moreover, who '[has] no words' and cannot 'speak grammar', who is given a long, important speech about the frustration of not being able to express oneself:

> 'Look the trouble there is when I have to only say what I *can* say, and so cannot ever say what it is really. Inside me it's like being crowded to death – ... I could more bear it if I could only say. Now she tonight [Stella], she spoke beautifully: I needn't pity her – there it was, off her chest. If I could put it like she does I might not be stealthy: when you know you only can say what's a bit off, what does it matter how much more off it is? ... I would more understand if I was able to make myself understood. (HD 245-246)

The narrative voice amplifies this naïve outpouring later, in a perceptive passage about the power and far-reaching effect of language. The blanks in Louie's vocabulary determine the way her mind works, we read, they 'operated inwardly on her soul' (HD 306); knowing only the words 'refinement' and 'respectability', she is incapable of recognizing any virtue divorced from those two, and her early hero-worship of Stella turns to moral condemnation when she sees in the papers a sensational version of her heroine's statement at the inquest: there has been an expensive flat, she reads, bottles, a lover, other men friends. Louie now sees Stella as a fallen woman, with the result that, having no one to admire, she drops back into her promiscuous habits.

The Heat of the Day is by way of being a key text in the matter of communication. We have often been told that political treason is the theme of the novel, and much ink has been spent in pointing to Robert Kelway's Nazi allegiances. Though these cannot be denied, I would suggest that they are in the long run of secondary interest. The near-identification of the two Roberts is too pointed to be ignored: not only do they have the same Christian name, they are also expressly linked in Stella's reflections about her lover's calculating attitude to their fellow-countrymen. He must have been spying on them all, she finally realizes, just as Harrison has been spying on him, and 'She now saw [Robert's] smile as the smile of one who has the laugh. / It seemed to her it was Robert who had been the Harrison' (HD 275). The use of the definite article before Harrison's name here confirms earlier suggestions that he is a type rather than an individual. His enigmatic personality, the uneven set of his eyes, his sudden comings and goings, his being in the know and apparently in a position of some power – all this contributes to giving his character an uncanny air of being not quite human. And since Old Harry is a nickname for the Devil, it is natural to see Harrison as an emissary from the Underworld (a role he shares with the sinister chauffeur Harris in *A World of Love*, as pointed out p. 47).

Coupled with the indeterminate nature of Robert's espionage, the link between him and Harrison suggests that the treachery on which the plot hinges is not essentially a betrayal of any one political system. It is something more universal, something that thrives in times of repression, and something that Stella herself is part of. The truth of Harrison's allegations is brought home to her during her trip to Ireland half-way through the book; but before that, the very first question she asks her lover about Harrison has been the beginning of what she later sees as her 'espionage' – her 'watch on Robert's doors and windows, her dogging of the step of his thought, her search for the interstices of his mind' (HD 172). In the most dramatic confrontation between her and Harrison she accuses him of having distorted love by making her spy on her lover – by making her like himself. To his 'You and I are not so unlike – yes, it's funny,' she throws out: 'Why? Below one level, everybody's horribly alike. You succeed in making a spy of me' (HD 138). Stella's words receive additional emphasis from their effect on Harrison: he winces when he hears them and walks away from her over to the window, where he stands 'headed into the curtain like an animal blindly wanting to get out of a room' (HD 138). The link between the two of them is underlined in this scene by the intimate ambience of her flat and the window embrasure where she joins him behind the black-out curtains, and sexual attraction seems part of that link. (Some verbal reflections of this are taken up in the next chapter).

All these things considered, *The Heat of the Day* may be read as a demonstration of the way confidence and trust between human beings may be stamped out by those in power, whether by democratic governments in times of national emergency or, by inference, by any authoritarian regime at any time. Bowen is no Orwell and her wartime novel no *Nineteen Eighty-four*, yet it does seem to me that in its insidious undermining of mutual trust and its pervasive mood of 'caginess' and lack of 'frankness', the book is fundamentally as pessimistic as Orwell's futuristic vision. It was said almost two thousand years ago by the Roman historian Tacitus, writing of the cultural and political totalitarianism of the Emperor Domitian, that the 'investigations of the secret police have deprived us even of the give and take of conversation', or, more literally, of 'the intercourse of speech and hearing'.[2] In betraying this essential human faculty, the Robert Kelways and Robert Harrisons of this world are equally guilty. They make traitors of the rest of us.

---

[2] The first is M Hutton's translation, revised by R M Ogilvie, of *adempto per inquisitiones etiam loquendi audiendique commercio* (Tacitus, *Agricola* 2.3), in volume 1 of the Loeb Classical Library edition of Tacitus, pp. 28-29; the second translation of *loquendi audiendique commercio* is from Ogilvie and Richmond's annotated edition of the *Agricola*, p. 135.

Eva Trout

In *Eva Trout* Bowen makes her final fictional statement about the limits and possibilities of communication. It is no longer, as in *The Heat of the Day*, a question of surmounting or surviving the deadening influence of totalitarian measures, but, rather, of people being by nature or upbringing or circumstances so inhibited that they cannot attain the supreme human good of making themselves understood by their fellow human beings.

Eva is presented as an outsider in the social world of the 1960s, one of her disadvantages allegedly being her 'cement-like conversational style' (ET 17). This is not necessarily the view of the narrator, or of the reader. The phrase occurs in a paragraph largely held in language alluding to the patterns of thought or speech of her teacher Iseult Smith, whose 'vivisectional interest' (ET 33) has originally drawn her to Eva:

> Iseult Smith had gone out of her way to establish confidence, for her own reasons – she proposed to tackle Eva's manner of speaking. What caused the girl to express herself like a displaced person? The explanation – that from infancy onward Eva had had as attendants displaced persons, those at a price being the most obtainable, to whose society she'd been largely consigned – for some reason never appeared: too simple, perhaps? Much went into the effort to induce flexibility. But Miss Smith had come too late on the scene; she had had to give up. Eva by then was sixteen: her outlandish, cement-like conversational style had set. Moreover – the discouraging fact emerged – it was more than sufficient for Eva's needs. She had nothing *to* say that could not be said, adequately, the way she said it. (ET 17; italics original)

The question in lines 2-3 in this quotation, 'What caused the girl to express herself like a displaced person?' reflects Iseult Smith's thoughts; some lines on, the question 'too simple, perhaps?' would seem to be the narrator's comment on the teacher's overly clinical approach. That Iseult Smith here is very much The English Mistress appears from the fact that she is now called 'Miss Smith'. 40 pages or so later the narrative shows the teacher-pupil relationship in action, so to speak, in a flashback to Eva's first term at the girls' school where she is sent after the disastrous mixed-schoool experiment at the castle. Miss Smith's own *noli-me-tangere* attitude does not prevent her from treating Eva in a way that is as manipulative as Miss Brodie's in Muriel Spark's *The Prime of Miss Jean Brodie* (1961); and, with a mind running in the familiar groove of English Literary History, she does not hesitate to divert Eva's nascent religious feelings into those well-worn channels:

'One thing,' declared Eva,' I *have* done.'
'Well – what?'
'Learned that religious poem.'
'*Religious* poem?'
'It is to God, I think.'
'Oh, one of the metaphysicals. Say it, then.' (ET 65)

Ignoring the religious content of George Herbert's verses then quoted in the text, and deliberately ignoring, likewise, any suggestion of erotic tension between Eva and herself, the apparently neo-critically trained Iseult Smith straightaway launches into her favourite subject: 'You see how pure language can be? Not more than two syllables – are there? – in any word' (ET 66). In her reading of Iseult's reaction as the 'ineffable emergence of lesbian panic', Patricia Juliana Smith posits that 'language' has by now become 'subliminally analogous with sexual desire' for both Eva and Iseult (116-117). Taking 'language' to mean 'verbal communication', perhaps more narrowly 'spoken communication', this is in line with an observation in *A World of Love,* allusively reflecting Lilia's thoughts about the future of her marriage: 'Survival seemed more possible now, for having spoken to one another had been an act of love' (WL 105). Iseult's obsessive interest in language also colours her initial reaction to Constantine Ormeau, whose letter she finds 'garlands of affection' (a style which she nevertheless adopts herself in her later letters) (ET 33). With regard to that conversational style of Eva's found so regrettable by her teacher, we may well feel that what Eva lacks is merely the airs and graces with which to embellish her own utterances, but that there is in fact nothing wrong with her actual meaning. This is apparent in the scene between Eva and Iseult in Broadstairs that I have referred to earlier (pp. 59-60). And we can hardly blame Eva for being suspicious of the false endearments and speechifying of many of the other characters – Eric Arble's repeated 'sweetheart', for instance. One endearment in particular haunts her for years, spoken by the mother of her sick room-mate Elsinore at the castle school: 'How is my darling?' (ET 47); but this, too, is merely a mechanical expression, for in spite of all her sweet words Elsinore's mother turns out to be just as flighty and uncaring as Eva's own. Eva has in fact a salutary habit of unmasking pretentious speech by asking the meaning of words she does not understand, as she does in her last words, spoken to her former guardian on the last page of the book; Constantine is making a wedding speech:

> 'Er – life stretches ahead. May a favourable concatenation of circumstances ... No, here I become a trifle tied up, I think. That is enough. – Henry, you'd better kiss Eva.
> Henry did so, lightly on the cheek.
> 'Constantine,' asked Eva, 'what is "concatenation"?'
> Her last words. (ET 268; punctuation original)

Eva's conscious or subconscious awareness of her reluctance to speak, brought about by years of virtual isolation, is given visual form in the communication devices with which she fills her drawing-room at Cathay, the house she has leased on North Foreland:

> Outstanding examples of everything auro-visual on the market this year, 1959, were ranged round the surprised walls: large-screen television set, sonorous-looking radio, radio-grammophone in a teak coffin, other grammophone with attendant stereo cabinets, sixteen-millimeter projector with screen ready, a recording instrument of B.B.C. proportions, not to be written off as a tape-recorder. Other importations: a superb typewriter shared a metal-legged table with a cash register worthy to be its mate; and an intercom, whose purposes seemed uncertain, had been installed. (ET 118)

When she returns briefly to Cathay after her stay in America, these installations have become obsolete and their futility is apparent. Perhaps we may take this to mean that there is in fact no substitute for the give and take of conversation. It is an open question whether Eva's killing at the hand of her adopted son suggests the failure of any kind of communication, even wordless, between people.

Eva's difficulty in communicating with others is magnificently symbolized in her adoption of a child who turns out to be deaf-mute. The eight years that elapse between parts I and II of *Eva Trout* are the 'inaudible' years of her life with Jeremy, when they have been cocooned 'as near as twins in a womb' (ET 188), hardly distinguishing between what went on inside and what went on outside the films and television they watch in silence. These seem to have been happy years, with Jeremy 'capering naked on Eva's bed like Cupid cavorting over the couch of Venus' (ET 189) in a Boucher-like image of Eva as the Temptress. But Jeremy is growing up. At the same time, Eva is beginning to conquer her innate suspicion of speech: she is 'ready to talk', though she senses that this will make her a traitor to the American years with Jeremy (ET 188). She has apparently been led to take him to

England by the sight of something approaching manhood in his eyes, not realizing the shock it would be to him. It is as though he has been brought into another dimension, and it makes her a stranger to him. There is even so much submerged hostility in his relationship with her that he gouges deep eye-holes in the clay head he is modelling of her: 'Out of their dark had exuded such non-humanity that Eva had not known where to turn' (ET 190). This is revealed in the text just before we hear that Jeremy has been carried off from the studio for some hours by an anonymous woman – Iseult Arble, it appears later. We are not told how Iseult and Jeremy communicated, but the text insists that they had a profound liberating effect on each other. They take a bus-ride to Westminster Abbey, where Jeremy traces the letters of monument inscriptions 'as though responsible for incising them for the first time' (ET 245; we recall that a beautiful handwriting is one of Eva's few accomplishments). Ever since this day Jeremy is withdrawn as never before, and the habitual contact between him and Eva changes: where Eva could earlier communicate with him even without lip-reading, she now has to touch him to get his attention. Their common universe is a thing of the past, and the location of their last weeks together is aptly Fontainebleau, a town redolent of past history.

That it should be French doctors who look set to cure Jeremy of his muteness and that French will thus be his mother tongue, as it were, adds yet a dimension to the book's concern with language (anticipated early in the book by Iseult's French translations). The issue of conveying meaning in what is not one's native tongue is not taken up, however, and Eva's long conversation with Dr Bonnard in the last chapter is conducted in English.

Silence
Jeremy apart, silence between Bowen's characters is as eloquent as words. It may be referred to as a 'vocabulary' (HD 187), and when Clare in *The Little Girls* chooses not to take up a bantering remark of Dinah's, the text tells us that she conveys her meaning by a 'formidable silence' (LG 168). Characters do in fact not always answer questions put to them, and our attention is often drawn to their silent responses. In *The Heat of the Day*, for instance, Stella's growing suspicion of her lover is mirrored in her silences: when he asks her whether she is influenced by what Harrison says, she tries to dismiss his question by

silence (HD 191); and to his 'You love me?' she 'eloquently' answers nothing at all (HD 200). Or silence may suggest that a character is fully aware of the unspoken emotions of others, as we realize that young Dicey in *The Little Girls* knows perfectly well how her mother feels about Clare's father, who puts in an apparently chance appearance at the beach picnic: on seeing him, 'the child said nothing, merely went back diligently to amassing shells' (LG 130). In *Eva Trout*, silence is palpably a cover for Eva's embarrassment on several occasions, e.g. when as a girl she evades a question of Iseult Smith's by 'examin[ing] the path's brickwork; then, down to its very roots, some near-by grass' (ET 59); or later when the talk veers dangerously near to her feelings for Henry Dancey, and she looks fixedly at a mobile in his room (ET 180), or into the distance (ET 231), or at some trees (ET 233), rather than speak.

As a characteristic woman's response, silence has been the subject of much discussion in feminist criticism, and since Bowen's protagonists are almost exclusively female it is usually women we hear of 'not answering' or 'remaining silent'. The blustering, bumbling Eric Arble in *Eva Trout*, who is occasionally at a loss for words, is one of the few exceptions: 'That's what comes of trying to talk,' he says early in the book, after a misunderstanding with his wife. 'Can anybody wonder I keep my mouth shut?' (ET 34). In *The Heat of the Day* there is a revealing glimpse of earlier generations of ladies at Mount Morris:

> Though seated together, hems of their skirts touching, each one of the ladies had not ceased in herself to reflect alone; their however candid and clear looks in each others' eyes were interchanged warnings; *their conversation was a twinkling surface over their deep silence*. Virtually they were never to speak at all – unless to the little bird lying big with death on the path, the child being comforted out of the nightmare without waking, the leaf plucked still quivering from the felled tree. (HD 174-175; my italics)

There is a subtle connection between the pregnant silences of Bowen's characters and the silence of her locations. In *The Heat of the Day*, Stella's silent responses and Robert Kelway's silence about his espionage are thus echoed in the silent London townscape, where 'silence mounted the stairs, to enter her flat through the door ajar; silence came through the windows from the deserted street' (HD 23); and the 'islands of stricken silence' (HD 91) formed by the roping-off of dangerous areas are a visual counterpart of the lovers' mutual silence and their 'hermetic world' (HD 90). In *Eva Trout,* Eva and her adopted son lead a 'cinematographic existence with no sound track' (ET 188), living in a visual universe of film and television that mirrors Jeremy's enforced silence. (Other instances of Bowen's thematic use of silent surroundings will be taken up in Chapter 8, 'Stages and Stage Properties').

Dialogue

In view of the many spoken exchanges between Bowen's characters, it may be appropriate to round off this chapter with a few observations about her handling of dialogue.

One may note, first, the use of stilted or meaningless dialogue to reflect the embarrassment or nervousness or withheld emotion of the speakers, as in this exchange between Dinah and Clare about a telephone conversation:

> 'What were you doing?'
> 'Well, I was in my flat.'
> 'Of course you were, else you couldn't have answered. What were you doing?'
> 'Thinking about you,' said Clare crossly. (LG 143)

Similarly, the first words between Iseult Smith and Constantine Ormeau in his office reveal the wary tension of the speakers:

> 'You're well, I hope?' he asked with renewed concern.
> 'Very. And you?'
> 'So-so. This is a treacherous time of year.'
> 'Though spring,' she suggested, 'is more treacherous, isn't it? In winter one at least knows what to expect.'
> 'How true. Yes, that is very true.' (ET 35)

Spontaneous or troubled thoughts on the part of the speaker are often expressed in sentences that may appear garbled in isolation but turn out to be perfectly idiomatic when read aloud, or with an inner voice, with the correct placing of stress. (Much of James Joyce's writing makes the same demands on the reader). Stella's enigmatic 'I don't think I think', for instance, makes perfect sense in the context: '"*You* think, in me this was simply wanting to get my hand on the controls?" / "I don't think I think "' (HD 273). A puzzling line or two of Robert's may likewise easily be cleared up when read aloud:

> 'When you didn't speak I thought you thought silence better.... There were other times when I was less certain you knew. But I did not know you did not know till you asked me.' (HD 271)

Such 'difficult' lines often involve a pun-like repetition apparently unnoticed or unintended by the speaker. This is particularly noticeable in *The Heat of the Day*, where such discourse may be seen as a colloquial variant of the book's general dislocation of language; it often occurs in passages whose style alludes to the ways of speech and thought of the characters:

> Here now was Louie sought out exactly as she had sought to be: it is in nature to want what you want so much too much that you must recoil when it comes. (HD 248)

This does not make for easy reading. But then, as William McCormack comments, speaking of a somewhat similar example in the underground café scene in the same book, 'Easy reading is not intended' (227).

Another recurrent feature of Bowen's fictional exchanges is equally easy to parody, but demonstrably functional in that it sets the pace for our reading and conveys a good deal about the the mood or character of the speaker: the use of syntactically intrusive speech tags of the type '"Do you think," she asked, "it's going to rain?"' (WL 137). On the one hand such tags undoubtedly encourage slow reading, but as against this they potentially speed up the reading process for the simple reason that an interrupted line of thought or an interrupted sentence naturally leads the eye of the reader on to its conclusion. Intrusive tags may reflect the hesitancy with which something is said, as in the conversation between young Roderick and the mentally disturbed Cousin Nettie in *The Heat of the Day:*

> 'I believe I am very odd. And you must not,' she said with a gesture, 'tell me I'm not, or I shall begin to wonder.'
> ....
> 'I thought,' she said, still in agitation, 'it had all begun again.'
> ....
> 'But,' said Roderick, having taken thought, 'I don't really think I'm like that.' (HD 208)

Similarly, the following lines from *The Little Girls* say a good deal about the guarded atmosphere at dinner-table conversation between Sheila and Dinah's sons:

> 'Who thought up those three extra-secret things?'
> 'That,' she said, having thought, 'I believe was me.'

'Neither of us,' said Roland – entitling himself, by a glance, to speak for his brother – 'now, of course, can ever hope to rest till we know what they are.' (LG 233).

Syntactically interruptive locutionary clauses like these are used frequently and with great effect in *The Heat of the Day*, where the pull of opposite forces is in keeping with the tension at the heart of the novel. Syntactic breaks range from a mild hiatus when tags coincide with the beginning of a subsidiary clause ('I'd no idea,' she said, 'you were going to feel like this' [HD 161]) to the startling separation of subject from verb or verb from predicate ('I don't,' she said, 'see anyone I have ever seen' [HD 233]). The hiatus is felt most violently when the locutionary clause is expanded, as it often is – especially in reporting the speech of Harrison, who is patently unsure of himself and consequently often acts up: '"Absolutely," he said with fervour, "not!"' (HD 221); "He might, of course," added Harrison, studying the short, clean nail of his right thumb, "fairly ask you what came over you" (HD 228); "Which was not," said Harrison, secretively fiddling with a cigarette but not lighting it, "unnoticed"' (HD 232).

This characteristic construction was one of the things that Daniel George, Cape's otherwise appreciative reader, singled out for comment in the manuscript of *The Heat of the Day*. Glendinning reports that he wrote four pages of notes on what he called 'snags in the crystal stream' for Bowen to think about (93:153). One sentence which came in for comment was the one I have just quoted: '"Absolutely," he said with fervour, "not!"'. George's remark was: 'Far, I diffidently suggest, fetched.' But Bowen did not amend the construction in *The Heat of the Day* (where it also occurs as '"Actually," he had to admit, "not"' [HD 137] – here, too, reporting a line of Harrison's), and she retained it even in her last novel: '"Evidently," he said, approvingly, "not"' (ET 166); this is spoken by Constantine Ormeau and aptly reflects his pompous, deliberate manner of speech, where every word is weighed separately and given its due.

Characterisation through speech thus combines with the dynamics of reading to forge Bowen's dialogue into a complex experience in which the active participation of the reader plays no little part.

* * *

In the texts I have been considering, instances of imperfect communication far outweigh those where people relate to one another in full understanding and openness. Lack of frankness is at the root of the tragic outcome of the Stella-Robert love-affair in *The Heat of the Day*, and even though the relationship between young Dicey and her mother in *The Little Girls* is in many ways idyllic, there is necessarily much that is unsaid between them (e.g. Mrs Piggott's love for Clare's father). Technical innovations of course do nothing to mitigate such psychological restraints, and they have their own disadvantages. Telephoning is attended with all kinds of drawbacks that go beyond the limitations imposed by the speakers' surroundings that I have instanced above (background noise, background company). A telephone call may come at a bad time or when people are simply unprepared for it, for instance: Clare sounds cross when Dinah calls her up, because, as she says, 'You made me jump, suddenly coming through like that' (LG 143); and some subjects seem unsuited to telephone conversation: 'What a thing to ask her over the telephone!' says Clare, when Dinah impetuously asks Sheila whether she has ever killed anyone (LG 150). Writing is 'hopelessly distant', as Iseult Arble remarks (ET 115) – and Bowen's narratives contain a good deal of 'writing' in the form of verbatim letters. The possible advantages of avoiding the constraints and embarrassments of a face-to-face interview by actually choosing to write rather than speak are not taken up. In the long run, non-verbal communication is no solution either, for the perfection of Eva's and Jeremy's 'cinematographic' life 'with no sound track' in America does not outlast the boy's growing need for independence. *Eva Trout* is the only one of Bowen's post-war novels to end on a significant note of finality: Eva overcomes her reluctance to speak only to be killed on the very last page by the flawed communication represented by her adopted son. The outlook for the future is bleak indeed in this last novel.

CHAPTER 6

Word Clusters and Interlinking Images

Though our understanding of both theme and plot in Bowen's fiction is naturally determined to a large degree explicitly by the individual words in the text, a lexeme will often work unobtrusively to suggest connections between scenes and characters, or to confirm parallels that may have been hinted at by intertextual references or by the speech of the characters or the patterning of the plot.

In *The Heat of the Day* the bond between Stella and Harrison thus goes further than the fact that they are both in fact spying on Robert Kelway, and in spite of her initial rebuffal of Harrison's advances it is clear that she feels sexually drawn to him and does not quite rule out the possibility of becoming his mistress (indeed, she invites him to stay the night in their very last scene [HD 321]). Their intimacy is subtly conveyed, e.g. by repeated occurrences of the verb 'to blot'. When they are standing in the window embrasure of her flat, behind the blackout curtains, they are 'blotted out' (HD 140); and 'blotted' was used a few pages earlier when Stella, walking home in the dusk, sees lovers kissing, 'blotted together' (HD 126). The erotic associations of the verb appear again in the final scene between Robert and Stella: Robert is 'blotted out' in the dark (HD 269), and when they embrace the text calls them 'the two blotted out' (HD 278). To take another example from the same book: it is in the air that the person waiting outside Stella's flat to catch her lover is Harrison, but not even this final sentence of the scene in question is explicit: 'In the street below, not so much the step as the semi-stumble of someone after long standing shifting his position could be, for the first time by her, heard' (HD 290). Step or semi-stumble is anonymous; our suspicion that it is none other than the counter-spy's is reinforced, however, by the use of 'shift', which is associated with him on several occasions; and we may also remember that in the beginning of the book Harrison was one of the first-time concert-goers who by chance 'stumbled' on to the music in the park (HD 9). In that very first chapter we are told that he looks up sharply as if the lawn has 'shifted' under his feet, and when he has lit a cigarette and let the match drop, he 'shifts' one foot to stamp it out. In the first scene we witness between him and Stella, he has not 'shifted' his look from her face during her long angry speech (HD 40), and when she thinks back to that Sunday, she asks herself whether he had 'more than discreetly shifted his eyes' (HD 172); for good measure, he is linked to the verb in his last scene with Stella, when he 'shifted his feet, equivocally, on the black hearthrug' (HD 319). But our conviction that it actually was Harrison standing outside Stella's flat on that fatal night is short-lived, for immediately after we have been told that he shifts his feet thus on the hearthrug the last time he is on stage, he himself reveals that he has been taken off the case the night before Robert's death. Whose then was the step on the pavement? Was it after all Harrison waiting jealously for some sign of the lovers, or was it some other counter-spy? The text has used Harrison's name about a role rather than a person when it seemed to Stella that it was Robert who had been '*the* Harrison' (HD 275; my emphasis); so perhaps not only Harrison himself, but anyone spying on someone else is *shifty*. There has been some talk in the novel of things being said in, or not in, 'so many words', and we may take this as a reminder that there is much that is unsaid in Bowen's discourse.

In looking at some of the characteristic lexemic aspects of Bowen's later fiction I shall focus on the novels, taking my point of departure in *The Heat of the Day*. I have found it practical not to treat figurative language separately: the image of Robert's sister moving restlessly around in a taxi 'like a ferret' (HD 182) will thus be of less interest for being a simile than for the lexeme 'ferret', which is used elsewhere as a verb ('every [shadow] had been ferreted out and killed' [HD 225]); 'ferret' is part of a whole cluster of words semantically related to the hunt and is thus central to the plot of the novel. In what follows I use *repeat/repetition* of lexemic repetition, as in act/acting/actor or die/dead/death, *echo* of a semantic or phonological link between lexemes, as in act/theatre or watch (timepiece)/watch (guard), and *verbal recurrence* of both repetition and echo, as distinct from the recurrence of tangible elements in the fictional world: landscape, houses, objects, and the like. I use *image* and *imagery* to cover all these forms of representation.

This is not an inventory of images. In the event of one being made, Bowen's fiction would probably be found to contain much the same imagery in varying degrees and with varying emphasis. Images of acting and the theatre occur in all four post-war novels, for instance, and also in some of the short stories; fish-imagery, which is so remarkable in *Eva Trout*, is found already in *The Heat of the Day*; chains and voodoo come into both *A World of Love* and *The Little Girls*, knives and scissors into *The Heat of the Day* and *The Little Girls*. It seems that Bowen had at her command a well-defined but not unlimited range of imagery which she applied lavishly to different contexts, in much the same way as she re-cycled other features from her own writings such as motifs (the young girl entering the adult world, for instance), vignettes (a paper boat cast on a stream, an uncurtained lighted window seen from without), scenes (meals, arrivals and departures), and types of character (the beautiful Edwardian widow, the slightly common Lawrentian male). What appears as recycling from one point of view, however, may from another be seen as the common intensifying device of repetition, especially when one considers a single work on its own. Identical imagery naturally has different functions in different texts. In 'Hand in Glove', for instance, locks on an attic trunk underline the fantasy aspect of the story, recalling the unopenable treasure-chest of fairy- and folktale. In *The Heat of the Day*, locks are primarily associated with the secretiveness of the spy mind; in *A World of Love*, with the idea of the Irish Big House, Montefort, as a fortress originally designed to keep out intruders. Locking in *The Little Girls* is first and foremost a means of preserving something for the future; it also connotes keeping one's feelings to oneself, much as in *The Heat of the Day*, though here it is not a question of espionage but of concealing one's sexual sympathies. Finally, locks in *Eva Trout* belong to the pervasive imagery of imprisonment that reflects Eva's feelings about Iseult and Eric Arble.

In the following pages I shall discuss some of Bowen's imagery in so far as it seems to me to be central to the novel in question. In *The Heat of the Day*, I will look first and foremost at the language of spy-hunting; in *A World of Love*, at images of fire and burning, which reinforce the emotional intensity of the story. *The Little Girls*, which is concerned largely with vestiges of the past and with one character's dominance of another, will be seen to be full of images of death and enchantment. In *Eva Trout*, the heroine feels like a prisoner rather than a paying guest in the house of her former teacher; in this novel I shall therefore consider imagery revolving on imprisonment, before moving on to related images of the underworld through which Eva illegally adopts Jeremy.

The Heat of the Day

Similar or identical scenes, gestures, and objects re-appear time and again, often highlighted by verbal repetition or echo: Stella *coils* the *cord* of a black-out blind round her finger, her son knots the *cord* of a dressing gown round him, her lover *coils* a piece of *string* into a hank, tightly bound *string* from a parcel cuts into Stella's finger, magazines are *corded* up into bales, pencils have frayed silk *cords*. The forbidding Mrs Kelway sits with her *knitting* just as Cousin Nettie and earlier generations of ladies at Mount Morris sat with their *embroidery*, and an expectant factory-girl clumsily *stitches* baby-clothes. We are given a gentle hint to keep our eyes open for such recurrences three pages into the book: when at the concert Harrison looks up at the end of every number, his fellow concert-goers begin to note this, and to expect it. In the novel's language of spy-hunting, his look has begun to be 'lain in wait for' and is at last to be 'trapped' (HD 10).

Verbal recurrence plays an important role in keeping the themes of the novel in our minds, or in the backs of our minds. Betrayal, for instance, is a central concept in the book: betrayal of love, betrayal of one's country. But the lexeme crops up in a quite innocuous context when Stella does not *betray* that she has forgotten the caretaker at Mount Morris though he so clearly remembers her (HD 165); and, nearer to the grain, when young Anne *betrays* her uncle Robert's nervous start by almost falling off his chair arm (HD 264). Similarly, in the scene between Cousin Nettie and Roderick at the mental home where she is confined, *conspiratorial* occurs several times in an ambience that is anything but criminal or treacherous, underscoring the general air of concealment that called forth the use of the same lexeme in an example early in the book, when doors are opened *conspiratorially* so that light does not escape into the blacked-out street (HD 46). We note, too, that cars outside Euston Station are parked *secretively* (HD 182). Recurrence also affects seemingly unimportant words, most noticeably perhaps those whose imitative quality links them to the notion of sound that runs through the whole book: Roderick *plonks* down his tin helmet

(HD 46), a maid *plonks* down a tea-tray (HD 212); Louie *flops* like a flatfish across her bed (HD 242) and gets out again with a *flop* (HD 243). *Flop* also connects with the many occurrences of *drop* and with Robert's fatal *fall* or *leap* from the roof, not only semantically, but also by sound: rhyme (*flop/drop*), half-rhyme (*flop/leap*), assonance (*plonk/flop*), alliteration (*flop/fall*), and by the liquid element (l,r) common to all these words. (Robert's fall is discussed more fully in Chapter 10, 'A Latter-Day Icarus').

It lies near at hand to think of verbal recurrences like this as semantic or phonological clusters or fields. One field would then consist of lexemes denoting sound and hearing: *bark, click, flop, hear, listen, plonk, sound, silence, snap, voice*. Language and meaning might form another field: *formulate, language, mean, name, put it, vocabulary;* communication, a third: *bridge, chat, communicate, conversation, speak, say, talk, telephone, tell;* treason and deception, a fourth: *accomplice, accuse, betray, conspirator, deceive, enemy, fear, frightened, hide, lie, secret, suspicion, threat*. The language of the chase might constitute a fifth word-cluster: *dog, follow, hunt, lie in wait, spy on, trap, to tail, watch; ferret* would come in here, and also *fishing*. The number of such loosely defined fields is of course arbitrary, and they are all to some degree overlapping. Words relating to treason and deception rub shoulders, for instance, with a whole set of theatrical words and phrases: *act, actor, audience, mask, make an entrance, play a part, theatre, set the scene, scenery, stage,* etc. These are often used in a non-theatrical context, as when windows are 'curtain-masked', and when Harrison hints at Robert's deceitfulness with the words, 'I should say, if a chap *were* able to act in love, he'd be enough of an actor to get away with anything' (HD 38). In this case, verbal recurrences have their counterpart in the tangible world of the novel, its furniture or stage properties: there is in fact a real theatre in the story, the open-air theatre where the concert in the first chapter takes place; the scene is set already on the first page, and the text points up the acting motif by referring again in the same paragraph to 'this tarnished bosky theatre, in which no plays had been acted for some time', and to the light as being 'so low, so theatrical, and so yellow' (HD 7).

The intertwining of verbal and non-verbal recurrence may also be illustrated by the verb *to dog*, which is part of the spy-hunting language already referred to. It is used figuratively by Stella to Harrison ('You did not have to dog me' [HD 137]), and she also uses it about herself: when she realises that she has in fact been spying on her lover, she thinks of the way she has been *dogging* his thoughts (HD 172). The essential meaning of the verb 'to dog', to pursue like a dog, is kept in the mind of the reader by the appearance of a number of dogs in the text. There is an actual dog in the underground café where Stella has dinner with Harrison, and there are several references to actual dogs: a labrador that had belonged to Robert's sister, Ernestine; Samoyed puppies bred twenty years before the story takes place; dogs at Mount Morris that Roderick hears about from the caretaker. On a different level again, Robert's niece Anne wears a pink plastic brooch of a dog, and among the many photographs of Robert there is one of him with his sister's dog. Dogs also come in for mention in the instruction-cards by which Cousin Francis regulates life at Mount Morris; one card reads: '*Hysteria, Puppies,* in case of' (HD 164); and among the odds and ends in his tray-like baskets there is a dog collar (HD 163; rather than a collar for a dog, this may of course mean the stiff white collar fastened behind worn by clergy, but the presence of the word 'dog' still holds good). Then there are the dogs that are used in metaphors and similes (here given in italics): 'Let sleeping *dogs* lie!' says Cousin Nettie (HD 216); Harrison slips round a door 'with the unobtrusive celerity of a normally outdoor *dog*' (HD 128); Ernestine looks 'rather like a *dog*', says the narrator, describing her long face and short body (HD 107); Louie thinks of 'that *dogged*, timid, unfaithfully followed hope' (HD 307), and Connie writes of Louie herself as 'straying about like a *dog*' (HD 327). Anne speaks '*doggedly*' (HD 263), Harrison makes his way '*doggedly*' to Stella's flat (HD 315). The phrase 'to *bark* up the wrong tree' is used several times, and there is also the '*bark*' of guns (HD 315) to link *dog* to the pervasive interest in sound throughout the novel, and to its wartime ambience.

Diagram of Clusters

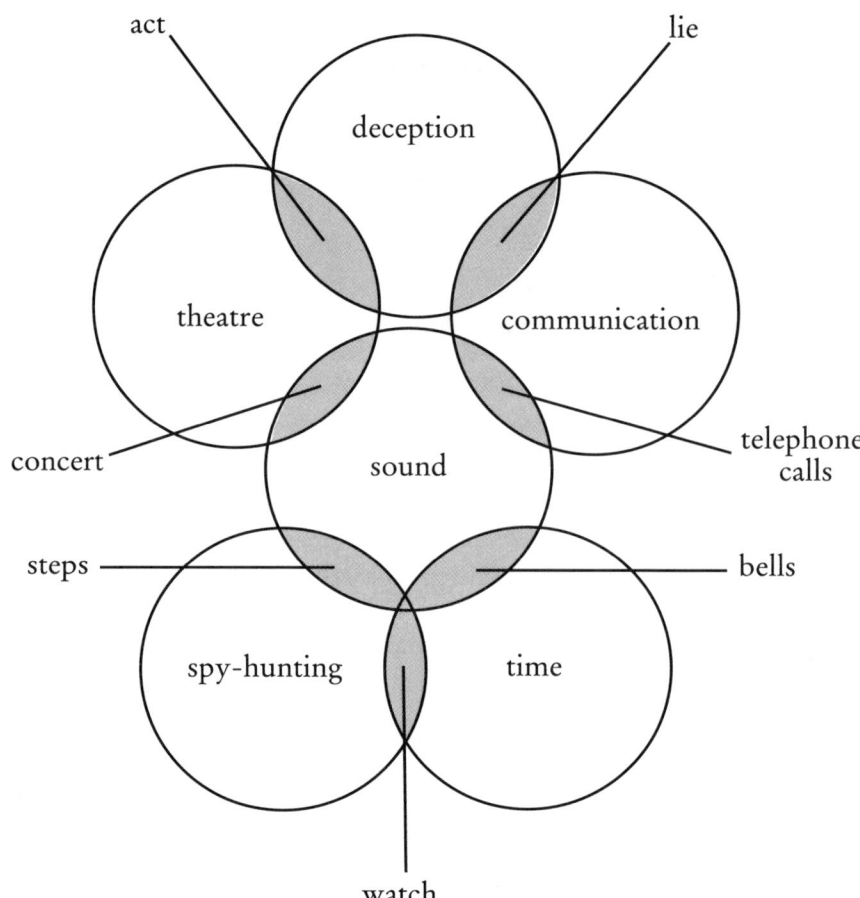

This rough sketch shows some of the different kinds of interrelationship between word-clusters in *The Heat of the Day* which also obtain between clusters in the other texts I shall be looking at. Some links are semantic: *deception* is linked to *theatre* through 'act' and to *communication* through 'lie'. Some are factual: *sound* links up with *theatre* by way of the concert in the open-air theatre, to *communication* through numerous telephone calls, to *time* through church bells, and to *spy-hunting* by means of steps heard outside doors. Finally, the link between *spy-hunting* and *time* through the two senses of 'watch' is (etymology apart) largely phonological.

A World of Love
Bowen's one novel of the fifties is an intense evocation of smouldering emotions. The heated atmosphere of its Irish Big House, Montefort, is reflected in the state of the weather, a June heat-wave with an imminent drought that is averted by the coming of rain at the very end of the book. Heat itself is carried over from the preceding novel in an arch reference in the first line: 'The sun rose on a landscape still pale with the heat of the day before' (WL 9).

Heat and burning are constantly kept in the mind of the reader by a group of recurring images, both verbal and non-verbal: *bake, blaze, burn, candle, char, cigarette, fire, glare, heat, hot, ignite, inflammable, kindle, lamp, match, oil-lamp, scorch, singe, smoke, smoulder, steam, sun, sweat, smoke, vesta, wax, hot tea*, the *lamp chimney*, the *steaming stew*, the enormous *kitchen range*. To these semantically related words may be added *burnish*, whose link to *burn* is primarily phonological. Examples of the semantic burning group would include the beautiful Jane being *kindled* by summer (WL 10), morning *blazing* into the bedroom of Antonia (WL 25), and the phrase 'to go to *blazes*' (WL 41). Jane's tendency to blush also belongs here; we read that she tries to hide her *burning* forehead, for instance (WL 25), that she *colours up* (WL 37), that she *turns red* (WL 117). In this verbal group we may also include the name of the nouveau-riche Lady *Vesta* Latterly, a 'vesta' being a kind of short match. (Chapter 4 on Identity has already had occasion to mention the naming of this upstart chatelaine). Antonia explicitly makes the connection between fire and emotional heat; 'If I'd started a fire, you'd know by now,' says Jane, referring to the way she has had a candle with her in the attics, and Antonia takes her up:

> 'We think we do,' said Antonia. 'That's what's the matter. We think we can smell burning; or at any rate the beginning of burning, smouldering. What have you done? You have an igniting touch'. (WL 40)

On a literal level, a moth is *scorched* by candles on the table at the castle dinner (WL 67); there is the smell of *singeing* hair at the hairdresser's (WL 89) and *sweat* and *heatedly* trodden grass at the Fête (WL 29). On Antonia's bedside table are *cigarettes, cigarette stubs, matches* and a *candlestick* (WL 10-11). Some of the characters are surprisingly careless in their use of open fire: Antonia herself goes to sleep with her *candle* burning (WL 12); she throws a *burning match* out of her car window, and Jane can actually smell the bracken *charring* (WL 72). Lilia repeatedly voices her fears that the house will *burn* because everything in the attics is *inflammable* and Kathie the maid takes her *candles* up there (WL 40). Even without the conflagration at the end of Bowen's early novel *The Last September* (1929) in mind, most readers will surely anticipate a similar outcome for this novel. But the expected fire does not break out; the only destruction is that of the letters, which Jane burns in the kitchen range – off stage, underplayed, but thus highlighted in a characteristically oblique move on the part of the author.

Another noticeable cluster of images in *A World of Love* revolves on the idea of Montefort as a fortress (as its name suggests) from which *sallies* may be made. Fire and fortress are both present in a cameo scene where Jane, coming back late at night from the castle dinner, finds her father trimming the oil-lamp in the hall, and shakes a small stone out of her sandal:

> The stone cast from the sandal spat like a shot on the floor; the lamp chimney around the urged-on lamp flame gave warning by an earsplitting crack, and the flame itself, spurting threads of itself and smoke stinkingly upward towards the ceiling, crimsonly stuttered inside the gloom it made like an evil tongue. (WL 76)

Antonia then locks up for the night:

> Not since Montefort stood had there ceased to be vigilant measures against the nightcomer; all being part of the hostile watch kept by now eyeless towers and time-stunted castles along these rivers. For as land knows, everywhere is a frontier; and the outposted few (and few are the living) never must be off guard.... when Antonia had done bolting and barring she remained, arms extended like another crossbar, laughing at the door. (WL 79)

The *chain knot* on the Montefort entrance (WL 28, 74) brings to mind Antonia tightening the slip-*knot* of her pearl necklace (WL 42). *Knot* recalls, too, the enigmatic figure of the long-dead master of Montefort, Guy, who had signed his love-letters with an almost illegible 'G' so difficult to read that Jane marvels how anyone could make such a *knot* of the letter (WL 42).

Guy's name resembles that given by Jane's sister Maud to her imaginary companion, Gay David,[1] thus providing a phonological link to Montefort's dead owner. Maud is a particularly obnoxious, even diabolical version of Bowen's horrible little girls, who bullies her schoolfellows, sucks raw eggs, and practises black magic and voodoo; characteristically, she has a pixie hood in the pocket of her raincoat.[2] The candle-wax she collects for making ritual figures links her to the central imagery of burning; and her communing with supernatural powers parallels Jane's sighting of Guy at the castle dinner, and Lilia's in the walled garden.

The Little Girls
In Bowen's next novel, a coffer is buried at night by three eleven-year-olds: Dicey (Diana/Dinah), Mumbo (Clare), and Sheikie (Sheila). The coffer is part of a central cluster of images revolving on death and burial, including *bones, bury, charnel, coffer, coffin, corpse, die, grave, lying-in-state, mortal, rot, skeleton, skull, tomb.*

On the level of verbal recurrence, the repetition of *die/dead/death* leaps to the eye. Coming into her house with wet feet, Dinah says she will *die* if the fire has not been lit (LG 19). Sheila reacts with theatrical exhaustion to Dinah's SOS in the press, speaking in a *deadened* tone (LG 34); her first reaction to the idea of the three girls meeting again is that she'd rather *die* (LG 38); spearing the slice of lemon in her tea, she runs it to *death* with her spoon (LG 38), and as a child she wears her pigtails with a *dead* straight parting (LG 72). The adult Sheila speaks lifelessly (LG 174) and stops *dead* when she unexpectedly sees her husband's car (LG 176). Her comatose father smoking a cigar in his leather arm-chair is called a *dead* man (LG 107); the High Street in Southstone bends to the right before *dying* out (LG 102). The tamarisks at the girls' school are *dead*-still (LG 86), and the old tennis balls they

---

[1] In Ireland Gay is a pet name for Gabriel, and it is characteristic of Maud's obsession with the Old Testament that she should call her familiar both Gay and David, seemingly from the already existing name of a cave on the Montefort demesne, 'Gay David's Hole'. Robert Tracy points out (247) that the name may be part translation from Irish, part anglicization, and that David 'like the Davy of Davy Jones, implies a conventional euphemism for devil'. 'Guy David's Hole' for 'Gay David's Hole' in the Penguin edition of the novel (46) is not in Cape's first English edition (1955) or in the Cape Collected Edition (1968), and would seem to be a misprint.

[2] A pixie hood is a pointed hood covering the ears and tied under the chin, formerly a common piece of girls' headwear.

play with seem to be *dead* (LG 88). These metaphors suddenly become very vivid when a visitor makes her appearance wearing a hat with magpie's wings, which to Dicey is not a hat-ornament, but a *dead* bird (LG 88). On a similarly non-figurative level, Sheikie volunteers that she knows of a wood with a *dead* sheep (LG 93), and a girl buying ants' eggs for her goldfish complains that one of them has *died* (LG 96). Dicey is sure she is *dead* when Mumbo topples her down on the lawn at school (LG 75), and later she wonders whether she might put one of her kittens in the coffer if it *died* (LG 109). In the final chapter of the novel, the bed where Dinah is lying after her breakdown looks like a *death* bed (LG 199).

Verbal recurrences of the *die/dead/death* lexeme are underlined by the mention of people who have actually died since the girls were at school. Some of them, like Clare's father and the elder brother of Sheila's husband, Trevor Artworth, were killed in the First World War; Dicey's mother died of the Spanish flu just after the war. Others also died young: Trevor's first wife, and Sheila's lover. The grandmother of Dinah's friend and neighbour Frank Wilkins must have died before 1914; before 1914, too, Dicey's father has thrown himself in front of a train, and a brother of Mumbo's has died of meningitis, in India. Sheila's sister dies towards the end of the book. The notion of dying is underlined by repeated warnings against driving in the dark or after too much drink (LG 165), as Clare warns Dinah that she will sleep in her grave rather than her bed if she insists on driving all the way home from Kent to Somerset at night (LG 164).

The charnel atmosphere is emphasized by references to smell: smells of chalk and ink and water slimy with rotting botanical specimens in the schoolroom; a house smelling of long-gone kittens; the humid, varnish-like smell of escallonia hedges; the 'knife-freshened but injured smell' of a newly cut privet hedge (LG 110); the smell of masks in Dinah's car, and the smell of hat-dye on a black straw hat (the one with the magpie's wings referred to above). There is always a smell of some kind in the air, and it is rarely a pleasant one. The bowl of sweet peas in Mrs Piggott's drawing-room is perhaps an exception, but Sheila's remark that the room 'always smelled like a hothouse' (LG 37) seems to annul any agreeable associations the reader may have. More unequivocally positive – a rare example – is the 'coarse, clean smell' of the shingle beach where the girls from St Agatha's go swimming, in a scene that serves to point up the birthday picnic that ends the childhood section of the book; parallels are suggested by the children 'ooz[ing]' through the gap in the parapet and 'pour[ing]' down the steps in their bathing suits and wraps (LG 86), much as they later 'cataracted' down off the wall on the day of the picnic (LG 120). The clean smell of the pebbly beach stands out by contrast with the unpleasant smells that are dominant throughout the book. *The Little Girls* opens in Dinah's garden in September, in the dying year, with 'steamy flower smells' (LG 17); in the last chapter it has become November, the fruit in the orchard that was merely bruised in September has rotted, and there is now 'a really nasty and musty smell' (LG 179; the words are those of Dinah's houseboy, Francis) from behind the mackintosh curtains covering the cave. In the Southstone section, the 'gloom' in Fagg's pet shop is 'smelly' (LG 94), and the Old High Street has

> deep-seated smells of its own, which, as none could be certified as downright insanitary, the denizens saw no reason to put a stop to. These mingled with smells always travelling up from the Old Harbour's fish-market, oily old engines and scummy puddles. (LG 98)

Nauseating smells may be said to culminate in the last chapter of the childhood section, where Dicey chases little Trevor Artworth up a rusty, sewer-like drainpipe on the beach. The drain is described in anthropomorphic terms with a mouth that is 'slimed on the lower lip' (LG 126), which in the context carries unmistakable associations of death in the trenches in the imminent war; and the stench is so awful that Dicey's accomplice quickly pulls her head out: '"Stinks," she said, making a *moue* at the grown-ups' (LG 126). (Other pointers to the trench warfare of the First World War are explored more fully in Chapter 12, 'Picnic on the Sands').

Semantically allied to the imagery revolving on death and emphasizing the theme of influence, another important word-cluster has to do with the supernatural: *apparition, Black Mass, Circe, devil, enchant, fetishism, fey, ghost, harpie, haunt, magic, mumbo-jumbo, obsession, omen, phantasmagoric, phantom, poltergeist, revenant, superstition, trance, visitant, voodoo, witch, witch balls,* etc. There is also Clare's nickname, *Mumbo,* and her claim that she, not Dinah, is the one who has exerted a *spell*. The note is struck on the very first page of the novel, when Dinah is intent on organizing the objects she has collected 'to the point of trance' (LG 9); the word *trance* reappears later, when Dinah is waiting for Clare, sitting *tranced* in her car (LG 45); later again it is applied to the customers in Clare's shop, who move about in a *tranced* state (LG 137). Frank sees Clare at the staircase window as an *apparition* or a *ghost* (LG 55), and the baskets of geraniums along the Promenade at Southstone are *bright-ghostly* (LG 110). The magpie whose wings adorn the black straw hat mentioned earlier is a bird of *ill omen* (88), and Clare and Sheila are thought of – by Francis, probably – as two birds of *ill omen* (LG 204). Houses at night are *phantasmagoric* (LG 173), Dinah's drawing-room is *haunted* (LG 227), and the text suggests that there was a *haunted* dimension to her life with her mother at Feverel Cottage (LG 77). People have *obsessions* about things (LG 15), and even as a grown-up Clare is *obsessed* by the Chinese puzzle that used to belong to Dinah's mother (LG 227). Though as a child she reacted against the twee poetry of Allingham's 'Up the airy mountain', it is characteristically this thoughtful Army daughter who later insists on quoting Meredith's poem 'The Woods of Westermain': 'Enter these enchanted woods / You who dare …' (LG 228). For Clare has become a mature adult of broad sympathies and tolerance, and she has learnt that it takes courage and love to understand Life. She has come a long way from the *unenchanted* garden of her unimaginative mother (LG 112).

Eva Trout
In the opening scene of Bowen's last novel, Eva Trout stands looking across the lake with her hands 'interlocked' behind her (ET 12). The wording serves to introduce a prominent word cluster revolving on capture and imprisonment: *ball and chain, cage, capture, catch, dungeon, executioner, grasp, grip, guard, handcuff, key, keeper, lock, manacle, power, prison, set free, take away, torture-house,* etc. The idea of capture crops up in the very first chapter of the book, when Eva herself is referred to as a *captor*; this is when she has taken the Danceys out for a drive and shown them the castle, and they can only think of when they are going to have tea. The imagery aptly reflects Eva's state of mind: it is because she feels imprisoned at the home of Iseult and Eric Arble, where she is a paying guest, that she takes flight from one end of the country to another, and from one country to another. She never leaves a forwarding address because she feels pursued, and when Eric Arble suddenly appears at Cathay she is afraid that he has come to *take* her

Fougasse: 'Strictly between you and me ...'
One of a series of posters by Fougasse (Kenneth Bird) that were a striking part of the campaign against careless talk in WWII Britain, the setting of *The Heat of the Day*. 'Everyone's so cagey,' complains the counter-spy, Harrison, himself an expert at deviously avoiding questions; and the lack of free and open speech largely determines the tragic outcome of the novel's love affair.
Courtesy of the Imperial War Museum, London.

Bruegel: The Fall of Icarus
The Fall of Icarus in this painting by Bruegel forms a telling subtext to Robert Kelway's 'fall or leap' from a high roof in *The Heat of the Day*. Robert's overweening pride and self-confidence are not less than those of Icarus, and the parallel between their deaths is borne out by echoes of W H Auden's poem, 'Musée des Beaux Arts'. *Musées des Beaux-Arts de Belgique, Bruxelles.*

Philippe Jullian: Dust jacket for *Eva Trout*
The dust jacket for the first English edition of *Eva Trout*, showing the mood-setting fake castle where Eva spent a few months at an experimental school run by a dubious friend of her guardian – 'Inspirational Kenneth of the unclouded brow and Parthenon torso', as the narrator calls him (ET 48). The jacket was designed, by Bowen's express wish, by the French art-nouveau expert Philippe Jullian, and leaves no doubt about the book's Gothic affinities. *Courtesy of Jonathan Cape, London.*

Sir John Millais: Ophelia
A late, idyllic scene between Eva Trout and Henry Dancey in *Eva Trout* is undercut by an echo of this painting of Ophelia by Sir John Millais. Eva had a friend at the castle school who had tried to drown herself and was referred to by another schoolfellow as 'Ophelia's illegit' (ET 56); her real name was Elsie-Nora (we learn much later), but at school she was called Elsinore. Now, towards the end of the book, Ophelia is recalled again through these allusions to the painter: '"Those are Millais wild roses at the edge of that wood," [said Henry] ... Against an overgrown larch plantation, the showering briar's crimped pink buds and corollas wide-eyed round tawny stems stood out translucently as though painted –' (ET 233). © *Tate, London 2001*.

away (ET 84), though when he has succumbed to fatigue and takes up her suggestion that he take a nap before driving home, it is again Eva who is called the *captor* (ET 98). In the Chicago episode, Eva's hand is *captured* in a *handcuff* grasp by one of Elsinore's friends (ET 136), who close in round her and shepherd her out of the coffee shop *under guard* (ET 136). The father-in-law of one of the friends, looking at Eva, holds her in a *grip* with his eyes (ET 138), and Elsinore stands in front of him as if she were *chained* (ET 137). Back in England, Eva wonders whether her adopted son Jeremy has *manacled* her (ET 190). In the last part of the book the idea of confinement is visualized in the *cage* of budgerigars that Eva and Jeremy have in Paley's hotel (we are not allowed to forget them, they are noisy birds that are repeatedly put away in the bathroom).

A closely related semantic field is constituted by lexemes referring to pursuit, including *chase, flight, hunt, pursue, take away*. Hunting is insinuated unobtrusively into the text as fox-hunting when Henry's brother and sister bicycle to a *meet* (ET 71); Henry himself refers to *blood sports* (ET 74), and he is within the same semantic field when he uses the expression *hold your horses* (ET 72). Estate agents are *on the hunt* for business (ET 76), in Chicago Eva asks Elsinore's friends not to accompany her *huntedly* (ET 136), and the lexeme is picked up later in her own *house-hunting* in London (ET 182).

Prison and hunt imagery link up semantically with a cluster of words belonging to the shady world of crime that Eva comes into contact with when she acquires Jeremy: *accomplice, assassination, blackmail, black market, collaborate, complicity, confederate, conspiracy, corrupt, crime, crook, defraud, delinquent, disguise, embezzling, extortion, gang, guilty, gun, iniquity, kidnap, in league, murder, marauder, poacher, parley, peccadillo, prey, racket, thief, threat, tip off, underworld, victim, villainy,* etc. *Racket*, for instance, is used originally of the castle school (ET 49). Later in the book, the more serious kidnapping *racket* in America is vividly described by Elsinore's father-in-law; to the reader, who is already aware or has begun to suspect, from Eva's cryptic telephone conversation with an anonymous speaker, that she is about to buy a child through that very *racket*, his diatribe is almost embarrassingly ironical:

'Of kidnapping, with extortion, I need hardly remind you; moreover, ma'am, there could be various persons for whom your family name spells top-bracket wealth: *At* a cost, your child could be likely to be recovered. But there's a racket more deadly – are you aware? There's a black market in infants, unknowing babies; are you conscious that they can be purchased, they can be traded?' (ET 139)

The novel is so full of examples of shady or underhand behaviour, however, that even without the mysterious telephone conversation Eva's illegal adoption of a baby boy can hardly come as a total surprise to the reader. The kidnapping involved in her acquiring Jeremy is echoed in a later episode in London when Iseult Arble carries off Jeremy for a few hours: *attempted kidnapping*, Eva's former guardian calls it (ET 227), and Eva herself admits that it is not the first time Jeremy has been *stolen* (ET 199). In part the air of criminality in the book is less than serious, however, e.g. when Constantine suggests to Iseult that they should *collaborate* (ET 44), begin to *concoct* something (ET 45), and when the text refers to a wine waiter where they are having lunch as an old *accomplice* of his (ET 39). In part it consists merely in being slightly on the wrong side of the law, as when Eva tries to dispose secretly of her car, and when she smuggles dollars out of America 'on her person' (ET 205). Young Henry's part in the proposed car deal suggests that he is not averse to cutting corners, either; this is confirmed on later occasions: he makes tea by starting the kettle off with the hot tap (ET 156), and leaves a book open face down (ET 149). Constantine is mildly suspected by Iseult of embezzlement; this is not taken up, but certainly the splendid lunch he gives her is on his expense account, and perhaps we should read the narrator's information that Constantine 'charged himself' with the financial aspect of Eva's living with the Arbles (ET 16) to mean not only that he undertook to pay her hosts, but also to suggest that he took a sizeable commission ('commission' is mentioned later in the text when Henry agrees to help Eva sell her car: 'I might act for you. On commission, of course' [ET 71]). Eric Arble, however, is flagrantly less than law-abiding: he lives with a Norwegian girl who has no immigration papers, and the two children he has with her are as illegitimate as Eva's adoption of Jeremy. (Much of this criminal and semi-criminal behaviour can be related directly to the pervasive Gothic mood of *Eva Trout*, which will be treated in Chapter 13).

* * *

Bowen's widespread use of verbal and non-verbal recurrences such as those I have singled out for notice in the preceding pages is one of many points where, for most of us, re-readings disclose meanings that we failed to pick up on a first reading. The effect of such recurrences is naturally cumulative, and later scenes owe much of their meaning to what has gone before. In *A World of Love*, for instance, the off-stage burning of Guy's letters towards the end of the book has in fact been prepared from the very first pages by the cigarettes and matches in Antonia's bedroom, and by Lilia's fear of seeing her go up in flames because she has gone to sleep with her candle burning. At first sight we may interpret this merely as an indication of the two women's characters; but as the book progresses, or as we read it again and pick up much of the fire imagery that may initially have eluded us, the letters and their final destruction emerge as important elements that invite closer examination in terms of theme and ultimate meaning, and which may lead us to a reassessment of the whole novel.

CHAPTER 7

Narrative Roles

By the 1940s Bowen's readership had grown accustomed to sharing the company of a mature, thoughtful narrator, grave and genially ironical by turns, who would give evidence of her reliability in passages of sober description and analysis, and in comments too general to be questioned. This is admittedly a simplified picture of a storyteller as sophisticated as Bowen. It remains, however, that with regard to narrative stance her early fiction is less complex than the novels and stories she wrote after the Second World War, whose narrator has become extremely self-conscious and at times adopts such a confusion of 'voices' that it may be misleading to speak at all of 'a narrator' as a single identifiable persona. Certainly such a composite persona is capable of numerous variations in the distance it keeps from the story and in its degree of self-consciousness, even self-advertisement. These objections notwithstanding, the narrative voice in Bowen's later fiction seems to me to be projected so clearly as a recognizable personal intelligence that I feel justified in speaking of 'a narrator', by which I understand the persona adopted by Elizabeth Bowen as soon as she puts pen to paper and begins to tell a story. Though in principle a concept, this individual intelligence is coloured so much by her own personality that it seems ungracious to speak of it as other than 'she'.

In the fiction I am considering, the roles adopted by the narrator range from that of meticulous craftsman to flippant punster, from judicious critic to deadpan ironist. In so far as these accents may be distinguished, it may be useful to look at some of them more closely before considering the works separately.

The Narrator in Exposition

Declarative statements that are not coloured by the attitude of the narrator seldom last for more than a few sentences. The purest examples are probably the 'editorial' notes concerning some of the letters in *Eva Trout*, e.g. the laconic italicised lines inserted in square brackets after the letter from Professor Holman that end chapter 11 of Part One:

> *[This unclaimed letter was in due course returned to the sender, Professor Holman, nothing further having been heard of the addressee since she telephoned cancelling her reservation].* (ET 129; original italics)

In most passages of exposition or analysis the tone is rarely so dispassionate; this also goes for Bowen's frequently anthropomorphic, 'atmospheric' descriptions of houses and landscapes. In the following example describing the early years of the war in *The Heat of the Day*, the inventive compounds 'stayers-on' and 'fled-from' immediately strike a playful note, which is confirmed by the use of informal dashes, the faux-naïf division of people into 'the wicked' and 'the good', and the un-warlike images of the last lines:

> Society became lovable; it had the temperament of the stayers-on in London .... These were campers in rooms of draughty dismantled houses or corners of fled-from flats – it could be established, roughly, that the wicked had stayed and the good had gone. This was the new society of one kind of wealth, resilience, living how it liked – people whom the climate of danger suited, who began, even, all to look a little alike, as they might in the sun, snows and altitude of the same sports station, or browning along the same beach in the south of France. (HD 94)

A similar voice lies behind many of Bowen's generalizing present-tense asides, which often seem deliberately banal: 'Nothing is more demoralizing than waiting about for someone one does not want to see' (HD 22), for instance, or 'The omelette, as sometimes does happen with those made under unfavourable conditions, turned out to be one of her best' (LG 195).

Where impassive exposition does exist, it soon veers into free indirect thought or speech allusion,[1] sometimes but not always ironically. This is what happens in the beginning of *Eva Trout*:

---

[1] The term 'speech allusion' is used by Leech and Short (349). The device is discussed by Stanzel (248 sqq).

> 'This is where we were to have spent the honeymoon,' Eva Trout said, suddenly, pointing across the water. She had pulled up the car on a grass track running along the edge of a small lake – *evidently, they were to gaze at the castle for some time.* (ET 11; my italics)

In like manner, what may seem at first glance to be a piece of neutral exposition often proves to reflect the viewpoint and style of a character. The flowery language of Constantine Ormeau in *Eva Trout* is thus discernible in the vocabulary and impersonal syntax of: 'Vibrations of heat invaded the table; covers were taken off – one disclosure being that Constantine was to partake of woodcock' (ET 43); in the same book, 'racket' in the following quotation is obviously the word used by the children about their school: 'Exactly how [Kenneth] proposed to run this racket, it was going to interest them to see' (ET 49). Speech allusion like this governs much of our response to the characters in *Eva Trout*; I return to this later.

The Narrator as Commentator

Speaking unmistakably from outside her fictive universe, the narrator may slip into evaluative or interpretive remarks, often with more than a touch of irony. The first lines of *The Little Girls*, for instance, immediately call forth a comment by a narrator-onlooker standing at some remove from her own story:

> A man came down the steps cut in the rock. By nature agile, he made the descent with unusual caution, placing each foot first tentatively then extra firmly. *He did well to* – the steps, inexpertly hewn at some unknown time, were no two alike, and were still slippery after rain. (LG 9; my italics)

Who expresses this approval of Frank Wilkins's caution? The same assessing voice, presumably, that is responsible for comments like the following: '"Put it that way," said Robert *with pardonable irony*' (HD 196); 'Antonia had felt this unfair, *as it more than was*' (WL 14); 'Lady Latterly *would have done well* to rearrange the room' (WL 62); 'She paused on its floor with a sense of being in beauty – and *she was right*' (ET 113; all italics mine).

The relations of narrator to fictional world are similarly that of a commentator when the narrative report takes up a remark made by one of the characters: '"You mean, the evenings are drawing in?" / *They were*' (HD 20); '"That's right," Clare told her, "go on, collect a crowd!" / *Sheikie was already doing so*' (LG 101); '"I fancy we can do better [than Chablis]." *So did the wine waiter*' (ET 39; all italics mine).

The Narrator as Craftsman

The narrator is distant, too, but her accent is less that of a bemused bystander than a conscientious professional writer, when she expresses some doubt about her own choice of words and offers alternatives. In *A World of Love*, for instance, Jane begins to 're-read' a letter, 'or, rather, ponder over what she seemed more than half to know by heart' (WL 10). Similarly, in *The Little Girls* Dinah looks 'with faint discouragement, or rather misgiving' at the objects she is collecting (LG 15), and in the same book the narrator corrects herself for having spoken of a 'gate' which is 'strictly, an ironwork door in the wall' (LG 84). The initially neutral and then openly critical attitude to the French doctors to whom Eva has entrusted Jeremy in *Eva Trout* is also expressed in self-correction, as if on second thoughts the narrator has decided to forego discretion: 'This had been suggested, it would not be unfair to say ordained, by the Bonnards' (ET 252).

This anxiety of the craftsman to find the most precise expression is also evident in Bowen's much criticised double negatives, which do in fact convey more nuances than the corresponding positive wording: 'Now the clock had struck, no step could not be his' captures the nervous expectancy with which Stella is waiting for Harrison in *The Heat of the Day* (HD 23); if she were not so nervous, she would realize that the next step she heard could very well be somebody else's. In *A World of Love*, the much-maligned 'Mush for the chickens, if nothing else, was never not in the course of cooking' (WL 21) emphasizes the sometimes exasperating monotony of the Montefort kitchen by implying that there *are* in fact kitchens free of these chores. And when a young boy in *Eva Trout* blows away a wisp of his comatose schoolfellow's hair 'not unkindly' (ET 56), we realize that he could well have been expected to have been unkind.

Though similes were included generally in the imagery discussed in the previous chapter, such explicit comparisons may also be mentioned among the stylistic devices openly revealing the hand of a precision-seeking perfectionist. They are, predictably, numerous, and predictably they are often used to underscore theme or motif or character. Similes in *The Heat of the Day* thus include Harrison looking about him in Stella's flat, feet apart, 'like a German in Paris' (HD 44), reminding us of the threat he represents as well as of the story's wartime ambience, and Ernestine 'bundling' around in a taxi 'like a ferret' (HD 182), reminding us of the book's pervasive hunt-motif. In *A World of Love* there is Jane, the not-quite-woman, 'like a boy actor in woman's clothes' (WL 10), and the 'commissar-like' figure of the sinister chauffeur (WL 53). There are also plenty of similes in *The Little Girls*, despite the fact that the narrator's role is played down in that book: cherries and angelica are set 'like jewels' in the icing on a cake in 'a sort of victory wreath' (LG 122), underlining the martial undertones in the party atmosphere of the scene on the beach; and the jagged trench landscape suggested by the location is sharply brought into focus when breakwaters are compared to 'teeth left in an otherwise broken comb' (LG 125). There are numerous similes in *Eva Trout*, too: Eva and Eric carry driftwood into her hideout, Cathay, 'like two thieves carrying loot out' (ET 96) – they must both be aware that their very being together is suspect; the hedge between Cathay and the road is 'like a fortification' (ET 97), and the Christmas crowds in Chicago are (mindlessly, incessantly) flowing 'like lava' (ET 130).

The Narrator as Word-Addict
The fascination with language apparent in the preceding examples often leads Bowen to juggle with words in such a way as to leave her open to the accusation of frivolity or mere showing off. Chapter 4 has already mentioned the inventive names she gives her characters, which are one indication of the way she loves to play with words. The hand of her narrator is particularly visible in pun-like language games; an extreme example is the first line of *A World of Love* quoted earlier, which picks up the title of the previous novel: 'The sun rose on a landscape still pale with the heat of the day before.' In *The Heat of the Day* this kind of language game may seem inappropriately frivolous given the seriousness of the context, but on the other hand it may also be seen to capture some of the devil-may-care humour of wartime. Examples would include the word 'bridge', which is taken up quite literally after Robert Kelway's remark that a lot of water has flowed under the bridges: 'There was no bridge for a mile up or down the river from Mount Morris' (HD 162); and 'know', which is carried over from a reflective

passage to narrative report: 'The significance of this drawing-room picture of Cousin Nettie's would never be known. / Stella woke up next morning not knowing where she was' (HD 176). This kind of juggling with words adds a curious dimension to the relations between narrator and reader. What kind of narrator is this, we may ask, who takes us into her confidence one moment, only to embarrass us the next with feeble attempts at schoolboy humour? If we find her unreliable, it is hardly the kind of unreliability that stems from wilful deception or forgetfulness, but rather a kind of ambivalence or volatility. This volatility becomes extremely noticeable in the last two chapters of *The Heat of the Day*, where the earlier empathetic treatment of Stella is abandoned (I return to this later). In a similar manner, immediate lexemic repetition is one of many distancing features in *Eva Trout*, as when 'Eva let Mr Denge let her into Cathay' (ET 79), 'the gloom ... consumed the gloom of his London overcoat' (ET 99), and Henry 'eased into ease in driving' (ET 237).

Bowen's frequently untraditional use of words includes agent nouns and prepositional adjectives. The effect is playfully hyperbolical when agent nouns (which generally refer to permanent qualities) are used for momentary, or at least temporary, roles: the narrative voice in *The Little Girls* calls Dinah 'the organizer', for instance, when talk is merely of the objects she is collecting for posterity (LG 16), and 'the visitor' and 'the smoker' when she lights a cigarette while visiting Clare's shop (LG 142).[2] Unusual prepositional adjectival compounds lend a similarly less than serious air to a text and may not always be explained as echoes of a character's way of thinking; they are a striking feature of Bowen's later style and recall the informal character of much of her feature writing. I have already quoted the 'fled-from flats' in London; other examples include 'his not-quite squint' (HD 86), 'her now in-shadow face' (HD 319), a 'put-about lady' (ET 148), and 'the at-large American years'(ET 189).

---

[2] Bowen's 'pervasive anxiety of naming', which leads the text to 'pick up an epithet from the preceding dialogue or from the surrounding situation', is exemplified and discussed by Bennett and Royle (133).

The Narrator under Cover: The Impersonal Passive Voice

As an indication of the distant position frequently adopted by the narrator, a few words may be said here about the use of passive rather than active verbal constructions. The remarkable wealth of instances in Bowen's fiction tends to give the overall impression that the characters are acted on rather than acting and to enhance the autonomous life of the story.[3] The passive voice even has recognizably feminist overtones in one or two examples from *The Heat of the Day:* though topicalization of Louie and Stella may be partly responsible for both women being 'married by' their husbands (HD 16 and 224), and for Stella being 'kissed by' her son (HD 294), these examples may well be read also as sly digs at male chauvinism. When the agent is left out, as it is in the following examples, the effect of narrative distance is marked: 'Feet ... could be heard walking with a hallucinated precision towards the window' (HD 269); 'Light long footsteps, though not harkened to, were none the less to be heard in the stable yard' (WL 105); 'An artist was to be seen in the act of sketching' (LG 102) (a finite form of the auxiliary 'to be' + the infinitive 'to be' + the past participle of the main verb, as in the last two examples, is a recurrent favourite). An agentless passive may tend to leave the reader asking 'By whom?' and is thus one of many details that force us think beyond the words on the page; these examples are from *A World of Love:* 'Of this arrangement it had not yet been decided whether it did or did not work' (WL 16); '[Antonia] was understood still to be making money' (WL 29); 'Lilia was slightly knock-kneed, as she had gracefully (it had been found, adorably) been as a young girl' (WL 85). Passive constructions sometimes combine with impersonal nominal subjects to introduce a note of ridicule into the text, as when Mrs Burkin-Jones in *The Little Girls* has emptied her watering can and is brought a full one by a menial soldier, whereby, with military precision of expression, 'exchange was effected' (LG 113); or, in the same book, when Dinah's omelette is eaten informally at the kitchen table and yet the text informs us, in a totally inappropriate elevated style, that 'claret was enjoyed' (LG 195).

* * *

---

[3] Bowen's preference for passive constructions is an obvious way of ensuring an impersonal voice in English, which has no quite neutral 3rd person singular pronoun like the German or the Danish *man*. These pronouns do not necessarily carry the familiarity of *you* or the mannered, upper-middle-class connotations of *one* that Bowen uses with such effect e.g. in the speech of Constantine Ormeau in *Eva Trout*.

In drawing attention to the language in which the story is told, a good many of Bowen's other stylistic devices share the aspect of metafictionality in the examples I have quoted. This holds good for innumerable instances of unusual word-order, convoluted syntax, disruptive speech-tags, hyperbole, and classical rhetorical figures like alliteration and zeugma: the list is as long as the inventories Bowen liked to include in her texts. Though by force of repetition such devices may acquire the unenviable label of 'mannerisms', they are in general far more than that when considered separately and in context. 'Any trick is justified if it adds a statement,' said Bowen in 1945, speaking of the cinema, which she found 'interesting study for the novelist.' 'In a good film,' she went on, 'the camera's movement, angle and distance have all worked towards one thing – the fullest possible realization of the director's idea, the completest possible surrounding of the subject.'[4] It is tempting to apply these remarks to her own fiction: most of her so-called mannerisms do in fact make a 'statement', in the sense of working towards the fullest possible realization of her idea – as e.g. the double negatives I have referred to earlier in this chapter say more than a positive wording would have done.

In addition to the narrative accents I have attempted to distinguish above, there are characteristic features in Bowen's individual post-war works that call for a few remarks: in *The Heat of the Day*, the dislocation of normal syntax and the fading out of the female protagonist in the last chapter; in *A World of Love*, the use of classical inversion and slow rhythm to mirror the meditative nature of the book; in *The Little Girls*, the preponderance of parentheses and the prevalence of dialogue and intertextuality as substitutes for narratorial explication; and in *Eva Trout* the widespread use of speech allusion, interrogative asides, and non-narrative elements like letters and telegrams.

The Heat of the Day
This first post-war novel is largely dependent on a traditional omniscient narrator who can provide information about past events and personal histories besides giving an inside view into the minds of the protagonists, and who may also invite us to laugh with her in passages of social comedy. A salient feature of the book is the dislocation of

---

[4] 'Notes on Writing a Novel'. *Orion 2* (Autumn 1945); quoted from *The Mulberry Tree*, 43.

normal sentence structure, which sits well with the strains and stresses of war and suspicion. In linguistic terms this may be described as iconicity,[5] the imitative principle whereby a text 'reflects' its object by sharing certain properties with it. Thus distorted syntax often palpably reflects a troubled state of mind in the characters:

> She shrank, even, from phrases in purple type on which, in the course of the listening, her eyes had from time to time lit.... She was not, therefore, then, in effect, again to see Robert until she *had* thought? (HD 57-8)
>
> He, looking put out, said he might or might not: evidently he felt that the situation, at this point, demanded something more from her. Concentratedly working towards this climax, he had not, as his tense fidgety blankness showed, envisaged it as it was to be. He had, as though to symbolize a sort of general coming-into-the-open, lighted the cigarette. (HD 233)
>
> Anne, stock still half-way across the lounge, fixed on him, one could not say how intuitively, her eyes. (HD 264)

The free indirect thought of the first quotation above is characteristic of the empathetic attitude towards Stella that is kept up through most of the book. But from Chapter 15 to Chapter 16 there is an abrupt change of tone. The long, emotionally charged Chapter 15 ends, after Robert has climbed up onto Stella's roof, with the prominent (and iconically stumbling) lines pointed to by Glendinning:[6]

> In the street below, not so much a step as the semi-stumble of someone after long standing shifting his position could be, for the first time by her, heard. (HD 290)

Already in the first lines of Chapter 16, immediately after Robert's 'fall or leap', narratorial empathy with Stella gives way to the word-play of a seemingly clumsy repetition, underlining the breaking in of the outside world: 'That day whose start in darkness covered Robert's fall or leap from the roof had not yet fully *broken* when news *broke*: the Allied landings in North Africa' (HD 291; my italics). The suggestion of narratorial distance in the punning of *broke/broken* in these first lines

---

[5] Iconicity is discussed e.g. by Leech and Short (ch. 7.7).
[6] Glendinning quotes this as an example of Bowen's contortionist manner of sentence construction, commenting, 'Contorted, maybe, but effective: one hears that slight shifting of the feet on the pavement' (93:152).

is intensified two lines further on by another play on words: 'Montgomery's *Order of the Day* to the Eighth Army ... became the *order of yet another day* for London' (HD 291; my italics). Furthermore, we are offered no comment on Robert's death; we are not even certain whether it was accidental or deliberate. And two pages further on we are given an outsider's view of Stella: travelling by train to visit Roderick, she is for several lines the 'woman in the corner' seen by the other passengers:

> Sunday short-distance travellers getting in and out, in and out of the carriage in which sat Stella found themselves being eyed with a sort of frozen attention by the woman in the corner; they shared an uneasy feeling that she was for some reason trying to learn their faces. She seemed to be someone for the first time finding herself alone among humanity. At the same time, the conveyance of that look of hers from one to another face was to be taken as the one sign of life: otherwise this person sat like an image, upright against the grime-impregnated tapestry of the compartment, dead gloved hands crossed in her lap, palms up. (HD 293)

Though 'this person' soon becomes 'Stella' again, her train journey and ensuing talk with Roderick provide the last reasonably intimate picture we have of her.

The externalization of our female protagonist continues unabashed in the dramatic form of the inquest in the next and last chapter, where we are left to infer the coroner's questions and remarks from her monologue. The effect is that of an interrogation in which answers are extracted forcibly from a witness – yet an element in the novel's ambience of espionage, and a graphic illustration of the ease with which Stella evades the truth:

> 'He had the idea that someone he did not name to me had followed us back and was in the street waiting to make trouble...I imagine that either he did not wish to give the person the satisfaction of an interview, or that he thought a quarrel outside my door might make embarrassments for me... Yes, I have other men friends, I suppose...I beg your pardon; I mean yes, I have other men friends.' (HD 302; elisions original)

After this dramatic monologue, Stella is seen through the eyes of Louie reading popular newspaper reports of Robert's death, and then by Harrison coming to pay her a final call, in a scene that is intensified by an ongoing raid (this is during the 'Little Blitz' of early 1944). This time we do not see Stella waiting for him, as we did in Chapter 2, but instead the text follows Harrison's movements: he stands in the street, walks to her flat, goes up by the rattling lift, and sees her open the door (wearing an overcoat – she is on her way out, and out of the story – and carrying a cat, like a witch or enchantress). The treatment of Stella is a practical demonstration of Bowen's insistence on the distinction between *seen* and *seeing* characters:

> Where is the camera-eye to be located? ... In the breast or brow of a succession of characters? This ... *must*, if used, involve very careful, considered division of the characters, by the novelist, in the *seeing* and the *seen*. Certain characters gain in importance and magnetism by being only *seen:* this makes them more romantic, fatal-seeming, sinister. In fact, no character in which these qualities are, for the plot, essential should be allowed to enter the *seeing* class.[7]

In the last scene between Stella and Harrison, their roles are reversed: no longer representing any threat, Harrison has become less 'romantic, fatal-seeming, sinister' than he has been hitherto, Stella more so. As she gradually recedes from the centre of attention and finally disappears from view altogether – iconicity, this, for people did actually go missing in wartime – there is a corresponding heightening of interest in Roderick and Louie, the prime survivors.

The progress of the war is reported ultra-briefly in this final chapter, sometimes in notes that are almost as disjointed as the hostilities appear to Louie and her fellow cinema-goers:

> February, the Germans capitulated at Stalingrad; March, the Eighth Army broke through the Mareth Line. North African spring teemed with pursuits and astronomic surrenders, with a victoriousness hard, still, not to associate with the enemy. July, the Sicilian landings; the Russian opening of their great leafy Orel summer drive. Mussolini out. September, Italians out, but leaving Italy to it. Landings, beach-heads, Russian tanks lurching across the screens in London; November, Italian rivers, however, being crossed by us in strength.... The day after Christmas we sank the *Scharnhorst*.... As early as January we broke the Gustav Line.... February, in Italy we encircled ten enemy divisions. (HD 308)

---

[7] 'Notes on Writing a Novel'. *Orion 2* (Autumn 1945); quoted from *The Mulberry Tree*, 42-3.

With the patriotic first person plural of 'us' and 'we', the narrative voice has slipped into a style allusively echoing Louie's way of thinking, a cinema-newsreel view of the war harking back more than 100 pages to the free indirect thought of her explicitly newspaper-inspired impressions:

> Left to herself she had considered that anything so dreadful as this last year could only in some way have been her own fault – Singapore falling the week Tom went away; the Australians right off even where they were getting that bad fright from the Japs; us getting pushed right on top of the Egyptians in spite of everything; the Russians keeping nagging at us to do something; the Duke of Kent killed who had been so happy; even those harmless ancient cathedrals not to speak of Canterbury getting bombed also; and us running out of soap and sweets till *they* had to go on coupons – one more headache…But once you looked in the papers you saw where it said, nothing was so bad as it might look. (HD 151; ellipsis original)

Nevertheless, to find the narrative voice in the last pages of the book speaking as 'we', however much this may allude to Louie's way of thinking, forces the reader out of a comfortable, accustomed identification with Stella and confirms the demise of the heroine.

A World of Love

The narrative voice of Bowen's next novel, *A World of Love,* is much like that of *The Heat of the Day* in respect of omniscience. Thus we are given a run-down of Fred's life previous to his establishment at Montefort, a glimpse of Antonia's career and marriage, and the story of Lilia's attempt to escape to London many years back. We are also offered longish passages of reflection on the part of the characters, sometimes, as in the following example, in direct thought. Here Antonia has just seen Jane hiding the mystery letters from Guy to an unknown woman:

> Antonia thought, so there *is* more to happen.
>   Life works to dispossess the dead, to dislodge and oust them. Their places fill themselves up; later people come in; all the room is wanted. Feeling alters its course, is drawn elsewhere or seeks renewal from other sources. When of love there is not enough to go round, inevitably it is the dead who must go without: we tell ourselves that they do not depend on us, or that they have not our requirements. Their continuous dying while we live, their repeated deaths as each of us die who knew them, are not in nature to be withstood. (WL 44)

Recalling the distorted syntax of *The Heat of the Day* but frequently different in kind and effect, there is a good deal of unusual word-order in *A World of Love*. It is very often a question of classical inversion, whereby certain words or phrases are given prominence by being placed at the head of a sentence and the rhythm becomes correspondingly slow: 'Endlessly was she to involve herself' (WL 15); 'Greatest of our denials to them is a part to play' (WL 44); 'Unmistakably was her stout shadow cast forward over the little garden' (WL 77); 'Stamped was the hour' (WL 77). The frequent inversions lend a solemn air of deliberation to the novel, harmonizing with its meditative character and recalling that its epigraph is taken from Traherne's *Centuries of Meditations*. The epigraph's sense of 'expectation and desire of some Great Thing' runs through the whole book and is heightened by the effect of timelessness, the 'almost total irrelevance of Time, in the abstract' to the Montefort kitchen (WL 21), which is broken violently at the end of the book by the strokes of Big Ben on the wireless.

There is also more robust writing in *A World of Love*, and the light of narrative irony plays hilariously on figures that are segregated, also by location, from the main plot: the nouveau-riche Lady Latterly less than graciously giving a dinner party at the castle, for instance, the village hairdresser in Clonmore blithely unworried about cutting Lilia's hair properly. It may be appropriate to dwell for a moment on such scenes, for this is the last Bowen novel in which comedy is reserved for subplot or minor characters; one might argue that it is the last novel to have anything like a subplot at all (if the Latterly passages may indeed be called a 'subplot'). Here is Clonmore's chatty, servile shopkeeper in free indirect speech, always a good vehicle for narrative distance:

> He would go so far as to say that this was heathen weather, in which but for God who was to predict what might happen next? They were demented with it, he had heard, in England – as for here, we were hardly to know ourselves. The advantage of having the hay saved early was less when you looked at cattle about to go mad with thirst – he hoped matters were not that way at Montefort? (WL 87)

More characteristically Bowenesque is the incongruous use of a word like 'applications' and the double-entendre of 'in still better spirits' in the following quotation:

The sole drawback of Miss Francie was her elusiveness: heart-whole applications of zeal and charm were interspersed by mysterious total vanishings. *In medias res* she had a way of flitting right off her premises, leaving a lady clamped down under a drier, steaming into a towel, or half-shorn (which was Lilia's predicament). Nor did another step in to take her place, Miss Maeve, her reputed partner, being never not known to be either indisposed or away on holiday. The *salon* ran therefore behind schedule: happily, however, time did not press – who could wish to hurry to quit this magic oasis of tinted mirror, enamel and bakelite? And Miss Francie never failed to return in still better spirits for having been away. Her smiling non-explanations were somehow flattering, and her goings, though inconvenient, left not a wound. (WL 90)

The Little Girls

Besides doing away with the traditional novelistic plot of courtship and romance, *The Little Girls* breaks new ground in respect of narrative approach. This was the consequence of a deliberate decision on Bowen's part, according to the Foreword that Spencer Curtis Brown wrote when he edited her posthumous *Pictures and Conversations*:

> In *The Little Girls*, she for the first time deliberately tried, as she said when discussing with me the writing of it, to present characters entirely from the outside. She determined never to tell the reader what her characters were thinking or feeling. She recalled that once when she had remarked to Evelyn Waugh that he never told his characters' thoughts, he had replied, 'I do not think I have any idea what they are thinking; I merely see them and show them.' In a way vastly different from Waugh's, she set herself the technical puzzle of writing a book 'externally'. (*Pictures and Conversations*, xxxviii)

Hence we now find the actions and words of her characters, and the comments of their friends, replacing psychological analysis – and much narrative report – on the part of their creator. The importance of dialogue is nothing new in Bowen, as her earlier fiction bears witness, and Glendinning tells how in 1942 Bowen spent a weekend in a country house where the talk was of writing, 'about how dialogue must always give clues, or counterpoints to clues; in that sense, Elizabeth said, every novel is a detective novel' (93:141). In *The Little Girls* dialogue becomes a mainstay of the narration, however, and even more than Bowen's earlier fiction this novel invites an attention to detail akin to the reading of detective fiction – a genre, incidentally, much appreciated by Bowen.

Dialogue is thus an obvious substitute for the 'stage directions' and character analysis otherwise provided by a narrator when Clare says to Dinah: 'Getting dark in here ... I can hardly see you' (LG 156), and when we understand that Dinah is deeply affected by the discovery of the empty coffer from Sheila's remark: 'You're as white as a sheet' (LG 162). When it comes to conveying information about past events, conversational exchanges are placed strategically. The death of Clare's father in battle is revealed by her to Sheila early in the book, for instance, in their teatime 'conference'; hence the parting in July 1914 between him and the woman he loves, Dinah's mother, receives full poignancy when it appears in the text a hundred pages or so later. Mrs Piggott is also dead when the novel opens, though we do not hear this in so many words before Part III (LG 145); but when her two needlework stools are mentioned as part of the furniture in Feverel Cottage in the childhood section (LG 77), we may readily think back to the faded stool we have seen earlier, in Dinah's drawing-room (LG 51), and we will then read the enchanting portrait of Mrs Piggott in the knowledge of her approaching death. The mystery surrounding the death of Dinah's father is likewise cleared up in Part III, perhaps putting to shame Sheila's suspicion that Dinah 'never did have a father, at the best of times' (LG 37). Here the use of having a forgetful chatterbox as a character is evident, for the reader is as much in the dark as Clare:

> '[The gun] may, of course, have been Father's; but if it was he can't have been keen on it. I mean, if he'd been keen on it he'd have used it, wouldn't he, instead of going under that train?'
> Clare's '*What?*' froze on her lips.
> 'I'm sorry – I'm terribly sorry, Mumbo!' cried Dinah, shaken. 'I thought you knew; I imagined everyone knew.' (LG 193)

One can see the felicity of Bowen's choice of major characters; apart from the talkative Dinah there is the malicious gossip, Sheila, and the eloquently taciturn Clare; all three very much alive to their surroundings and to each other, and any two of them not averse to talking about the absent third. Clare and Sheila discuss Dinah's press advertisements in Chapter I, 3, for instance, and manage *en passant* to convey a good deal of information about their friend's childhood; Dinah unfolds the mysteries of Sheila's character to Clare with similar advantages to the reader (LG, Ch. III,1). The choice of the three women is not merely practical: they correspond remarkably well to the triad of 'blood, brain and spirit' in George Meredith's poem 'The Woods of Westermain' (1883), which is recalled when Clare quotes from it, meaningfully repeating the line 'Enter these enchanted woods, you who dare' (LG 228). These are the lines referring to the triad:

> Pleasures that through blood run sane,
> Quickening spirit from the brain,
> Each of each in sequent birth,
> Blood and brain and spirit, three
> (Say the deepest gnomes of Earth),
> Join for true felicity.[8]

The sensuous Sheila corresponds to the poem's 'blood', the intellectual Clare to its 'brain', and the sensitive Dinah to its 'spirit'. Just as, according to the poem, all three must be present for 'true felicity', so the novel insists that they should be there all three: 'Three it was, so Three it should be,' as Dinah has it (LG 48). Mrs Piggott also draws attention to the threesome, finding them 'tiresome' when they are all together (LG 81)

Dinah will serve to illustrate how Bowen manages to convey depth of character without resorting to explicit analysis in the narrative voice. As we have met her as child and adult, this main character is impulsive and bossy, capable of cajoling her friends into joining in her fanciful schemes, both then and now; and she does not hesitate to spend enormous sums on putting advertisements in the press to get in touch with Clare and Sheila, or to trespass in a suburban garden to find the coffer they buried as children. It may therefore come as a surprise at the end of the book to hear her son say, 'As a rule, as you know, she's so very placid' (LG 232). 'Placid'? Sheila feigns exaggerated interest in her finger-bowl rather than answer this. And yet, thinking back some thirty pages or so, we may perhaps remember how Dinah reacted when Clare turned down her invitation to spend the night at Applegate: '"Very well," said Dinah *gently*, turning away' (LG 198; my italics). It is immediately after Clare's departure that Dinah knocks her head so violently that she loses consciousness. Whether this is in effect an accident or, as Patricia Juliana Smith suggests, the result of 'striking her head against the wall in her frustration and shame' (2), it certainly belies

---

[8] *Selected Poetical Works of George Meredith*, 51.

any 'placidness'. We may recall the narrative's wording in a childhood scene where Dinah is also the sufferer:

> Clare snatched at [Diana's] leg and expertly jerked it away from under. Down came Diana, without even a shriek. Not doubting she now was dead and in Heaven, she stayed as and where she had fallen, *placidly* wide-eyed. (LG 75-76; my italics)

So the adult Dinah's unruffled surface is not without precedent. How far it is a deliberate cover for emotional turmoil is for the reader to decide.

In the absence of narratorial analysis, intertextual references play a particularly important part in this book. Parallels to *Macbeth* are the most obvious. The idea of three women meeting for clandestine purposes bears a marked similarity to Shakespeare's three witches; the similarity is pointed out by one of them (Clare) and taken up immediately by another:

> 'This ... could be quite a Macbeth meeting-place, could it not?'
> 'Bubble-bubble,' said Dinah instantaneously. 'Not quite a heath, this, or exactly the weather, but near enough. The main wrong thing is, being one short. First Witch, Hail. Second Witch, Hail. Third Witch ...?' (LG 47)

The witch imagery is echoed in a remark by Dinah's friend, Frank Wilkins: 'What is this [potion] you two've been brewing up?' (LG 58); he later refers to the mask-maker as 'our local witch' (LG 191). The Macbeth reference is taken up again when Dinah calls Clare her 'Weird Sister' (LG 139), and when she speaks of their meeting place as 'the blasted heath' (LG 140). The play is also invoked at length later when, musing on anticipations of pleasure that are often disappointed, Dinah forces Sheila to quote Banquo's line, 'This guest of summer, the temple-haunting martlet' (LG 209). On a more concrete level, the handle of the butter-knife that Dinah inveigles from Clare is a visual reminder of the pilot's thumb in Shakespeare's witches' brew; it is 'gnarled and dark and with a knuckle bend in the middle' (LG 152). The pilot's thumb comes to mind again at the end of the novel when Sheila startlingly reveals that the secret object she has put into the coffer is a deformity she has been born with: a witch-like sixth toe. Equally remarkable is the sight of 11-year-old Dicey emerging with rust-reddened hands from an insanitary drain she has just chased little Trevor Artworth into (LG 127), recalling the blood on Lady Macbeth's hands (*Macbeth* 2 ii 64 and 5 i 33-49), and preparing us for the book's parallel to the queen's madness: the adult Dinah's final breakdown.

Bowen's decision to give up explicit character analysis when writing *The Little Girls* does not prevent her from letting her narrator 'intrude' frequently into the text, as she does in some of the examples at the head of this chapter. The ironical presence of the narrator is also unmistakable in stylistic devices like hyperbole. The text refers to Sheila as 'the traveller', for instance, when she has, after all, only 'travelled' from Kent to Somerset; often an exaggeratedly complimentary adverb will strike a mock-heroic note:

> Frank, with an emphatic roll of the eyes, said: 'Mrs Artworth has had a rocky journey, you'll be sorry to hear.'
> 'It's not that, so much,' said the traveller *pluckily*. (LG 51; my italics)

> 'So I ended up in a taxi,' said Sheila *bravely*. (LG 53; my italics)

A remarkable feature of this novel is its profusion of parentheses, in themselves an early idiosyncrasy of Bowen's which is kept up in her last novel, *Eva Trout*. They tend to establish an intimate relationship between narrator and reader and generally lend an impromptu air to the narration, which in *The Little Girls* chimes in with Dinah's extremely informal way of speaking and writing; the connection is pointed up by her page-long telephone conversation with Sheila (quoted p. 69 above), where her asides to Clare (sitting next to her) are given in parenthesis.

Sometimes the parenthetical texts convey factual information that might well have been left to straightforward narrative report:

> A portion of the Old High Street (that exactly across the way from the picture shop) reflected itself not only in the shop window but in the glass of these numerous pictures of itself. (LG 98)

> Her village (no great distance from Dinah's) was famed in this part of Somerset. (LG 181)

At other times the text inside the parenthesis offers a comment on the wording of the text outside and is not very different from metafictional asides of the type quoted above, p. 103, which needed no parenthesis:

> Today, in spite of (indeed, because of) the heat, Miss Ardingfay strolled outdoors after lunch. (LG 72)
>
> Something about the destruction (for so it seemed) of the moment of the candles let loose ... an element of scrimmage. (LG 122)

Or the reader may be addressed directly, sometimes with a question:

> If Dinah's regard more rested upon than examined the new-found Clare, Clare's in return (out of habit?) was inventorial. (LG 46)
>
> The cut of the jib of Mrs Artworth (whom, recall, he'd taken to be *the* lady) had caused him at once to whisk out the lace mats. (LG 57)

Parentheses apart, the text has many such questions inviting reader participation, often with a note of irony:

> Cuth Barnes pocketed the hankie – whether from knightly love, out of fetichism or with some idea of blackmail, who was to say? (LG 111)
>
> Their marriages had not only rejoiced her but seemed to allay some fear – had she perhaps feared to outstay her welcome? (LG 201)

The presence of the narrator thus makes itself strongly felt in *The Little Girls*, and though explicit analysis in the narrative voice is rare, it has not quite disappeared. Anticipating Dinah's musings about disappointed expectations noted a couple of pages back, the narrative voice has thus told us that Mrs Piggott was 'smiling at the beginnings of so much pleasure' when she arrived at the birthday picnic – little knowing that this was to be the last time she would see the man she loved, and that in a few years they would both be dead (LG 120). Here are other examples where the narrator steps in to explain the workings of her characters' minds:

> [Clare's] known objection to scenery had been hardened by years which had shown her how sound it was. By now, she resisted many things; or, should she fail to, acted as though she did by affecting an extra nonchalance or jocosity. To be sardonic could be a refuge also. (LG 47)
>
> (The sons' adoption of a would-be repressive policy towards Francis was a sign not of overbearingness in their natures but rather of the optimism of which their mother had spoken). (LG 202)

The liberal use of irony and the many grotesque scenes in which the main characters take part lend this novel a playful, throwaway air that belies the seriousness of its themes and may be linked to the general foregrounding of the textual surface referred to in my introduction. Along the same lines, and with her special interest in the lesbian tensions of Bowen's work, Jane Rule has this to say:

> Because the book is so elaborately teasing, it diverts the attention from its basic emotional statement while at the same time it creates the climate for it. Dinah will finally have everything, including Clare. (121)

Eva Trout

The narrative style of *Eva Trout* is coloured by the Gothic mode of the book, which will be discussed separately in my final chapter. Imagery is often violent – Eva is thought of as a 'she-Cossack' (ET 81) and her speech 'cement-like' (ET 17) – and there are formulaic forays into the register of fairy-tale: 'For two-and-a-half hours, up hill, down dale, they had been rushing through cold scenery' (ET 11-12); 'How fared the benighted Jaguar, over hill and dale?' (ET 18).

In this last novel, the decision Bowen made when writing *The Little Girls*, to present her characters from the outside, is not so much modified as refined. True, there are few passages where the voice of the narrator explicitly analyses the minds of the characters, but their thoughts and reactions are amply revealed in other ways that are hardly 'from the outside'. Eva's half-awake memories or fantasies, for instance, are given in a dreamlike mixture of direct speech and free indirect thought that presupposes access to her mind, and in the image of the 'broken pieces of time' such narrative report as there is unmistakably bears the mark of the narrator:

> What are you doing, Eva, lying in the dark?
> Lying in the dark.
> Supposing somebody came in softly, saying, 'How is my darling?' She *had* heard somebody saying, 'How is my darling?' – but when? where? Some other child had been present, a very sick one: 'Darling.' Eva searched through her store of broken pieces of time, each one cut out more sharply by fever, looking for an answer. The voice had come in as a door opened – but what door? where? (ET 47-48)

A salient feature of this last novel is the widespread use of speech allusion, whereby words or turns of phrase associated with a particular character or a commonly held point of view are incorporated into a seemingly impassive narrative. I have earlier quoted allusions to Louie's way of speaking and thinking in *The Heat of the Day*, and in *Eva Trout* to Constantine's flowery language and the slangy speech of the castle school pupils. Speech allusion effectively determines reader reaction in the case of a character like Eric Arble, who changes inexplicably from the patient, understanding husband of Chapter I,2, who does not even openly blame his wife for her part in the failure of their fruit-farm, to the domineering vulgarian who tries to fetch Eva back to Larkins in Chapter I,7 – inexplicably, that is, until we realize that the hostile picture in Chapter I,7 reflects Eva's fright, and that Chapter I,2 in fact gave us Eric's own self-image in terms that he himself might have used, with questions that might have been his own:

> Eric had profited, hands down, by his military service – he came out of three years with a mechanized unit a first-rate mechanic: clearly, he'd been a born one. (And good with men). Possibly that should have been his line from the start? – from, that was, when he first came out of the army? He might have had a garage of his own by now, who knows? Anyway, no good thinking ... As it was, he nowadays daily caught the seven-thirty a.m. bus into town, intercepting it at the crossroads, and usually made it home on the six-thirty p.m. In the Larkins barn sat an old Anglia, bought when they'd sold the van – but if *he* took that, what was Izzy to do all day? (ET 22-23)

His wife is given a different but similarly allusive presentation. As a teacher we see her first in theatrical silhouette, holding forth to a breathless class of adolescent girls:

> Supremacy set apart this wonderful teacher. She could have taught anything. Her dark suit might have been the habit of an Order. Erect against a window of tossing branches she stood moveless, but for the occasional gesture of hand to forehead – then, the bringing of the finger-tips to the brain seemed to complete an electric circuit. Throughout a lesson, her voice held a reined-in excitement – imparting knowledge, she conveyed its elatedness. (ET 58)

To a reader of today, this classroom performance would admittedly have profited by more modern teaching methods; and the 'wonderful' in the lines just quoted does not seem to be shared by the narrator, who has already referred to Iseult hyperbolically as a 'dazzling' teacher (ET 17). Nevertheless, the almost journalistically fulsome praise is not really qualified until much later in the book, when it is recalled, and unmasked as a piece of self-promoted hearsay, in Constantine's 'You still teach marvellously?' (ET 226)

We have met Iseult Smith in exposition before we see her actually functioning as a teacher, however, and her too-easy disparagement of Eva's speech is even then pinpricked by a recurrent stylistic move on the part of the narrator: an interrogative aside that invites us to share her reservations about Iseult Smith:

> What caused the girl to express herself like a displaced person? The explanation – that from infancy onward Eva had had as attendants displaced persons, those at a price being the most obtainable, to whose society she'd been largely consigned – for some reason never appeared: *too simple, perhaps?* (ET 17; my italics)

Later, Iseult is again under a similar kind of attack:

> Even Iseult (then Smith) had, during the great research, uncovered practically nothing on that subject [Eva's first school] – *she had perhaps not probed deeply enough?* (ET 48; my italics)

The fragmented structure characteristic of much Gothic writing appears in *Eva Trout* in the extraordinary dependence (even more than usual in Bowen's fiction) on extra-narrative features like letters and telegrams, which are used not only to reveal character but also to carry the plot along. The text thus reproduces numerous letters – from Constantine, Eric, Iseult, Henry, and from Eva herself, plus telegrams between Henry and Eva and several pages of Iseult's reflective, character-revealing diary. We understand much of what is actually going on from these communications, but understanding does not always come easily. In the second part of the book, for instance, it takes a good deal of concentration on the part of the reader to follow the movements of Mr and Mrs Dancey in Paris. By thus being forced to scrutinize the text in order to follow the plot, we are led to examine also its revelations or suggestions about what has been going on in the minds of the characters. Apparently Henry's father did not meet Eva in Paris, for example, but we are not told whether this was because he deliberately avoided her; most readers will very likely see their non-meeting as a sign of his disapproval of the Henry-Eva relationship – again, the interpretation is up to us.

The epistolary form is also used for one of the comic highlights of the novel, Eva's journey by air to America to pick up Jeremy. We read about the flight in a letter from a fellow passenger of hers, the self-important Professor Portman C Holman. He appears to be quite taken with Eva's nonchalant behaviour and 'unencumbered physique' (ET 123; she is apparently bra-less), and in between bouts of narcissistic self-pity he gives a graphic picture of her, putting a generous interpretation on her bovine silences and slow speech:

> In my academic capacity I give forth constantly, when not to my students then to my colleagues; existence would be insuperable without that. What a gulf between that and our intercourse. To you I *spoke*, Mrs Trout, to a comprehension latent within your silence. You in return granted me observations which to one not in key with you could have seemed enigmatic: each was, on the contrary, *you* revealed. The exactitude of your diction, its slow purity –. (ET 125)

First Person Narratives
The preceding pages have dealt exclusively with third person narratives. The first person narrator is a rare bird in Bowen's fiction, and there are only two examples among the works I am looking at. One is the late wartime story, 'The Dolt's Tale', where a seedy criminal ambience is seen through rose-coloured spectacles by a 'dolt' who is being exploited by a gang of black marketeers. The other is 'A Day in the Dark', the last story to be included in *The Collected Stories of Elizabeth Bowen* and a considerably more sophisticated example of Bowen's writing. This story of an adolescent girl's encounter with adult cynicism is told by herself many years after the event with an extraordinary degree of narrative over-emphasis, including the too-neat setting up of contrasting characters, glaring metaphors, and dramatic paragraphing and linear spacing. Yet it is precisely because the narrator is so heavy-handed, so obvious in her striving for effect, that we as readers are disposed to take at face value the artless way she tries to convince us that there was no element of sexuality in her relationship with the charming, easy-going uncle at whose farm she was staying as a young girl. Because she is so often less than subtle, we do not suspect her of being designing.

* * *

There are many different ways in which Bowen colours the story she is telling. The chapter entitled 'A Summer's Day' in *Eva Trout* may serve as a representative late example where the hand of the author appears felicitously in the choice of narrative mode. In this failed reconciliation scene between Eva and her former teacher, there is much free indirect thought and speech allusion on the part of Iseult Arble, revealing both her nervous anticipation at meeting Eva and her lightweight literary interests; there is also a good deal of direct speech, where we see Eva's stubborn refusal to be drawn out. With such built-in indicators, we hardly need the narrative voice to interpret the scene for us.

But Bowen's narrator is never quite silent, not in any of the texts I am considering. Perhaps paradoxically, the overall effect is arguably to enhance the credibility of her fiction. On the one hand, the metafictional aspects of her narrative moves serve to stress the fact that someone is merely telling a story – worrying about finding the right words, supplying similes, giving deadpan comments on the characters: the garden gate to Feverel Cottage is 'strictly, an ironwork door in the wall' (LG 84), Jane is 'like a boy actor in woman's clothes' (WL 10), Robert says something 'with pardonable irony' (HD 196). On the other hand, the texts often suggest that the narrator herself is an onlooker like her readers – involving us in her own frequently ironical assessments, inviting us to share her scepticism: Sheikie's room is 'surely the prettiest in Southstone? – probably England, possibly the world?' (LG 108), the never-given explanation for Eva's unfortunate conversational style is 'too simple, perhaps?' (ET 17). In other words, by making us forget that she is actually writing about a fictive universe, Bowen may also make us forget that her narrative persona is part of the fiction.

CHAPTER 8

Stages and Stage Properties

In employing a theatrical metaphor of Bowen's own as the heading of this chapter I do not mean to suggest that there is anything particularly *stagey* in her universe, but that the characters in her fiction move and speak in a space as sharply visualized as any theatre set, containing objects designed to suggest the meaning of a given episode or an entire text. I take my point of departure in two quotations from Bowen herself. She speaks of the *novel* in one and *stories* in the other, but this is clearly because of the context; the world of her novels and short stories seems to me to be fundamentally the same, and even the futuristic landscape of 'Gone Away' has the same kind of stage properties as traditional Bowen 'terrain'.

The first quotation refers to the use of objects in fiction, and since Bowen includes trees and mountains as 'objects' I take it that her remarks also apply generally to features in a landscape. 'It is a good main rule,' she wrote in 1945,

> that objects – chairs, trees, glasses, mountains, cushions – introduced into the novel should be stage-properties, necessary for 'business'. It will also be recalled that the well-set stage shows many objects *not* actually necessary for 'business' – but that these have a right to place by being descriptive – explanatory. In a play, the absence of the narrating voice makes it necessary to establish the class, period and general psychology of the characters by means of objects that can be seen. In the novel, such putting of objects to a descriptive (explanatory) use is excellent – alternative to the narrator's voice.[1]

My second quote is from the posthumously published *Pictures and Conversations:* 'Am I not manifestly a writer for whom places loom

---

[1] 'Notes on Writing a Novel'. *Orion 2* (Autumn 1945); quoted from *The Mulberry Tree*, 47-48.

large?' Bowen asks, wondering at the lack of critical interest in the localities of her stories. She goes on to explain that she is not a 'regional' writer, for her terrain is unspecific and cannot be found on any map. She continues:

> Ireland and England, between them, contain my stories, with occasional outgoings into France or Italy: within the boundaries of those countries there is no particular locality I have staked a claim on or identified with. Given the size of the world, the scenes of my stories are scattered over only a small area .... Since I started writing, I have been welding together an inner landscape .... A writer needs to have a command of, and to have recourse to, a recognisable world, geographically consistent and having for him or her a super-reality.[2]

Though Bowen's terrain is largely 'unspecific' (somewhere in the west of England, somewhere in the Home Counties, somewhere in or around County Cork in Ireland), one or two places are particularly associated with her: in the fiction I am considering, there is both Regent's Park (in 'I Hear You say So' and *The Heat of the Day*) and the Kentish coast – a fictional Folkestone appears as 'Southstone' in 'Ivy Gripped the Steps' and *The Little Girls*, 'Wanchurch' in that book is patently modelled on Dymchurch, and North Foreland is the site of Eva's miserable villa in *Eva Trout*. There are certain well-known public places like Shannon airport and the main-line departure stations in London, but one rarely finds actual buildings described as minutely as Dickens' study in 'Bleak House' in Broadstairs, whose dead, insipid atmosphere, with its dreary mementoes and its early paperback editions 'set out in a grubby fan' (ET 113), is well calculated to inspire in the reader a gloomy sense of mortality in keeping with the Gothic mood of Bowen's last novel.

Objects and features in a landscape (or seascape, or townscape) do not necessarily have to figure by more than mere mention for them to influence our understanding of a text – much as, for example, the actual dogs mentioned in *The Heat of the Day* link up with various uses of the word 'dog', and so emphasize the thematic aspect of spy-hunting in that book. In this respect the treacherous Goodwin Sands off the east coast of Kent, though only thought of and talked of in the Broadstairs scene, contribute unmistakably to the sense of doom running through *Eva Trout*.

---

[2] *Pictures and Conversations*; quoted from *The Mulberry Tree*, 282-83.

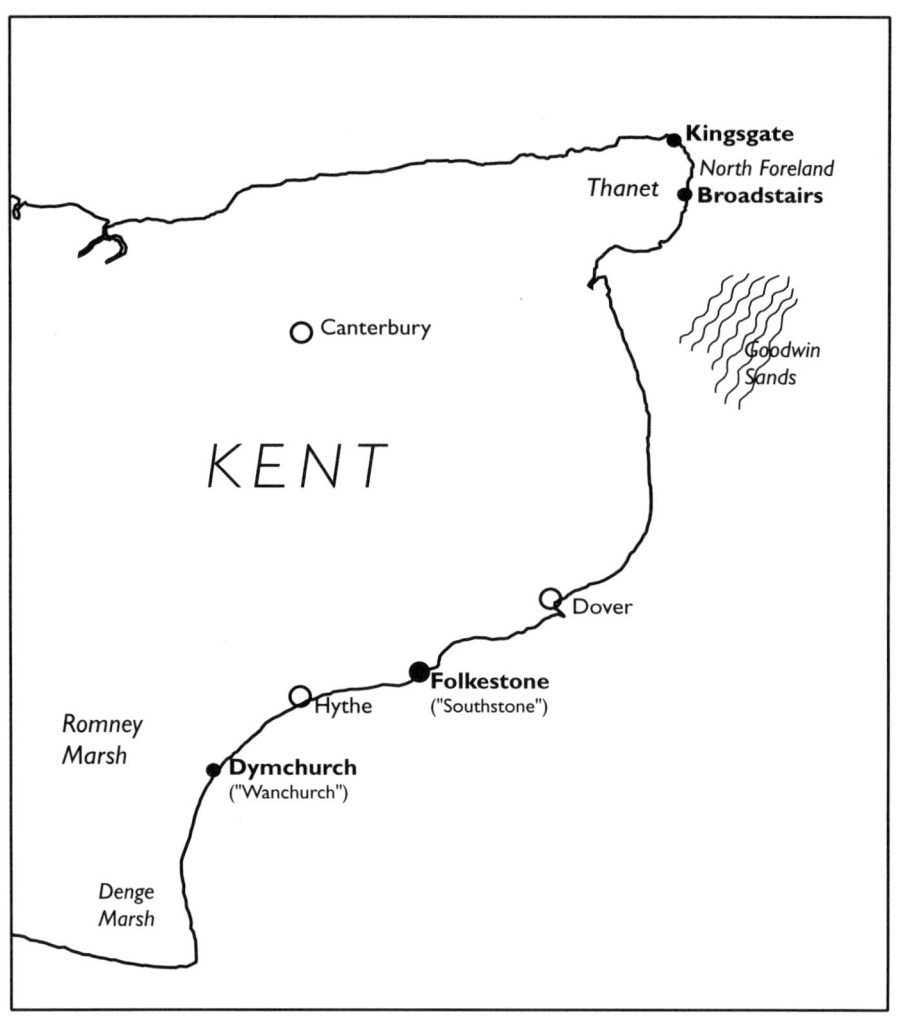

This map shows some of the real-life and fictionalized places that come into Bowen's later fiction. The Kentish coast belonged to what she called her 'terrain'. Some places are lightly fictionalized: Folkestone as 'Southstone', Dymchurch as 'Wanchurch' - Bowen herself said she had 'taken liberties' with the Folkestone landscape in her fiction (letter to William Plomer 18 June 1963; quoted Jordan 182). Other locations are not disguised, e.g. Broadstairs with the Bleak House Museum shown p. 60.
Map by Museum Tusculanum Press.

Movement

A characteristic Bowen type of location invites special mention: the moving scenery in which she frequently places her characters – an airliner, a car, a train compartment. Space is often constricted, as in these cases, which recall on the one hand the many other kinds of constricted space in her books, on the other the almost compulsive travelling she puts her characters through and the recurring sense of movement and speed in her fiction.

Cars, for instance, are not only natural attributes of their owners, as Clare in *The Little Girls* has a business-like Mini and the estate agent Mr Denge in *Eva Trout* drives an eminently respectable Rover, Eva herself an ostentatious Jaguar. Cars also serve as a location for much dialogue, which is given a sense of urgency by the movement of the vehicle and the proximity of the speakers; examples include Antonia furiously driving Jane home from the dinner party at the castle in *A World of Love*, and, in the same book, Jane and Maud and the chauffeur in uneasily close company on the front seat of the castle van on the way to Shannon Airport. One of Bowen's most remarkable moving scenes is set in the airliner that takes Eva to America in her last novel. In tune with the excesses of the book's Gothic mode, the Biblical story of Eve makes a sudden appearance in these airborne surroundings: Bowen's Eva drops an apple; the fatuous professor whose letter tells the story hands it back to her; then she apparently falls asleep.

Lighting

It will be natural to mention another characteristic feature of Bowen's locations: their lighting. Before adopting the career of a writer she had in fact had hopes of becoming an artist, and when she was twenty she spent two terms at an art school in London. She found that she did not after all have the necessary talent, but her early interest stayed with her:

> It seems to me that often when I write I am trying to make words do the work of line and colour. *I have the painter's sensitivity to light.* Much (and perhaps the best) of my writing is verbal painting. (My italics)[3]

Glendinning has noted that this sensitivity to light is 'most striking when she writes about the effects of the outside, disorderly world on the

---

[3] An autobiographical note from c. 1947, quoted by Glendinning (93:41).

inside world, light filtering through the boundaries of this and that' (98:30). In the present context the play of light and dark in many Bowen landscapes comes to mind. There is for example the open-air theatre in Regent's Park in the beginning of *The Heat of the Day:*

> The light was so low, so theatrical, and so yellow that it was evident it would soon be gone. The incoming tide was evening. Glass-clear darkness, in which each leaf was defined, already formed in the thicket behind the orchestra and was the other element of the stage. (HD 7)

Or there is the early morning in the first lines of *A World of Love*:

> The sun rose on a landscape still pale with the heat of the day before. There was no haze, but a sort of coppery burnish out of the air lit on flowing fields, rocks, the face of the one house and the cliff of limestone overhanging the river.... This light at this hour, so unfamiliar, brought into being a new world – painted, expectant, empty, intense. (WL 9)

The many dominant night-time scenes in *The Heat of the Day* are rendered particularly intense by taking place in the wartime blackout; and on this background the very different lighting at the end of the novel – there is a day of sunshine followed by one of 'white quiet light' (HD 329) – goes to reinforce the ironical, cliché-like impression I have referred to earlier, where Louie holds up her new-born son to see swans flying towards the west (HD 330). Symbolic associations are never far below the surface, and not least in interiors: the lurid café scenes in *The Heat of the Day* (Ch. 12) and *Eva Trout* (Ch. I,12), for instance, and Antonia's dusky bedroom in the first chapter of *A World of Love*, with sunlight coming in through rents in the curtains (the bright light of day ousting the shadows of the past). The use of light and dark is not always unambiguous, however. A case in point is the short story 'A Day in the Dark', where the obnoxious Mrs Banderry's sunless house has thick lace curtains and a screen of trees that make it a suffocating contrast to the farm where the adolescent protagonist-cum-narrator is staying; there, butterflies fly in and out of the open windows. In spite of its emphasis on 'dark', and in spite of its title (with its play on being 'in the dark', as the narrator is in her youth), the story does not leave a final impression of darkness, for the evil aura of Mrs Banderry is far outweighed by the radiance of the young girl's first experience of love.

Recycled Objects

In discussing Bowen's imagery (Chapter 6) I have included locks as an example of objects that appear in all the novels under consideration. In the present context I may mention one or two further examples of recycled properties that belong on all her fictional stages. Bells, for instance. The sound of bell-ringing is rarely pleasant. The bells rung to celebrate Montgomery's victory at El Alamein in *The Heat of the Day* might have been thought of as bells of joy, but they lose their attraction even before they have come to a climax (HD 291). In the dining room at Montefort in *A World of Love*, the first of Big Ben's nine o'clock chimes on the wireless is enough to make the room 'a struck ship' (WL 129). The church-bells in *The Little Girls* are almost diabolical; Dinah's car, darting to and fro in an attempt to escape from their 'pandemonium', becomes 'a thing trapped' (LG 181). The Christmassy sleigh-bells in *Eva Trout*, 'gusted' out of the revolving doors of big stores, are as synthetic as everything else in that book (ET 130). There are countless door-bells, too, and attention is frequently drawn to ringing or knocking on doors, heightening the effect of 'proper' bell-ringing and the pervasive interest in sound in Bowen's fiction.

Among recycled objects one might also instance curtains. In *The Heat of the Day*, they are at first a natural part of the blackout in wartime London. But as the novel progresses, the common fear of showing a chink of light also becomes a metaphor for hiding one's feelings; in the final show-down it merges into Robert's very real fear of capture, and he knows that someone is waiting outside Stella's flat to take him when he says: 'Stella! Don't touch the curtain!' (HD 286). Elsewhere curtains are often mentioned as an indication of economic standing, but rarely only that: in *The Little Girls*, for instance, Mrs Piggott's bay window is 'tangled with muslin curtains' (LG 77) that have come down to her from a larger house – besides revealing her poverty, the tangled curtains are also a metaphor for the entanglement of the spell cast by Dinah's mother. In *Eva Trout*, the straitened circumstances of the Arbles are immediately visible in arty curtains that have been 'skimped by economy' and have between them 'strips of vacuous darkness' (ET 19); at the same time we are made aware of Iseult Arble's artistic aspirations, and her inadequacies outside the classroom. And with characteristic lack of subterfuge, for all her persecution mania, Eva herself gladly leaves the drawing-room uncurtained at Cathay – willy-nilly, for the material has rotted and the runners are rusted onto the rail (ET 96).

Short stories

Before considering Bowen's post war novels separately, I might note that locations and objects in her shorter fiction are quite as meaningful as those in her novels. I have already drawn attention to the houses in 'A Day in the Dark'. One could also instance the ivy that chokes the once-distinguished house in 'Ivy Gripped the Steps', epitomizing the strangled emotional life of the protagonist. In 'Gone Away' the location *is* the story: a picture-book village complete with church and vicarage and pond with stuffed ducks, preserved as a showpiece in the middle of a ghost town where machinery is the only sign of life, and where conveyors with plastic platefuls of frozen salad still circulate past empty rows of stools in the cafeterias.

The first paragraph of 'Hand in Glove' offers a good example of a well-set fictional stage, with a style allusively reflecting the attitude of a mother with marriageable daughters ('favourably', 'prettily-wooded', 'still better', 'lively', 'auspicious', 'the military', 'advantage'). The objects singled out for mention are more than enough to establish the class, income-level, and mental make-up of the characters:

> Jasmine Lodge was favourably set on a residential, prettily-wooded hillside in the south of Ireland, overlooking a river and, still better, the roofs of a lively garrison town. Around 1904, which was the flowering period of the Miss Trevors, girls could not have had a more auspicious home – the neighbourhood spun merrily round the military. Ethel and Elsie, a spirited pair, garnered the full advantage – no ball, hop, picnic, lawn tennis, croquet or bathing party was complete without them; in winter, though they could not afford to hunt, they trimly bicycled to all meets, and on frosty evenings, with their guitars, set off to *soirées*, snug inside their cab in their fur-tipped capes. (CS 767)

By now we already know that this will be a story about two impoverished sisters aggressively on the look-out for a husband. They have clearly been on the market for some time, setting out in a hired conveyance with their inevitable guitars, and 'trimly' cycling to meets of the hunt they cannot afford to take part in. The sisters put a brave front on their poverty, and the last line reads like a reflection of their own speech; for a merely fur-*tipped* cape never made anyone 'snug'.

The Heat of the Day

The townscape of wartime London forms a natural setting for *The Heat of the Day,* and the novel begins with a scene in Regent's Park, a favourite part of Bowen's terrain. There are relatively few place names in the story, in keeping with the universal tenor of the theme. Here is a characteristic passage; the narrator is talking of 'that heady autumn of the first London raids', the autumn of 1940:

> Never had any season been more felt; one bought the poetic sense of it with the sense of death. Out of mists of morning charred by the smoke from ruins each day rose to a height of unmisty glitter; between the last of sunset and first note of the siren the darkening glassy tenseness of evening was drawn fine. From the moment of waking you tasted the sweet autumn not less because of an acridity on the tongue and nostrils.... All through London, the ropings-off of dangerous tracts of street made islands of exalted if stricken silence, and people crowded against the ropes to admire the sunny emptiness on the other side. (HD 90-91)

The metaphor 'islands of stricken silence' in this quotation is also a latent metaphor for the isolation of the lovers. Stella Rodney lives in different rented flats, which are the closest she gets to a home of her own, reflecting both the impermanence of wartime conditions and her own rootless nature. Her flats are on the top floor of tall buildings, reached either by laborious staircase or cranking lift (she is an attractive women, and a sexual interpretation of such staircase wells lies near at hand). The two houses in the book that come in for lengthy description are not Stella's: her lover Robert Kelway's family home, Holme Dene, and the Irish Big House inherited by her son, Mount Morris.

Holme Dene is a sordid parody of the English upper-middle-class country house, which is shown up in all its tasteless narrow-mindedness, with imitation oak beams and twisting passages,[4] and fancy-shaped flower beds in an over-furnished garden complete with tennis pavilion, pergola, sundial, rock garden, dovecote, gnomes, seesaw, rusticated seats and bird bath. The very name 'Holme Dene', silly and pretentious, suggests the isolation of the house. *Holme* may mean low-lying land near a river or, very appositely in this context, a small island (cut off from its surroundings just as much as the Kelways' house is); it is tempting also to think of *holm*, meaning the holly or evergreen holm-oak. A *dene* is a valley, often a wooded valley. 'Holme Dene' is thus a fitting name for a lonely house surrounded by evergreens and hidden

---

[4] The passages are called 'swastika-like' (HD 258), with an open allusion to Robert's Nazi sympathies.

from the road, contrasting with the more openly (but equally pretentiously) named 'Fair Leigh' where Robert's unfortunate father would have preferred to live. Behind its evergreen barricade, Holme Dene is permeated by an almost police-state surveillance with a highly effective 'intelligence service' (HD 256): everyone always knows what everyone else is doing, and one cannot even look out of a window or up the stairs without being asked what one is up to. It is, as Glendinning has it, 'a house of spies, a house to breed spies' (93:150).

The oppressive atmosphere of Holme Dene is intensified by its silence: the grandfather clock in the hall has stopped, and there are no rooks in the sky or in the trees. The sterile silence of the Kelway mansion is diametrically opposed to the nighttime stillness of the Irish Big House, 'something more than silence', where there is not even the 'rustle of a sleepy rook' (HD 311) – for of course there *are* rooks at Mount Morris. Though its master may be dead, the Irish house is very much the opposite. The building itself is like a living being whose colour changes with the changing light; the landscape, too, is almost alive, and the verbs used to describe it are active: the cliffs *drop* their reflections into the water, trees *top* or *clothe* the cliffs, the river *sweeps* towards the house and *traces* the boundary of the land, and woods *run* down in a series of promontories (HD 162). With its river valley, overgrown cliffs, and fringe of meadow land, the Mount Morris demesne has all the trappings of the pleasance or *locus amoenus* of classical rhetoric. It becomes a welcome place of refuge from the emotional turmoil of the previous scenes; and it is here that Stella begins to see the plausibility of the assertions made by Harrison about her lover's treason which gives her the moral strength to confront Robert.

Along with houses, restaurants offer obvious symbolic possibilities as locations and are exploited in much of Bowen's later fiction, their meaning often pointed up by the effect of lighting. A case in point in *The Heat of the Day* is the sleazy underground café or night-club where Stella has dinner with Harrison, a meal as unappetizing as their relationship: lobster mayonnaise on a 'bed of greenstuff knifed into dripping ribbons' (HD 226) followed by a fruit flan onto which ashes drop from Harrison's cigarette (HD 233). The lighting is 'more powerful even than could be accounted for by the bold white globes screwed aching to the low white ceiling' and makes all human details stand out with uncompromising clarity: 'there survived in here not one shadow: every one had been ferreted out and killed' (HD 225). The entrance to the restaurant has a dimmed sign saying 'Open', and light comes up a flight of stone stairs down which Harrison takes Stella. An earlier reference to the 'Danteësque' features of the caretaker at Mount Morris (HD 164) makes it natural to associate this underground café with the Descent into Hell in Dante's *Divine Comedy*. In the same novel an emptying restaurant – lights being put out, table-cloths taken off – serves to suggest an inevitable end to Stella's affair with Robert after her illuminating trip to Ireland and their near-quarrel in the taxi (HD, Ch. 10). The scene is reminiscent of the last scene in James Joyce's 'Araby', where the half-dark hall of the closing bazaar is a forceful icon for the disillusionment of the protagonist.

One aspect of Bowen's descriptions of location that I have only briefly touched on earlier, the notation of sound and silence, makes itself felt conspicuously in *The Heat of the Day*. Sound and its absence are an integral part of the wartime London setting and form a running accompaniment to the story, which is framed in sound, so to speak: it opens with an open-air concert in Regent's Park, and it ends with the drone of homecoming bombers and the sound of flying swans over the south coast of England. On the evening Harrison first calls to see Stella, bringing with him an end to her peace of mind, stillness – the quiet before the storm – is an all-permeating force that mounts the stairs to enter her flat at the half-open door and comes in through the open windows from the deserted street (HD 23). The early days of her love-affair with Robert are associated for her with the 'icelike tinkle of broken glass being swept up among the crisping leaves' (HD 93) in that heady autumn of 1940; their actual meeting in a bar or club is orchestrated by an air-raid, where the text's drawn-out verbs and twice-repeated 'detonation' stand out with full force against a startling array of short violent verbs and nouns:

> Overhead, an enemy plane had been *dragging, drumming* slowly round in the pool of night, *drawing* up *bursts* of gunfire – *nosing, pausing, turning*, fascinated by the point for its intent. The barrage *banged, coughed, retched*; in here the lights in the mirrors *rocked*. Now down a shaft of anticipating silence the bomb swung whistling. With the *shock* of *detonation*, still to be heard, four walls of in here *yawped* in then bellied out; bottles danced on glass; a distortion ran through the view. The *detonation* dulled off into the cataracting *roar* of a split building: direct *hit*, somewhere else. (HD 96; my italics)

A World of Love

Bowen often signals the importance of her locations by placing them at the head of a text, as *The Heat of the Day* begins with a description of the open-air theatre in Regent's Park. The following example is from the first page of *A World of Love;* as in the previous novel, active verbs are applied to both house and landscape:

> Montefort stood at a right-angle to the nearby gorge, towards which it *presented* a blind end – though in this the vestige of a sealed-up Venetian window was to be traced. In its day the window had *overlooked* the garden which, broken-walled, still *projected* over the river view. A way *zigzagged* steeply down through thickets and undergrowth to the water's edge: the cliff *arose* from the water, opposite. (WL 9; my italics)

Meaning is also embodied in the name of the house, Montefort, which appears throughout as a fortress from which 'sallies' are made (WL 28); attention is frequently drawn to the gate with its 'warped white spears' (WL 74) that has to be unchained and chained again whenever anyone passes through, and to windows that must be bolted and doors locked at night. The 'sealed-up' window in the quotation above prefigures the pent-up emotions and conflicts of the people living in the house. It is interesting, too, to see the garden mentioned so early, for it proves to be the location of a turning-point in the husband-wife relationship in the novel. It is one of the most symbol-laden locations in a generally symbol-laden book, complete with apple-tree, sundial, box-hedge, briars, thrush, and lizards.[5]

The beauty of the adolescent Jane is captured in the night landscape she cycles through after the fête at the castle:

> Music followed her over the empty country as she bicycled home through the lanes between there and Montefort; dust wraithlike rose from under her wheels. Honeysuckle sweetened the deepening hedges, from beyond which breathed distances cool with hay. The land had not yet composed itself quite to sleep, for light was not gone and might never go from the sky. The air through which she was swiftly passing was mauve, and tense with suspended dew: her own beautiful restlessness was everywhere. (WL 26-27)

---

[5] Martha McGowan points out (61 sqq.) that the imagery of the Montefort garden recalls the *hortus conclusus* of Christian iconographic and related literary traditions.

Elsewhere the landscape has more unequivocally sexual overtones, as in a central passage (WL 77) where Antonia, standing in the front doorway at Montefort, feels the presence of Guy's and her own past rushing towards her from the obelisk and avenue and woods and river. The obelisk comes in here, of course, for this powerful erotic symbol runs through the whole novel. The monument appears already in the second paragraph of the book: even before Montefort itself is described we read of the obelisk standing on a rise of grass and casting its long shadow towards the house. It is mentioned in Guy's old love-letters; Jane reads them leaning against its base; her Lawrentian father enters the story sauntering down the rise on which it stands; and the castle chauffeur Harris finds a four-leaved clover near its foot.

I have mentioned above some of the moving locations Bowen uses. I might also draw attention to the potential sexual associations of the motion of a car, which are exploited, and perhaps parodied, in *A World of Love,* when Fred and Lilia seal their reconciliation by going for an almost unprecedented drive in the old Ford. The 'blow of air' Lilia speaks of twice in the following lines readily lends itself to an erotic interpretation, as does 'going for a spin'. We note, too, that the obelisk is mentioned here, in no uncertain terms:

> Antonia ... begged to know: 'What are you doing now?'
> 'We thought of going for a spin.'
> 'You and who?'
> 'I and Fred – for a blow of air,' amplified Lilia, fanning her brow to show the need. She opened the fence gate into the elsewhere of the evening: up stood the obelisk over floating light; sunset kindling the belt of trees dissolved into others the faint elder – from which like a cry came the sadness of something gone. 'Like we sometimes used to,' Lilia continued.
> 'Fred needs a blow of air?'
> 'It was his idea.' (WL 125-126)

This is Joan Hassall's woodcut for *A World of Love* in the Cape Collected Edition of Bowen's works. It shows the heroine leaning against the obelisk in front of Montefort, the Big House that has lost its former grandeur. She is wearing an old muslin dress she has found in the attic, and reading one of the letters that fell out of the dress – a packet of old love letters from the charismatic Guy, Montefort's former owner, which pass from one character to another through the book until their final burning puts an end to his dominance. *Reproduced by kind permission of Mr Brian North Lee, London.*

The dilapidated (and sexually evocative) state of Montefort is contrasted markedly with the sterile ambience of Latterly Castle to which Jane is invited. At Montefort the water-colours on the wall in the drawing-room are obviously there to cover stains, the Gothic hall chairs are unsteady, the best bedroom has rents in the curtains and its pillows shed their feathers. Lady Latterly's bedroom at the castle, on the other hand, is a costly replica of 1930s furnishings, and there is no sign that anyone has walked on the silver bloom of the carpet apart from 'footprints like tracks in dew' (WL 56).

As in *The Heat of the Day,* sound and silence are used with great effect in this novel; here the silence is not that of fear before an air-raid, however, but the held breath of expectancy. The noise of the tractor in the fields (WL 20, 45) brings in the haymaking backdrop to the story, and sounds come across strongly in the silent landscape: a bird, a door creaking, a dog barking. In the following quotation, unusual word-order, striking images and a deliberate rhythm build up a hush of anticipation in the Montefort yard, an anticipation of rain and of sexual fulfilment:

> [A] visible silence filled the place – long it was since anyone had been here. Slime had greenly caked in the empty trough, and the unprecedented loneliness of the afternoon looked out, as through eyelets cut in a mask, from the archways of the forsaken dovecote. Not a straw stirred, or was there to stir, in the kennel; and above her [Jane] something other than clouds was missing from the uninhabited sky. Nothing was to be known. One was on the verge, however, possibly, of more. (WL 43)

The loudest sounds in the book are the nine o'clock chimes of Big Ben referred to above, with the volume turned up to the full by the fanatical Maud (WL 129). Their effect is the more violent, and more meaningful, against the silence of the location; and they have been foreshadowed throughout the book by numerous occasions when the handbell on the dining table has been rung for Kathie.

The Little Girls
Objects are eminently necessary for 'business' in Bowen's next novel, in which the whole plot revolves around objects – objects that are buried in a coffer, and objects that are intended to be sealed away in a cave for future generations to find. 'Explanatory' objects and landscape

features also seem particularly important in this novel, following Bowen's deliberate decision to play down the narrative voice that she had hitherto used to analyse her characters. We do not need to be told of Dinah's closeness to her mother, for example, when we see Mrs Piggott's embroidered stools and china figurines and clock at her daughter's house, Applegate, many years after her own death. And we do not need to have the easy-going atmosphere of the Piggotts' Feverel Cottage spelt out for us when we read of its garden, a marked contrast to the orderly, well-tended garden of the Burkin-Joneses: Mrs Piggott's lawn is already 'growing up into seed', the 'meagre delphinium lean[s] through ferns', and the cabbage roses are 'ungirt' (LG 84-85).

The cave introduced in the first scene is the thematic focus of the whole plot, and with its traditional associations of female sexuality it is among the most suggestive of Bowen's locations. This real cave in the adult Dinah's garden is replicated in other cave-like interiors, and incongruously picked up in the name of the suburban dream of glass and light built in their old school grounds, 'Blue Grotto' (LG 155, 158). Shopping in 1914 for a chain to put in their coffer, the three girls enter the 'awesomely smelly gloom' of Fagg's pet shop, which is 'more than sunless' and 'dark as a cellar' (LG 94) – the name 'Fagg' bringing to mind Fagin's unsavoury den in Dickens' *Oliver Twist*. In later life Clare has a gift-shop in a similarly constricted space: the street frontage is narrow, but the original interior has been lengthened by a glass-roofed extension, where, when Dinah enters, 'misty October sunshine [comes] wandering in, to be met by lit though seductively shaded lamps throwing glow on the wares on shelves and tables' (LG 137). In this stylish décor customers move about as though in a trance. The word *trance* itself occurs on the very first page of the book, where Dinah is intent on what she is doing 'to the point of trance' (LG 9), and it links up with a whole cluster of words concerning magic and the supernatural (see pp. 95-96 above). Quite specifically, it points to the drawing-room in Feverel Cottage where Dinah as a child lives with her mother (the name of the house recalling Meredith's *The Ordeal of Richard Feverel* [1859], a novel about secret courtship and marital unfaithfulness). Mrs Piggott is an enchantress like her daughter after her, and her room is a veritable enchantress's cavern whose curtains make of the bay a 'muslin window-cave' (LG 77). Mumbo is entranced by Mrs Piggott, just as her father is, and it is no coincidence that as an adult she makes a similar cave of her gift-shop; given her unarticulated lesbianism, it is likewise no coincidence that she does not want to go down into the cave where Dinah is making her collection of objects for posterity (LG 62).

The unworldly, even escapist nature of Mrs Piggott is reflected in the objects she surrounds herself with, the novels she is forever immersed in and the china crowding every surface in her drawing-room; and her poverty is obvious from the fact that the china has been much mended and the voluminous muslin curtains have come down to her from a larger house. But there is another side to Dinah's mother. We may link the facts that her new novel is called 'scarlet' rather than 'red' (LG 78), and that her china is flawed (LG 76), to the tea-gowns she wears and the (undescribed) pictures on her drawing-room wall that make Sheikie giggle (LG 37). Recalling also the word 'geisha' (the 'Geisha Café' [LG 94]) and the 'uncle's eye' (LG 110) of the Cousin Roland who apparently paid for her novels and flowers and for her daughter's schooling and took a house with them during the war, and after whom Dinah called her first son, we may pick up also the extra-marital associations of 'Feverel', and all in all we may perhaps feel justified in seeing Mrs Piggott as a woman of comparatively easy virtue. Dinah herself prompts a conclusion along those lines in the adult section of the book:

> '[Cousin Roland] thought of everything. He paid my school bills, I *think*; but also, which was still nobler, all those years he kept Mother in flowers and new novels. From which I suppose there may have been those who manfully tried to argue he kept Mother; if he had, she could hardly have cost him more.' (LG 193)

To what degree Mrs Piggott's easy-going ways were responsible for her husband's suicide (revealed also LG 193) must remain forever a speculation; Cousin Roland's sexual tastes are uncertain ('His friend had gone down on the *Titanic*' [LG 110] ... 'friend'?), and we may equally well put the blame for Mr Piggott's death on some same-sex proclivities of his own. Thinking ahead to *Eva Trout*, we may even find that the suicide of Dinah's father is of a kind with that of Eva's, who apparently takes his own life because of Constantine Ormeau's philandering.

The fragile china belonging to Dinah's mother holds a surprising attraction for the clumsy, seemingly robust Mumbo and is a measure of her love:

> Scenery motifs spoke in particular to Clare. Their miniature vastness was of a size for her; their look of eternity could be taken in in less than a minute. She had lived within them. That she knew each landscape, to her a planet, to be linked in destructability with the cup, bowl or plate upon which it was, added peril to love. One saw, here, how china could break. One foresaw also how, one day or another, it must do so beyond repair. (LG 77)

Curtains, masks, coffers, china figurines and personalized dog dishes, cress sandwiches and rock cakes, chalk and ink-wells and a magpie's wings on a lady's hat: the novel is a veritable storehouse of objects that are either necessary for 'business', or explanatory, or both. In the pre-1914 section, for instance, a chest of some kind is necessary for the girls' project, and the search for one is responsible for a good deal of the action in those chapters. The Beakers have two coffers, which is not only fortunate for the project but also says not a little about the family's middle-class taste in interior decoration: one coffer is in the hall next to an enormous brass gong, the other on a landing, under a table with a chenille cloth and Oriental fern pots; it appears later that Sheila has inherited the one that was not buried, along with her parents' values. Likewise, masks occasion some of the action in the book, when Dinah and Clare visit a mask-maker's village and then leave a mask at Frank Wilkins' cottage; at the same time they suggest the masked or suppressed attraction between the two women. The text often points out the symbolic dimensions of an object, in an unmistakable invitation to readers to do a bit of symbol-hunting on their own. An illustrative example would be the butter-knife Dinah asks Clare for: its handle, to one or two of the characters and surely also to the reader, is disturbingly phallic in appearance. On a conscious level, Dinah covets it because she feels it to be like the pilot's thumb in *Macbeth* (to which earlier references have been made), and she blithely (naïvely, perhaps) writes: 'And you need not worry if it is a symbol, as practically everything is, as we now know' (LG 152).

Shakespeare apart, intertextuality is encapsulated in several of the tangible objects in the novel. Dinah has two books with her in the car while she is waiting for Clare: Tennyson's *In Memoriam* and John Wyndham's *The Midwich Cuckoos* – one a lament for a dead (same-sex) friend, the other a horrific vision of future inhabitants of the earth; this latter 'object' may be taken as a wry comment on the whole idea of burying things for some unknown posterity which may not even exist.

Intertextuality also comes into the book by way of a gramophone record that Frank Wilkins is fond of playing, with the song 'The Runaway Train':

> The runaway train went over the hill,
> And she blew – she blew.
> The runaway train went over the hill,
> And she blew – she blew.
> The runaway train went over the hill,
> And the last we heard she was going still,
> And she blew, blew, blew, blew – (LG 195)

This American song is quoted twice in the book and highlighted by several occurrences of the verb 'to blow' in other contexts, also as 'to blow on' = 'to defame', perhaps also playing on the slang use of 'to blow' = 'to leave,' and on the erotic connotations of blowing. Attention is thus drawn to the novel's emotional climax, Dinah's shock on finding the coffer empty, and her ensuing breakdown: Sheila pointedly tells her that her home won't 'run away' merely because she stays in Southstone for a drink, but Dinah's reaction is: 'That's what it *has* done, Sheikie.... Everything has. *Now* it has, you see. Nothing's real any more' (LG 163).

Not surprisingly, stage properties are used to emphasize the homoerotic tension that builds up towards the end of the novel. Bearing in mind the possible same-sex overtones of the colour yellow, much in Dinah's sickroom thus calls for attention: her yellow dressing gown (mentioned three times), the fire, the lamplight, the 'mustard yellow' chrysanthemums, and the curried eggs she speaks of twice. This all goes to confirm the sensual atmosphere of the room conveyed by the sleeping patient:

> Deep into the curtains' shelter, the head of the sleeper was invisible. Sleep so gave this room a sensual climate that to enter was to know oneself to be in the presence of an embrace. (LG 235)

That the 'embrace' in this quotation is not between Dinah and Frank Wilkins is made quite clear, for he has earlier thrown himself down on her bed but is out of her reach: 'Between them existed the great distances. She again reached a hand out, this time sideways. But the bed was as wide as it was long' (LG 226).

Eva Trout

The sham, pseudo-Bavarian pile that appears with 'dramatic suddenness' on the first page of *Eva Trout* is a blatant announcement of the Gothic mode of that novel. The castle is mirrored in a lake of 'probably artificial water' (ET 11) and looks 'as though cut out, flat, from a sheet of cardboard' (ET 13); the reader is thus well prepared for the falsities and surrogate relationships of the plot. Characteristically, Eva herself has no permanent home and lives mostly in hotels; she is a 'displaced person' even more than Stella in *The Heat of the Day*. When she does acquire – unseen – a house of her own, it turns out to be a dilapidated once-chic villa with temperamental plumbing, dangerous electric wiring, and a legacy of grease-marked furniture from its previous tenants. The imperfections of the house anticipate another, more tragic unseen acquisition of Eva's: a baby boy who turns out to be deaf-mute.

One object has particular relevance for the plot of *Eva Trout*: an old army gun belonging to Eric Arble, which makes its way into a box of discarded toys found by Jeremy, and which becomes the means of Eva's final destruction. There are explanatory objects galore in the book, too. Thus Eva's inability to organize her life is given visual form in the jumble of luggage she arrives with at Southstone station: a suitcase and a duffle bag plus a number of corded bundles and mesh bags. Eight years later the pile of luggage she assembles at Paley's hotel is a similar reflection of her confused state of mind – though in this case it is only fair to add that the sudden move to Paley's has been forced on her, very inconveniently, by the French doctors into whose care she has entrusted Jeremy:

> Round her lay everything, everything, like a fallen city: huge or little hide suitcases, canvas ones, copperbound tea chests and packing-cases, duffle bags, nylon string bags, cartons with flap-topped lids open at angles, the scooter, overcrammed-hampers dwindling to waste-paper baskets, rugstraps, at least one extraneous parcel, objects half-clad in twiddles of paper ... (ET 253; ellipsis original)

Eva's imperfect grasp of other practical issues is made evident. Cooking seems quite beyond her, for instance: early in the book, at Cathay, she panics on realizing that she would not know how to boil a kettle even if there was one,[6] and the freedom she feels at having made her escape

---

[6] Kettles are mentioned also in the vicarage scenes, among others the fish kettle (used to boil

is reflected in the way she can enjoy her first meal in her own house, though it is only a Swiss roll and milk drunk out of a cocktail glass. Other food plays a similar role in conveying meaning and character. The macaroons brought home for tea in a paper bag are an obvious treat in the impoverished Dancey household; at the other end of the scale is the gourmet lunch given to Iseult by the ostentatiously wealthy Constantine Ormeau (oysters, riz de veau and profiteroles). The chichi Father Clavering-Haight is not above helping himself with a mere 'May I eat one of those?' to Eva's box of sugared apricots (ET 183); on their outing to the castle Henry likewise helps himself to her strawberries and cigarettes, thus establishing a link between the two male characters and suggesting the ambivalence of Henry's sexuality.

The strawberries provided by Eva call for more than passing mention. In Christian art the strawberry is the symbol of perfect righteousness, and the Virgin sometimes appears in a dress overstrewn with strawberries.[7] The association of Eva with strawberries may thus be seen to suggest the essential uprightness of her character, which is further confirmed by the early sympathy between her and Henry's stern father. Her upright carriage is likewise a sign of her upright character, and arguably her fundamental righteousness is only superficially at odds with her acknowledged habit of lying, and with the lordly disregard of petty rules like parking restrictions and currency regulations she shows when she inserts her Jaguar 'masterfully ... into a park long placarded FULL' (ET 116) and flies in 'wads of dollar bills' from Chicago to Paris 'on her person' (ET 205). It is also possible, I think, to reconcile her graver crime of illegal adoption with a fundamental righteousness; paradoxically, one of the reasons she gives for resorting to illegal adoption is that she does not wish to be 'immoral' (ET 222). Blunt of speech she may be, and deaf to irony, but her words and actions reveal a natural consideration for other people: she upbraids Henry for inconsiderate parking, for instance ('Henry, this was a wrong place to stop the car, just round the corner, unfair to other traffic' [ET 237]), and she commiserates with his father for the loss of Louise (ET 156). All in all, we may well find ourselves agreeing with Mrs Dancey, who says to Eva: 'By nature, you are as honest as the day!' (ET 75).

---

handkerchiefs in) which links up with the pervasive fish-imagery in the novel.
[7] See e.g. George Ferguson, *Signs and Symbols in Christian Art*.

Fontainebleau, the home of the doctors who bid fair to cure Jeremy, offers a good example of Bowen's thematic use of location. The town lies some 60 kilometres south of Paris; the extensive forest is still a reminder of the neighbourhood's early popularity as a royal chase, and the impressive *château* has notable associations with French royalty and with Napoleon, who took final leave of his guard in 1814 on its famed antler-shaped staircase. Inside the castle, the Napoleonic bees on the furnishings in his apartments fascinate Jeremy. Since bees are associated with resurrection because of their hibernation, this may be seen to presage the boy's 'rebirth'; more immediately to the point, perhaps, the historical associations, and particularly Napoleon's leave-taking, confirm the fact that Eva's life with Jeremy is now a thing of the past.

In spite of the Bonnards' idealism – 'dedicated zealots', the narrative voice calls them (ET 252), and 'the noble Bonnards' (ET 255), with more than a touch of reservation – they seem naïve in other respects than their calling and have little regard for the psychological make-up of either Eva or Jeremy. They are childless themselves, and that they are out of touch with reality is suggested in their rather old-fashioned country home with its white doves and louvred shutters and 'patriarchal' wistaria (ET 215); the house is best reached by walking through the Fontainebleau forest – the 'tapestry of the forest', as the text has it at one point (ET 216), bringing in a touch of fairy-tale. The doctors' blindness to the depths of Jeremy's character appears when we read that they give him a room overlooking the dovecote; surely this cannot but remind him of the ever-present cage of budgerigars at Paley's hotel and thus of the 'cage' of his deaf-muteness, and it is tempting to transfer the birds' 'emotional tumult' (ET 255) to the boy's state of mind. It is curious that in the last scene at Paley's he himself occasions the birds' commotion by trailing a finger over the bars of their cage; as he can hardly have been blind to the visible effect of this 'greeting' (ET 255), we may perhaps draw no uncertain conclusions about the latent cruelty of his nature, and recall his sudden outburst of violence when he throws a potted gloxinia out of the hotel window.

The castle park at Fontainebleau is the location of a long talk between Eva and Dr Bonnard. He walks over to see her on the first evening Jeremy is to sleep away from her, believing (says the narrative voice) that Eva's solitude might be intensified by the beautiful summer evening, whose sensuous atmosphere is pointed up by a reference to Cythera, the legendary birthplace of Venus, and a glimpse of lovers embracing by the pool. Well aware that Eva is brimful of sexual desire and feeling that he should make her aware of it herself (as to any other possible personal motivation of the good doctor's, the text is silent), he talks to her feelingly on the subject of love. Their conversation reads almost as much like an interrogation as Eva's earlier talk with Father Clavering-Haight, however. Though Dr Bonnard as interrogator is gentle, flattering and infinitely more empathetic than the High Anglican priest, it is clear to the reader that he is intent on drawing Eva out on subjects which she does not want to talk about, and we may easily feel his questions as an impertinence – what business is it of his whether Eva has ever been to bed with anyone? The dialogue is introduced by words that might stand at the head of the minutes of some meeting or interview: '*Gérard Bonnard began by thanking* Eva for her confidence' (ET 221; my italics); their conversation is an object lesson in listening technique:

> 'Had you or had you been given reason to think you could not give birth to a child? Otherwise, what made you prefer mimicry to what could have been the actual continuance of a flesh-and-blood? You were young eight years ago, you are young still. You shrank from something?'
> Eva looked waitingly at the doctor, hoping he might assist her to answer. But in return he looked waitingly back at her. (ET 222)

The boyishly charming doctor seems well experienced in talking to patients, and possibly also to other, unwilling talkers; we would do well not to discount the fact that he has been prominent in the Resistance. If his talk with Eva has affected him at all, it can only have been to whet his sexual appetite: he walks 'quickly' through the 'gathering dark' of the forest to his home, where his doctor wife has assumed the role of a womanly woman and sits sewing by a lighted window. A fitting tableau to end a tableau-like scene (ET 225).

* * *

In concluding these observations on the locations of Bowen's later fiction it may be appropriate to consider briefly the places where some of her characters live. These are in many respects bound up with the themes of identity and communication I have discussed in Chapters 4 and 5, since much of a person's identity is reflected in his or her home surroundings, and the hospitality of an open, caring home is an indication of a wish to relate to, to communicate with, one's fellow human beings. Well-run homes are rarities in the dislocated universe of Bowen's post-war fiction. In the adult sections of *The Little Girls*, for instance, only Dinah's 'Applegate' has in any way a feeling of hospitality or 'at-hominess' (LG 51); Clare is less than encouraging when Dinah asks if she may see her flat, and Sheila's elegantly appointed drawing-room with its thought-out colour scheme and too brilliant but indirect lighting is a mirror image of the hostess, but not a place where guests feel at home – 'Ravenswood Gardens was what it always was: a place to be left to go back to one's own home' (LG 165), says the text, harking back to pre-1914 days in the same house, when the unlocked door did not indicate hospitality but served rather 'to direct attention to the law-and-order imposed by Beaker rule' (LG 106). Genuinely open homes like that of the Danceys in *Eva Trout*, on the other hand, though 'well-run' only in a Pickwickian sense, are signs of both hospitality and a wish to talk to other people – in direct contrast to the Arbles' old home, whose door is closed in Eva's face. Matching the Kelways' reluctance or inability to communicate, the lack of hospitality at Holme Dene in *The Heat of the Day* that I have looked at above is captured in the grotesque tea provided for their guests (a stale cake, and no butter): yet another instance of the abortive host-guest relationship that is used, as John Coates has pointed out in speaking of *The Death of the Heart*, as an 'index to the failure of a culture' (98a:12). In *A World of Love*, the panic occasioned by the sudden appearance at Montefort of the Latterly chauffeur (echoed in the wary attitude of Sheikie's father to 'callers' in *The Little Girls*) is an unhealthy sign of an obsessive concern for privacy; and it is a serious failing of the present state of Montefort that 'the door no longer knew hospitality' (WL 9).

Barrage balloons were a familiar sight on the London skyline in the Second World War. In the first chapter of *The Heat of the Day* there is a seemingly irrelevant snippet of conversation involving a balloon which has apparently 'come all untied' (HD 17); later in the novel this turns out to be a visual metaphor for the life of the heroine, Stella Rodney, who has also 'come loose from her moorings' (HD 114). *Photograph courtesy of the Imperial War Museum, London* (HU 3725).

The absence of a permanent home is revealing. The identity-seeking Stella has 'come loose from her moorings' (HD 114) and seems even grateful to the war for having provided her with an opportunity to 'free herself of her house' (HD 25); the equally rootless Eva Trout never succeeds in finding a house that might have bolstered her identity – 'Cathay' is a dismal failure, and house-hunting in London comes to nothing. The identities of both spy and counter-spy in *The Heat of the Day* are so indistinctly defined that we are not surprised to hear that they apparently have no home of their own: 'He never did seem to me to be living anywhere very particular,' says Roderick of Robert (HD 298), and Harrison is evasive when Stella asks him exactly where he lives: '"There are always two or three places where I can turn in." / "But for instance, where do you keep your razor?" / "I have two or three razors," he said in an absent tone' (HD 140). On many occasions the positive connotations of the word 'home' are cancelled out by its ironical use, as when the over-heated, over-furnished apartment in Chicago in *Eva Trout* is referred to as 'the Anapoupolis home' (ET 136). The pronunciation of its name leads one to expect Holme Dene in *The Heat of the Day* to be a real, permanent home – an expectancy that is soon belied not only by its inhospitable atmosphere but also by the revelation that the house has for years been for sale. Similarly, the phrase 'to make one's home with someone' implies a surrogate existence that can hardly have been enjoyed by Mr Anapoupolis, who is 'making his home' with his son (ET 136), or by Mrs Beaker in *The Little Girls*, who 'made her home' with Sheila's elder sister (LG 165). And that Harrison should feel 'quite at home', as he says, in Stella's impersonal flat (HD 128), is a caustic comment on both their identities.

CHAPTER 9

Time

Along with place, time was for Bowen more than an element in her fiction, it was one of the actors.[1] In *A World of Love*, for instance, the past appears in the form of the love-letters from Guy to an unknown woman. The letters are found by Jane, who reads them and then hides them under an elder-tree. They are discovered there by Maud and offered by her (for a consideration) to Fred, who confiscates them and wants to give them to Lilia. They are rejected by her unseen, left lying about to be found and, having 'run their course' (WL 123), finally burnt. The letters are thus as much a part of the plotline as any fictive character.

Time appears in various guises in the novels: historical time, childhood influences, timing, contemporaneity, heredity and posterity, the relationship of the living to the dead (in a recurrent phrase, 'the wall between dead and living is very thin'). There is throughout a careful notation of calendar time and clock time that serves both as a constant reminder of the concept itself and a practical framework for the course of events; this is in accordance with Bowen's dictum: 'The passage of time, and its demarcation, should be a factor in the plot.'[2] Her own practice in this respect far outstrips that of Virginia Woolf, who lets the chimes of Big Ben accompany the protagonist on her walk through London in *Mrs Dalloway* (1925).

Demarcation of Time
The time of year is invariably noted in the novels I am considering, and seasonal weather not surprisingly carries a good deal of symbolic

---
[1] 'I am, and am bound to be, a writer involved closely with place and time; for me these are more than elements, they are actors.' Preface to second US edition of *The Last September* (1952); quoted from *The Mulberry Tree*, 123.
[2] 'Notes on Writing a Novel'. *Orion* 2 (Autumn 1945); quoted from *The Mulberry Tree*, 45.

content: the sweltering summer of *A World of Love*, for instance, and the ice-cold January at the beginning of *Eva Trout*. Bowen is only remarkable for the obviousness with which she uses this common device.

More unusual in the general run of fiction is the constant interest in the time of day that is shown by Bowen's narrator and characters alike. Hours and minutes may even be specified: thus in *The Little Girls*, as part of the mocking air of conspiracy that surrounds the meeting of two of the women, we are told that it took place at '3.45 of an afternoon by now some way on into September' (LG 29). Narrative distance is likewise signalled in *Eva Trout* by the fact that the emotionally charged interview between Eva and her teacher takes place 'at five ten in the evening, by the library clock' (ET 61). In the same book this precise registration of time ludicrously parodies itself when, in explanation of the fact that there are very few biscuits left, Mr Dancey admits to having eaten several 'at two o'clock in the morning' (ET 156).

In all four post-war novels there are countless clocks and watches, and verbal references to clocks and watches, to serve as reminders of one aspect or another of time. The clock golf at the Hunt Fête and the sundial in the garden in *A World of Love* also fulfil this role; more eye-catching is the restaurant clock in *The Heat of the Day*, in a scene from the early days of the lovers' courtship:

> The gilt-faced clock in the sunburst on the restaurant's wall had, like others in London, been shock-stopped. When she began to feel about for her gloves and he began to push out the table, their two wrist watches – which, in the time to come, were to come at some kind of relationship of their own by never perfectly synchronizing – found it, respectively, to be a minute before and a minute after half past two. Half past two of a day which, having begun late for her, finished late for them both. (HD 99)

Time-pieces singled out for mention are naturally and often emphatically related to theme and character, in addition to being indicators of time. We are thus told more than once that the projecting clock in the hall at Montefort in *A World of Love* is next to where a photograph of the former owner in uniform used to hang, reminding us of his long-dominant presence (WL 76, 136); in *The Little Girls*, Mrs Piggott's clock in Dinah's drawing-room recalls the enchantress mother she so much resembles; and the location of the last scene in *Eva Trout*, the Continental Departures section at Victoria Station in London, is rendered particularly sinister by being 'dominated by its own clocks' (ET 258). Then there is Eva's own wristwatch which she has characteristically left on the train, forcing her at one point to borrow Eric Arble's, and in *A World of Love* there is Fred's watch which he keeps glancing at, a reminder of the almost obsessively strict time schedule by which he runs the Montefort farm.³ 'Watch' is a key word in *The Heat of the Day*,⁴ and the two senses of the word (time-piece, guard) are brought together in the text itself, in some of the hero-cum-villain Robert Kelway's last remarks: 'This thing locked up inside you ... In the night, how did I not hear it ticking under your pillow like your watch? ... So you've always been watching me while we've been together?' (HD 191). In *A World of Love* time is brought resoundingly on stage by young Maud's worship of Big Ben, whose nine o'clock chimes ring the knell of Guy's dominance:

> Maud ... increased the volume. At the full, the first of the whanging blows struck down upon quivering ether, the echo swelling as it uprose. Repetition, fall of stroke after stroke where stroke after stroke had already fallen, could do no more than had been done: once was enough.... The sound of Time, inexorably coming as it did, at once was absolute and fatal. Passionless Big Ben. (WL 129)

Meals are important time-keepers, and their rigid observance is an amusing illustration of an extremely regular way of life even amid the hardships of *A World of Love* and the excesses of *Eva Trout*. In the first chapter of this last book, the children's worry about when and where they are going to have tea provides a down-to-earth corrective to Eva's honeymoon fantasies. In *A World of Love* the fanatical Maud, a stickler for the observance of mealtimes as of any other ritual, purposefully leaves her favourite spot by the river, stuffs her frock into her drawers and laboriously picks her way homeward through the shallow water merely because her instinct tells her that 'it's teatime' (WL 49).

---

³ Their watches and the way they are referred to provide a tangible link between these two Lawrentian characters: Fred's is 'strapped inexorably' to his wrist (WL 21), Eric 'unstrapped' his to give to Eva (ET 98).
⁴ 'Watch' belongs to a cluster of words related to spy-hunting discussed in Chapter 6, 'Word Clusters and Interlinking Images'.

The attention drawn to the passing of time inevitably affects the mood of the novels. As Hoogland points out, the 'emphatic presence' of time thus builds up 'an overall atmosphere of tension' in *The Heat of the Day* (120). In *A World of Love* the atmosphere of timelessness is reflected in the useless time-keepers in the following description of the kitchen at Montefort:

> On the dresser, from one of the hooks for cups, hung a still handsome calendar for the year before; and shreds of another, previous to that, remained tacked to the shutter over the sink. These, with the disregarded dawdling and often stopping of the cheap scarlet clock wedged in somewhere between the bowls and dishes, spoke of the almost total irrelevance of Time, in the abstract, to this ceaseless kitchen. (WL 21)

The timelessness of the Montefort kitchen is echoed in the datelessness of the letters Jane finds, which are only headed 'Tuesday', 'Saturday', etc. It is also replicated in timeless elements in the landscape, which is 'at all times open and great with distance' (WL 9). Jane thinks of the land as 'poetically immortal' when she sees, like a vision, the very same features Guy had written about in his letters so many years before: the clown's face in the limestone cliff on the opposite side of the river, and the crooked thorn tree that she rubs 'propitiatingly' (WL 48-49).

Characters in Time

The relationship of people to the moment of time in which they are living is highlighted in a key passage in *The Heat of the Day*. The time is that of the Second World War, which determines the course of the love-affair between Stella and Robert – making a spy of him, blighting their relationship with a lack of frankness, sitting always 'in the third place at their table':

> [T]hey were not alone, nor had they been, from the start of love. Their time sat in the third place at their table. They were the creatures of history, whose coming together was of a nature possible in no other day – the day was inherent in the nature.... The relation of people to one another is subject to the relation of each to time, to what is happening.... Could these two have loved each other better at a better time? At no other would they have been themselves; what had carried their world to its hour was in their bloodstreams. (HD 194-195)

The classical notion of one time being more 'right' than another – what the Greeks referred to as *kairos* – is expressed later in the same book by the clairvoyant Cousin Nettie, talking to Stella's son:

> 'There *are* purple roses. Nobody believes me, but I could lead you to the very place in the garden and show you the bush. There is only one; it's not my fault if there are no others in the world; there is one at Mount Morris – an old Persian rose, only ever blooming for a week, and no sooner are they open than they die. So you must look for them at the right time.' (HD 216)

The idea recurs more than once in Bowen's last novel: when Eva reasons with herself against taking her newly found childhood friend with her, she thinks, 'You came back too late, Elsinore. I cannot. You came at the wrong time' (ET 143); and when Iseult carries Jeremy off for a few hours, thus beginning his liberation from his handicap, she speaks of coming 'at the right time' (ET 245).

Being on time, or late for an appointment, or off schedule is related to this more philosophical concept of correct timing. In *The Little Girls* the business-like Clare proudly arrives 'on the dot', for instance, for her rendezvous with with her old schoolfellow Dinah (LG 45). In *The Heat of the Day* Stella's son Roderick is earlier than expected when he visits Cousin Nettie (HD 203); Harrison is 'a few minutes late' when he comes to see Stella (HD 26); she herself arrives late at Cousin Francis' funeral (HD 71); and her train to London is 'running late' (HD 180). Similar examples occur with remarkable frequency in *A World of Love*: Fred sets off too late to fetch Lilia and Maud from the Fête (WL 30), Lady Latterly is down late for her dinner-party, after her guests have arrived (WL 59), Jane is late for supper (WL 126), Maud predicts that her mother's hairdressing appointment will make them late for dinner (WL 86) and wonders whether the Latterly van will be too late to meet the plane from America at Shannon (WL 146), Lilia is down late on the last morning (WL 133).

In this novel the idea of being late is linked to Jane's feeling that she is living at the same time as Guy; the narrative voice, allusively reflecting Antonia's thoughts, thus remarks that Jane 'had come late enough (had she not?)' (WL 45) – late enough, that is, not to share the disadvantage of her elders, who, more than anything else, are painfully aware of the loss that Guy's death meant to them. Jane feels Guy's presence so strongly in his letters that 'Seeing how brief all time was it seemed impossible she could be too late.... Between him and her dwindled the years: where indeed was he if not beside her? They could not now miss one another, surely?' (WL 48). We will be the more ready to accept this illusion of hers if we have picked up an early hint of the narrator's that, in a muslin dress like those worn by the girls of Guy's youth, Jane does indeed look as if she belonged 'to some other time' (WL 10).[5]

The feeling of Guy's continuing presence culminates in a central chapter (Ch. 6) half-way through the book, where Jane comes home late and finds her father waiting up for her in the hall with a glass of milk. The preceding chapter (Ch. 5) has been taken up by the phantasmagoric dinner-party at Latterly Castle. In one sense this is an incisive satire on the modern money-making mind, but in terms of the fiction itself it is traumatic experience for Jane, who feels Guy's presence so strongly that she almost sees him sitting opposite her at the table. The following chapter (Ch. 7) will show Lilia having her hair cut (a momentous decision for her, one that symbolizes her break with the past, and with Guy). In between these two chapters comes the night scene at Montefort (Ch. 6), which alternates between realistic details – a glass of milk, the reek of an expiring lamp, a stone that Jane shakes out of her sandal – and a profound sense that the land is still permeated by the energy and passion of its long-dead owner. The narrative voice follows Antonia in this passage:

> Going to stand in the doorway, she was met at once by a windlike rushing towards her out of the dark – her youth and Guy's from every direction: the obelisk, avenue, wide country, steep woods, river below. No part of the night was not breathless breathing, no part of the quickened stillness not running feet. A call or calling, now nearby, now from behind the skyline, was unlocatable as a corncrake's in uncut grass. A rising this was, on the part of two who like hundreds seemed to be teeming over the land, carrying all before them. The night, ridden by pure excitement, was seized by hope. All round Montefort there was going forward an entering back into possession: the two, now one again, were again here.... Ghosts could have no place in

---

[5] In English literature, a well-known expression of contemporaneity is the beginning of T S Eliot's 'Burnt Norton' (1936): 'Time present and time past / Are both perhaps present in time future, / And time future contained in time past. / If all time is eternally present / All time is unredeemable'. *Four Quartets*, 7. It bears noting that the rose garden of Eliot's poem is recognizable in the walled garden at Montefort, though the roses in the Irish garden have run to briar and its thrush takes fright.

this active darkness – more, tonight was a night which had changed hands, going back again to its lordly owners: time again was into the clutch of herself and Guy. (WL 77)

It is some time after this, in the afternoon of the following day, that Lilia thinks she sees Guy in the enclosed garden where she sits sewing, musing on their parting more than twenty years earlier, and accepting the fact that he was not faithful to her though they were both 'deep in love' (WL 98). The creaking garden door she hears is not Guy, however, but Fred, coming to bring her the packet of letters in the belief that they were written to her. Serene and majestic in her true knowledge of Guy, Lilia can now run towards her husband and reject the letters without reading them: 'What's it all about? What he's saying here well might not make sense to me any longer, whether it *was* to me or to who knows else. No, Fred, thanks: give them back to Jane' (WL 101). Thus is the past dismissed out of hand by the character whose life has been most blighted by its memory.

The Anglo-Irish Past
The part played by the past in *A World of Love* invites closer attention. Such action as there is takes place around 1950 on the Irish estate of Montefort, which used to belong to Guy and has fallen into near-ruin since his death in 1918; the now impoverished demesne, with its decaying Big House, moss-grown carriage sweep, rutted drive, and garden running wild, is a fitting emblem for a bygone era, more particularly for the carefree days of the book's dead hero, before the First World War. That this should be so is suggested also by Guy's name, which phonetically recalls the name given in the book to Maud's familiar, Gay David – to all appearances a malign spirit, if only because he is associated with the witch-like, almost inhuman Maud. It is tempting to transfer this malignity, and the corollary negative overtones of the word 'gay', to the speciously idyllic pre-1914 days of Guy's lifetime, the 'former gay days', as one character has it, '... you know, before it was 1914'; this was long before Jane was born, which would be 'true of any gay days,' as she herself says (WL 62). 'Gay' is used almost contemptuously by the obsequious shopkeeper, Mr Lonergan, when he asks Jane, 'Was it gay enough for you last night at the castle?' (WL 87); and 'gaiety' seems to be a word that can now be used only mockingly, much as if it were in inverted commas, as Antonia uses it when speaking of the Hunt Fête:

'And how are we all, after all that?' she genially asked, looking round the table. – 'You, for instance,' turning to him, 'Fred?'

He blinked at having been singled out, swallowed, and asked her: 'After all what?'

'Our gaiety.' (WL 36)

The location of the story in Ireland makes it natural to see Guy and the Montefort of his day not only as representative of an anonymous gracious world before 1914 (a role also filled by Mrs Piggott and Sheikie in *The Little Girls*), but specifically as a symbol of the Anglo-Ireland that did not long survive the First World War; as Robert Tracy points out (250), 'Gay Days' is the title of a chapter in Bowen's book about the Shelbourne Hotel in Dublin, that describing the high point of the Anglo-Irish Ascendancy at the end of the nineteenth century. The figure of Guy is in many respects an embodiment of that Anglo-Irish 'fatal lack of connection between enthusiasm and resolution, between the heart and the guts' that Bowen pointed to in *Bowen's Court* in discussing the failure of Grattan's parliament at the end of the eighteenth century: 'We could envisage general reform, but not face the details of sacrifice ...' she says. 'Had we truly come up to scratch, Grattan might not have failed' (*Bowen's Court* 153). The ambition of those earlier generations of Anglo-Irish to 'give life an ideal mould' that she speaks of in the same paragraph is well matched by Guy's lofty idealizings, which are so divorced from reality that he neglects to make a will. It is worth noting that Guy and Antonia are not only Anglo-Irish, but absentee landlords at that. They are deeply and sentimentally attached to Montefort but prefer to live permanently elsewhere, and it may be argued that the visible crumbling of the estate after Guy's death is in part due to the failure (notably Antonia's) to establish healthy working relations with the neighbouring community, such as Fred demonstrably has. Before he turns up, Antonia simply cannot cope with unco-operative grazing tenants and a decaying, empty house. Absenteeism may have been acceptable in the old days, the text seems to say, especially in the person of a charismatic young master, but there is no room for it any longer. Characteristically, it is only after Guy's death that the roses in the Montefort garden have 'undeniably' run to briar and stones begun to fall out of its wall:

> Now it was not so much that the decay was more rapid or widespread, but that it was apparent – out it stood! Nothing now against it maintained the

place. Struggle there was, as not in his day; but never a heedless victory – gone was the master-touch of levity, nerve or infatuation. The crazed perfection he saw, once, into the place left a trace of itself, but in such a way as to make it the more to be felt to be gone, with him. Yes, in his way he had kept Montefort up – up, that was, to his own high idea of it (WL 97; these are Lilia's musings).

Moreover, the time-honoured Big House tradition of patronage has become disastrous in Antonia's hands: by virtually adopting his fiancée when Guy died, his cousin (the Danbys' 'patroness' [WL 14] and Lilia's own 'former patron' [WL 18]) ruins her chances of ever standing on her own feet, as she later ruins Jane's chances of a happy family life at Montefort by carrying her off to London and assuming the responsibility for her education.

The dangers of the past are represented tangibly in the novel by the junk cluttering up the attics at Montefort, both a very real incendiary danger and a metaphorical one – who knows what flame the past might ignite? It is in an attic trunk that Jane finds Guy's letters, and they do in fact ignite new passions and rekindle old ones. For it is through the figure of the long-dead Guy that the past determines the present lives of the characters, and not until his spirit is exorcised by the burning of his letters is Lilia free to give herself whole-heartedly to her husband, and Jane to enter into womanhood and exchange a real-life lover for her vision of a dead one. Because his cousin Antonia was so close to him in childhood and Lilia in love with him at seventeen, and because he becomes the object of Jane's passion, the reader may be equally inclined to fall under his spell. Piecing together facts given at different places in the text, however, we find him a fickle lover and an irresponsible landlord, and we, too, may feel the burning of his letters as a release.

'Let Sleeping Dogs Lie'
As these remarks about *A World of Love* will have suggested, Bowen's attitude to the past was not nostalgic; her fiction is frequently concerned to demonstrate the dangers of seeking refuge or confirmation in the past, as in a phrase used by more than one of her characters: 'Let sleeping dogs lie'. The plotline of *The Little Girls* will serve as further illustration. Dinah's final breakdown ostensibly occurs because the three friends have discovered that the coffer they buried as children is now empty; in her own view, her past has 'run away' (the notion of

'running away' having been introduced into the text in quotations from the song 'The Runaway Train'). Dinah's low-key relationship with the rather anaemic Frank Wilkins also seems to rest on false premises: with his fear of future generations and his fondness for 'talking over old times' (LG 191), and his old-world cottage complete with Welsh settle and Jacobean loose covers, Frank is a living epitome of a worship of the past that is both false and dangerous (and we see the danger or evil clearly in the shape of his fierce, teeth-baring 'black beast' of a labrador, more hell-hound than house-dog [LG 184]). The cottage reminds Dinah of Feverel Cottage, where she had spent her childhood in complete love and trust together with her mother, and Frank's cottage is characteristically the only place where she says she feels 'safe'. But a climactic scene in the book shows that her feelings about the past are not yet fully resolved. This is when the three women gather in Sheila's drawing-room to wind down after the discovery that their coffer is empty. They talk about a large picture on the wall depicting Southstone's long-gone Old High Street, which Dinah in her worked-up state sees as a kind of lie, saying: 'It might be better to have no pictures of places which are gone. Let them go completely' (LG 169). Her remark receives a good deal of prominence by being the final words in the chapter, and it anticipates the very last words in the book (quoted above, p. 56), where she rejects Clare's childhood nickname 'Mumbo' and calls her 'Clare'. It seems that Dinah has at long last grown out of her childhood past and into the present.

Dinah's final rejection of the past is in line with the opinions Bowen expressed in an essay from 1950, 'The Bend Back': in the face of the contemporary demand for 'novels set back in time, picturesque biographies, memoirs, diaries dated long ago, books about old homes, collections of family letters from generations back', she ends her essay with a plea to writers not to dwell exclusively on the past at the cost of the present day, but to 'examine the stuff of our own time to see if, through it also, there does not run some gold vein.'[6] Though she was unhappy about the post-WWII world, and though she willingly wrote about her own childhood and family history, it is consistent with these thoughts that she does not escape into easy historicism in the novels she went on to write in the 50s and 60s, where the past is always subservient to the present.

---

[6] 'The Bend Back' was first published as 'Once Upon a Yesterday' in *Saturday Review* 33 (27 May 1950); reprinted in *The Mulberry Tree*, 54-60.

Childhood and Heredity

A significant aspect of Bowen's interest in time is the relation of her characters to their own past. In *The Heat of the Day*, for instance, it is made quite clear that it is Stella's willingness, 20 years or so prior to the story, to go along with the generally accepted explanation of her early divorce that is responsible for her later awkward position vis-à-vis her former in-laws, and which contributes not a little to her outsider status. In the same book, the seeds of Robert's defection were sown (on his own authority) in childhood and in his parentage: 'I was born wounded; my father's son,' he says (HD 272). The childhood we read of in *Eva Trout* is the very opposite of Dinah's loving upbringing in *The Little Girls*, and Eva's hunger for love and her marriage fantasies are clearly a result of her loveless upbringing; this is signalled by the heading of the first part of the novel, 'Genesis'. Eva's peripatetic early years with her father are topped by a series of curiously blind teachers, who write her off as a 'displaced person' or a 'case' without probing further into the causes that have made her different from other children. With the pampered, secluded upbringing Eva gives him, Jeremy does not fare much better at her hands: we never hear of her trying to find any playmates of his own age for him, for instance, or letting him meet other children that share his handicap. The spectre of a tainted heredity comes into this novel even more than *The Heat of the Day* or *The Little Girls*: Eva's mother, according to Constantine Ormeau, was '*not* normal ... frankly, she was maniacal' (ET 41); her father, we are told elsewhere, was suicidal. Constantine seems to be afraid that Eva is like her mother (not, we note, her father, the lover to whom he apparently was unfaithful). In the figure of Jeremy, the concept of heredity surfaces as a question of Nature versus Nurture, and we shall never know whether it is some heritage from his unknown parents or his homeless, movie-dominated upbringing that determines the boy's penchant for violence.

Continuity of character from childhood to adulthood appears clearly in *The Little Girls*. The long middle section devoted to the eleven-year olds is given not as a flashback from a later narrative stance, but as a separate narrative present; any feeling of continuity is thus not posited by the text but comes from the reader's own assessment, helped not a little by the talkative Dinah. The grown women are the same kind of people they were in childhood: Dinah sensitive, impulsive, bossy; Clare morose, introvert, taciturn, bookish; Sheila spiteful, acquisitive, unintellectual, ultra-feminine; they even revert to their old nicknames: Dicey (Diana, later Dinah), Mumbo (Clare), and Sheikie (Sheila). Dinah, their ringleader, is in later life still fey, and still bossy; Clare is still clumsy and reticent, a 'freak intellectual child' who has become a successful business woman; and Sheila is as self-centred and calculating as ever – spiteful, even: the fashionable woman whose spoon gores a slice of lemon in her tea 'without mercy' (LG 38) is recognizably the child who splits leaves with her finger-nails and lobster-pinches her friends. Their personalities go back to the previous generation: Dinah is an enchantress like her mother (and as careless about money as she is); Clare is as commonsensical as her mother and as intuitively intelligent as her father, Sheila as snobbish and compulsively respectable as her mother and as 'dead' as her father. Heredity having thus been given its full due, there is also room for less than serious treatment in Sheila's catty speculations about Dinah's family: 'They were none of them mental, by any chance?' and in Clare's answer: 'Not that I heard, ever. The bishop may have been' (LG 37). In a similar vein Dinah refers to the early deaths of her father and her husband with the fanciful 'Widows ... run in families' (LG 194); it is tempting to put this whimsicality down not only to her obvious pleasure at making a witty remark, however, but also to self-protection, and to suggest that Dinah herself has in some respects become just as 'barnacled over' as she accuses Sheila of being, or just as adept at hiding her thoughts and feelings.

Time Future
Of the four novels dealt with in these studies, only *Eva Trout* ends on a note of finality; with differing degrees of irony, the endings of the three others allow for their stories continuing into the future. The open closure of *The Heat of the Day*, where the promiscuous Louie holds up her new-born son to see swans flying westwards, is perhaps best seen as a wry comment on the cliché of a 'happy ending', for it is difficult to imagine a happy future for the characters after the moral chaos of wartime that the novel has depicted; the most optimistic outlook for the future would seem to lie in Roderick's full-hearted acceptance of his new role as master of the estate he has inherited in neutral Ireland – though, as I have suggested earlier, the less than realistic picture of the Irish demesne may well annul any confidence we may feel. *A World of Love* does not end when Guy's letters are burnt, as we might perhaps

have expected, but the book is rounded off by eight pages describing Jane and Maud's run to Shannon airport in the Latterly van and their wait for the arrival of the plane from America. (This coda brings to mind *The Heat of the Day*, which similarly does not end climactically with the death of Robert Kelway). The route to Shannon is new country to the two sisters:

> [T]hough for some way yet to the girls' eyes nothing intrinsically was new or failed to resemble something they'd seen before, the unmistakable breath of the unknown came to meet them ever more strongly, and pure strangeness lay over the opening country. (WL 142)

If we are tempted to interpret this unfamiliarity of the countryside in a broader sense to suggest that our heroine's life is now changing, this is sanctioned by Jane's surprise that 'the world could change so fast – where they had been, where was it now? And still more, what was to come?' (WL 146), and by the narrative voice explicitly telling us that the turn off for the airport, a cement causeway, 'looked like the future, and for some was' (WL 146). Casting our minds back, we can see that we have in fact been prepared to read this eight-page coda in terms of the future by Antonia's peremptory decision to leave immediately for London with Jane (WL 127), and by the last remark she makes in the book (highlighted by the following extra line spacing), when the van has just left for Shannon: 'But for the future ... we'd have nothing left.' (WL 141). That the future will be different from the past has been apparent more than once from Jane's musings. It has become clear to her that she cannot go back to London, and to her dependence on Antonia. And the fact that she lets her eye be caught by 'a profusion of roses' in one of the gardens they are passing (WL 145) suggests that she is now ready to fall in love, as she does in the last lines of the book.

The question on which *The Little Girls* ends ('Clare, where have you been?') gives that book a closure so open as to be nearly parodic. In another sense, too, the strands of time reach into the future in *The Little Girls*: in the recurrent talk of future generations and the posterity for whose benefit mementoes are being buried in the 1960s, and were so in 1914. The very notion of a future and its relation to the present is questioned when Clare doubts the rightness of digging up something that was intended for posterity, to which Dinah remorselessly retorts: 'We are posterity, now' (LG 63). Behind much of the novel's talk of the future lies the fear of nuclear extinction: 'We may all go with the same bang,' in the words of Frank Wilkins. It is hinted on several occasions that there may possibly be no posterity to find the buried objects, and the terrifying world of science fiction is brought into the universe of the novel by a book belonging to Dinah: John Wyndham's *The Midwich Cuckoos*.

'Broken Pieces of Time'
I have earlier quoted a passage from *Eva Trout* where Eva, in bed with a feverish cold, searches through her 'store of broken pieces of time' to try to remember where she has heard the words, 'How is my darling?' (ET 48). 'Broken pieces of time' might well serve to describe the fragmentary nature of time sequences in Bowen's fiction. There are extreme examples of time gaps in *The Little Girls* and *Eva Trout*; but *The Heat of the Day* and *A World of Love*, whose story-lines range from two years in one case down to four days in the other, also present instances of whole lifetimes – indeed, the lives of more than one generation – which we must construct for ourselves from the 'broken pieces' offered by the texts. In *A World of Love*, the course of Guy's life is a case in point. He appears briefly in the narrator's introductory run-down apropos of Lilia's position at Montefort, and this is where we hear of their love-affair and his death in action (WL 14-15). It is not until much further on (WL 45) that Antonia reads the War Office telegram telling of his death. That he had dined often at Latterly Castle and that he had had a studio photograph in uniform taken for Lilia also appears later (WL 67, 68, 78), though both must have been prior to 1918. Guy's close boyhood comradeship with Antonia comes into the text after this (WL 78). Then we are in 1918 again, when Lilia gave him a lock of her hair before he went back to the Front, and she saw him off at Charing Cross (WL 91); we hear more of this leave-taking scene some pages later (WL 95-96), and on the very last pages of the book Antonia imagines the situation some time after Guy's death, perhaps still in 1918, when the stranger he wrote to came to Montefort and left his letters there. It is not until Chapter 8, almost 100 pages into the novel, that we are given to understand, from Lilia's memories, what exactly happened when she said her last good-bye to Guy. In this intertwining of different layers of time, *A World of Love* thus offers a striking example of the iconicity that informs much of Bowen's fiction: as past and present are apt to be confused in the minds of the characters in this book, so they are easily confused in the mind of the reader.

III

INDIVIDUAL STUDIES

CHAPTER 10

A Latter-day Icarus

(*The Heat of the Day*)

Elizabeth Bowen was thirteen in 1912 when the loss of the *Titanic* sent a shock through the unruffled Edwardian world of her childhood; 'the first black crack across the surface of *exterior* things' was how she later described it (*Bowen's Court* 314). The disaster became a generally accepted icon of man's presumptuousness and arrogance, what the Greeks called *hubris*. As such, many years after the event, Bowen brought it into *The Heat of the Day* (1949): in a corner of the shuttered drawing room of a Big House in Ireland, Stella Rodney finds a picture torn out of an old magazine, stuck crooked into some frame – the liner 'going down in a blaze with all lights on, decks and portholes shining, ... one half already plunged in the black ocean, the other reared up against the sky' (HD 176).

The *Titanic* catastrophe prefigures the fate of Stella's lover, the debonair, self-assured Robert Kelway, who, having come out of Dunkirk totally disillusioned with the British version of democracy, has now switched sides and is passing information to the enemy. Ever since the novel was published, criticism has been eager to find fault with the figure of Robert Kelway; he has been called unreal, a construct, a mere plot-device, a woman's idea of a man. Perhaps this negative view may be partly explained by the fact that the reader chiefly sees him through Stella's eyes; if we feel that we never get to know him as a person, then neither has Stella really known him. And perhaps he does become more alive when we see him briefly without Stella towards the end of the book, when he is expecting arrest at any moment and cannot seriously enter into his family's debate on whether or not to sell their house. But our view of him both as a person and a fictional character can hardly be other than prejudiced, since he is given many pages of largely negative build-up – and the counter-spy, Harrison, early sows the seeds of suspicion in the reader's mind as well as in Stella's – before he appears on the scene himself, in the fifth chapter of the book.

Robert is a central figure in the novel, however, in terms of theme as well as plot; in Bowen's own words, he is the 'problem character' and 'touchstone' of the book.[1] Our uncertain reponse may perhaps be most satisfactorily resolved if we accept that he is indeed the abstraction that many see in him – not an abstraction in any negative sense, but a universal type, rather, an allegorical figure: the spoilt, proud son hankering for something greater than himself that might give some meaning to his life. Classical mythology provides a well-known prototype in the story of Icarus, whose pride and folly made him fly too near the sun, so that the wax melted on the wings his father Daedalus had made for him and he fell into the sea; this was when Icarus and Daedalus were fleeing from Crete, where Daedalus had been employed by King Minos to construct the labyrinth associated with his name. It is tempting to see in *The Heat of the Day* a reflection of this ancient myth. Robert's 'fall or leap' alone might suggest a reading along those lines; besides, his hubris is certainly on a par with that of Icarus, much is made of his relations with his father, and it is suggested more than once that he has never really grown up. Even more telling is the novel's counterpart to the labyrinth in the myth, the twisting passages of Holme Dene, Robert's family home, where 'corridors, archways, recesses, half-landings, ledges, niches, and balustrades combined to fuddle any sense of direction and check, so far as possible, progress from room to room' (HD 256).

Robert Kelway would not be the first ambitious young man, in or out of fiction, to be compared to Icarus. 'I was ever sorry your Lordship should fly with waxen wings, doubting Icarus' fortune,' wrote Francis Bacon in 1600 to Queen Elizabeth's fallen favourite, Robert Devereux, Earl of Essex (*Letters and Life* II, 191); Devereux was of an age with Bowen's fictive character when he was executed for high treason in 1601. It does not seem impossible that something of the earl went into the making of Robert Kelway besides his name and his fall; like Kelway,

---

[1] Letter from Elizabeth Bowen to Charles Ritchie, quoted by Glendinning (93:151).

Essex was the strikingly tall son of a weak father and a domineering mother, and he was by all accounts as arrogant and moody as Bowen's character.[2] Essex's sister was reputedly the 'Stella' of Sir Philip Sidney's sonnet-sequence *Astrophel and Stella* (1591).

In the present context, Robert Kelway's death is in itself therefore less interesting than the fact that he dies by falling from a height. Falling is an important motif in the novel, from Stella's reputation as a fallen woman – she is rumoured to have asked her husband for a divorce after only two years of marriage and is 'officially known to have quite a heart' (HD 40) – to the general theme of betrayal and underlying associations to the Fall of Man. The motif is foreshadowed in the falling leaves in the very first paragraph of the book: 'already leaves were drifting on to the grass stage – here and there one turned over, crepitating as though in the act of dying, and during the music some more fell' (HD 7); and Robert's fatal fall is anticipated when he is first introduced, discharged from hospital with a wounded knee which makes him 'pitch' along when he walks (HD 90).

Textual Reflections of Falling
The motif of falling is kept in the mind of the reader throughout, partly by non-verbal repeats of scene and character, and partly by the repetition of lexemes belonging to the same semantic field: *fall, flop, pitch, drop, teeter, dive, plunge, knock down.* These words recur in different contexts and uses. The loss of the *Titanic* referred to above is a case in point, both for its non-verbal icon (the magazine picture) and its verbal echo (*plunged*). Again, there is an actual bunch of snow*drops* in Stella's flat, and *drop* recurs in a number of metaphorical uses: it is a trick of Harrison's to *drop* his voice for emphasis (HD 29), he talks of *dropping* in to see Stella (HD 29, 43), and *dropping* her a bottle of milk (HD 132). The air-raids on London and their wake of falling buildings are responsible for numerous occurrences of the word *fall* itself, and there are several references to the *fall* of France. Both *drop* and *fall* are also brought in quite naturally when rain is mentioned. In the most intimate scene between Stella and Harrison, when they are standing in a window embrasure watching the rain, the text finds occasion to use *fall* or *fell* five times in less than a page; this follows immediately after

---

[2] See e.g. G B Harrison, *The Life and Death of Robert Devereux, Earl of Essex*.

a striking foreshadowing of Robert's fall or leap: 'the silence could not have been more complete than if Harrison had walked straight on out of the window' (HD 139).

The movement of falling is visualized in several tangible details, like the drifting leaves in the very first lines of the book I have just mentioned; petals fall from a bowl of roses, ash falls from a cigarette. Falling is also highlighted in one or two graphic scenes. The first is the grotesque, and grotesquely elaborated, meeting of Louie and Connie referred to earlier: coming home laden with vegetables one night, Connie falls down the stairs, and Louie is brought out from her first floor front in her pink nightdress by the sound of carrots and potatoes and turnips and an electric torch 'bouncing down step after step of flight after flight or dropping plumb through the banisters into the hall below' (HD 149-150). Later in the book Robert, on his last visit to Holme Dene, starts so violently at the sound of the telephone that his young niece falls off the arm of his chair; the slight accident is dwelt on:

> 'Knocking the child off the chair,' went on Mrs. Kelway [Robert's mother], further tried by having to raise her voice above the demoniac ringing of the telephone, 'though she had no business to be sitting on the arm.'
> 'I simply fell off, Grannie.'
> 'You should not sit on your uncle when he is nervous.' (HD 264)

After Robert's death, falling is again brought to our attention in a warning given to Stella's son, who wants to take a look around his newly acquired property in Ireland on the night he arrives, even though it is after dark. The caretaker tells him, picking up both *drop* and *pitch*:

> 'There's a more deceptive drop from here to the river than you might think. ... I even heard how once a carriage and pair of horses pitched over it in the darkness before we had the parapet – and again there's a rocky drop from the Alpine Walk, if you should be thinking of going that way.' (HD 310)

Indifference

Robert's fall thus brings to a head a motif that runs through the whole novel. It is coupled with another motif that becomes prominent in the last two chapters: the indifference of both natural and social environments. The truism that 'Life must go on' has surfaced occasionally in the novel. A newspaper report triggers off a childhood memory of Louie's, for instance. She remembers seeing birds gathering on telephone wires, and Connie explains why migratory birds are now in the news: 'They do keep on doing what they always did do.... They go to show how Nature pursues her course under any circumstances. Birds like that wouldn't notice there was a war' (HD 154). Quite early in the book, people themselves have become insensitive to the ruins around them. The 'heady' autumn of the first air-raids on London in 1940 has given way, two years later, to a 'deadening acclimatization':

> The first generation of ruins, cleaned up, shored up, began to weather – in daylight they took their places as a norm of the scene; the dangerless nights of September two years later blotted them out. It was from this new insidious echoless propriety of ruins that you breathed in all that was most malarial. Reverses, losses, deadlocks now almost unnoticed bred one another; every day the news hammered one more nail into a consciousness which no longer resounded.... This was the lightless middle of the tunnel. (HD 92-93)

At the end of the book, in the remarkable coda after Robert's death, the motif of Nature's indifference comes to the fore. It is reflected in the narrative stance, which in these last two chapters is quite different from the rest of the book, as I have discussed in Chapter 7. Having up till now given us an empathetic inside view of Stella, often very intimately in the form of free indirect thought, the narrator now becomes a dispassionate onlooker: at one point Stella is described from the point of view of other passengers in a railway compartment, as 'the woman in the corner' (HD 293), and the inquest after Robert's fall is given non-narratively, as dramatic monologue. Lack of concern on the part of the narrator also appears in the off-hand, almost flippant form in which the progress of the war is now reported, in Louie-like style: 'July, the Sicilian landings; the Russian opening of their great leafy Orel summer drive. Mussolini out. September, Italians out, but leaving Italy to it' (HD 308). This distancing from wartime events is parallelled in the lives of the characters. After the inquest, everything in the last chapter points forward, and everyone is making plans: visiting his Irish property, Stella's son talks of taking an agricultural course and making the estate a going concern; Stella herself has thoughts of getting married; Harrison, who has been attempting to blackmail her into sleeping with him, realizes that she will never love him, and that he had better stick to making plans; Louie gives birth to a son. The very ordinariness of these events signals a return to normality after the heightened emotions of the previous chapters, just as the fortunes of war herald a return to peace; and the Allied victories in France now even make it possible for the flighty, promiscuous Louie to return to the scenes of her childhood, hitherto out of bounds on the south coast, as an 'orderly mother' (HD 329). The novel ends with Louie holding up her baby son to see three swans flying towards the west. They are all survivors, and they all, even the swans, have some purpose in life, 'somewhere to get to'.

Auden and Bruegel

I have borrowed this last phrase from a poem that W H Auden wrote in the late 1930s, 'Musée des Beaux Arts', which provides an explicit link between the motif of fallen pride and that of Nature's indifference. The poem is a meditation on the impassivity of the natural world suggested by Bruegel's *The Fall of Icarus* in the Musées royaux des Beaux-Arts in Brussels. The painting shows a hilly landscape on a seacoast. In the foreground a ploughman is intent on turning the earth into elaborate parallel lines; in the centre is the smaller figure of a shepherd, on the right a man fishing with his back to us, and further back an elegant ship heading out to sea. Ploughman, shepherd, and fisherman all appear in Ovid, whose *Metamorphoses* is the traditional source of the story.[3] But while the *Metamorphoses* has all three figures look at Daedalus and his son flying in the air, in Bruegel's painting only the shepherd looks up, into a sky where no Daedalus is to be seen;[4] ploughman and fisherman are both looking down, and Icarus is no more than a pair of legs disappearing into the sea.

Auden's poem goes a step further than the painting in making no mention of the observant shepherd. It begins with general reflections:

> About suffering they were never wrong,
> The Old Masters: how well they understood
> Its human position; how it takes place
> While someone else is eating or opening a window or just walking dully along;

After meditating on the indifference shown by old and young alike to

---

[3] *Metamorphoses*, VIII, 203 sqq.; also, but without ploughman and fisherman, *Ars Amatoria*, II, 21 sqq.
[4] In a slightly different version of the painting in the D M van Buuren collection in New York, Daedalus appears in the sky near the top of the picture.

both miracle and martyrdom, the poet turns to Bruegel's picture to illustrate his point:

> In Brueghel's *Icarus*, for instance: how everything turns away
> Quite leisurely from the disaster; the ploughman may
> Have heard the splash, the forsaken cry,
> But for him it was not an important failure; the sun shone
> As it had to on the white legs disappearing into the green
> Water; and the expensive delicate ship that must have seen
> Something amazing, a boy falling out of the sky,
> Had somewhere to get to and sailed calmly on. (69:123-124)

Whether or not Bowen had Bruegel's picture and Auden's poem consciously in mind, the mood of her last chapter is much the same as that in the painting, which the poem picks up and develops. There are similarities of detail, too. On the last page of the novel Louie finds that the scars of war are already being obliterated on the site of her parents' bombed-out house, and its foundations are overgrown with grass; the very wording, 'the ridges left by the foundations' (HD 329), seems to recall the elaborate ridges and furrows in Bruegel's picture. Painting and theme are echoed in the upward look Louie gives in the last lines of the book: her baby boy sleeps through the sound of returning bombers that has gone just before, but his mother wakens him to see the flying swans. Most striking, perhaps, is the light suffusing both painting and poem and novel, with the sparkling sea in Bruegel and the sun shining 'as it had to' in Auden, and the air 'full of today and sunshine' in the novel (HD 329). The indifference of the natural world is made quite explicit in Bowen's text less than a page from the end in a bald statement that receives full emphasis by being given a whole paragraph to itself:

> The sea, there, glittered as though nothing had happened. (HD 329)

This echoes the 'all-day glittering in the sun' of the gate in Regent's Park in the very first chapter (HD 20) and may well be read as an oblique comment on the novel's title: on the long view, the physical and emotional upheavals – the 'heat of the day' – that have held our attention for 300 pages or so are as nothing compared to the permanence of the natural world.

Other Intertextuality
The structural parallel to the story of Icarus I have suggested chimes in with other elements of intertextuality to lend resonance to the novel: direct quotation, character reference, scenic and verbal echo. This also includes the title, a much-quoted line from the biblical story of the husbandman who paid those labourers who were hired at the eleventh hour the same as those who had worked all day and 'borne the burden and heat of the day' (Matthew 20:12). Other examples are references to Shakepearean and Dickensian characters – Hamlet, Lady Macbeth, Mr Dick – that point up the motif of madness which runs through the story; for Robert's defection, like his hubris, is perhaps a kind of madness. Shakespeare is mentioned by name in an obvious invitation to read significance into the novel when Roderick says to his mother, 'I couldn't bear to think of you waiting on and on and on for something, something that in a flash would give what Robert did and what happened enormous meaning like there is in a play of Shakespeare's' (HD 300). Wordsworth's 'Lucy' poems are quoted, in an apposite reminder of man's humble place in the universe: 'Rolled round with rocks and stones and trees,' thinks Stella, '– what else is one?' (HD 274). Childhood reading also comes in, with allusions to Lewis Carroll and A A Milne. Both crop up in the chapter that is played out at Holme Dene, where they underline the distorted values and cramping indoctrination of Robert's upbringing that are posited as part of the reason for his disaffection: Robert and Stella retreat smiling from an upper window 'leaving grins behind them on the air in the window' (HD 122-123) like the Cheshire cat in *Alice in Wonderland,* and a young Kelway soldier-nephew much fussed-over by his mother and grandmother is called Christopher Robin, like the little boy in *Winnie-the-Pooh.* A broader cultural inheritance is invoked by the 'Danteësque' features of the caretaker on the Irish estate (HD 164), encouraging us to associate a lurid underground café some chapters further on with the Inferno of Dante's *Divine Comedy*, and to recall Dante's poem again later when Louie thinks of Stella as 'a soul astray' (HD 248, 249). Stella herself thinks in terms of classical mythology when, looking out for Robert to meet her when she arrives at Euston Station, she is reminded by the crowded scene on the platform of the 'arrival of the shades in Hades, the new dead scanned dubiously by the older' (HD 181) – a barely veiled suggestion that Robert himself is already a shade in Hades, and Stella (who is still considering Harrison's offer) well on the way to becoming one.

These are some of the literary allusions and echoes that go hand in hand with the classical story of Icarus to nudge us into a deeper understanding of the book and an awareness of the tradition in which it was written. The intertextuality of *The Heat of the Day* may not be as signposted as the often cited example of James Joyce's *Ulysses,* or indeed as Bowen's own use of literary parallellism in her short story 'Mysterious Kôr' (1944), which describes London on a moonlit night with reference to the hidden city of Kôr in Rider Haggard's *She*. Intertextuality works in a similar way in *The Heat of the Day*, however, encouraging a wider interpretation of a story that ostensibly deals with a particular conflict at a particular moment in history. Kelway's overreaching arrogance becomes the arrogance of a self-centred malcontent in any age; his treason, more than the mere transfer of allegiance from one political system to another, becomes the ultimate betrayal of love and trust between human beings, and a negation of the supreme good of free and open speech. On this level, the novel touches the springs of human tragedy.

Chapter 11

Doors and Entrances in *A World of Love*

There are doors and doorways, gates and gateways, in many of the texts discussed in these studies – often, but not exclusively, with sexual connotations. In *The Heat of the Day*, for instance, there are street doors that are opened 'conspiratorially' because of the wartime blackout (HD 46). In 'A Day in the Dark' there is the porch of the hotel bearing its name in gold lettering that forms a theatrical frame for the princely figure of the protagonist's uncle (CS 782). Dinah's 'nice white gate' in *The Little Girls* is one of the places where, much to Clare's disgust, she runs 'for cover' (LG 198). In *Eva Trout* the open door of the Danceys is a sign of their generous hospitality; when Eva visits them with Jeremy it stands 'ajar, by about three inches, indicating, "Out, but back in a minute"' (ET 149). It is in *A World of Love*, however, that doors and gates come in for the most sustained attention in Bowen's post-war fiction,[1] appropriately enough for a story that is, in her own words, 'on the periphery of passion';[2] a story, moreover, where the boundaries between present and past, between sensory and extra-sensory perception are repeatedly crossed as the long-dead Guy, the 'creature of extra sense' (WL 69), manifests himself to the three women who have loved him: Antonia, the cousin who was as a sister to him; his fiancée Lilia, 'at seventeen a wonderful golden willow of a girl' (WL 14); and now Jane, his 'latest love' (WL 79), the golden-haired changeling who might have been his daughter. Some aspects of the book's concern with the past have been discussed in Chapter 9; here I shall be looking at doors, gates, and archways as entrances into different worlds, different

---

[1] Though it is beyond the scope of these studies to discuss Bowen's early fiction, it will be natural to recall the innumerable doors in *The Last September* (1929) that lead up to the final image of the burning Big House of Danielstown: 'Above the steps, the door stood open hospitably upon a furnace' (Penguin ed., 206).

[2] Letter from Elizabeth Bowen to May Sarton, quoted by Glendinning (93:200).

types of reality. The recurrent mention of these images, particularly on the Montefort demesne – front door, kitchen door, outhouse doors, garden door, doors to drawing-room and dining-room and the bedrooms of Antonia and Lilia; the gate of the little front garden, the gate of the Horse Field, the white gates of the drive that must at all times be kept closed because of the cattle; the stone archway leading into the yard, the archways of the deserted dovecote – all this contributes to the overall impression of thresholds to be crossed and new worlds – new experiences, new loves, new lives – to be explored.

Lilia, Fred, and Jane

Lilia and Fred are those most conspicuously associated with doors and door-openings, and their story is a textbook example of the sexual connotations of such images. A few pages into the book we meet Lilia 'inching' into Antonia's bedroom and then stopping 'with a look at once of uncertainty and affront'; when the door swings to behind her she seems 'glad to have the decision made' (WL 11; Lilia's ability to make decisions is reserved for later in the book). Fred is early on a great hesitater in doorways. When he first saw Lilia more than twenty years before the story begins he 'came in as far as doorways, where he lingered taking oblique notice' (WL 16); now in the narrative present, hoping to hear news of his beloved daughter Jane who has forgotten to come out to help with the hay, he prolongs his exchange with his wife by 'plucking away at an old nail loose in the lintel of the door' (WL 20); finding Lilia lying down in the drawing room after the trials of the Fête he stands 'fidgeting in the doorway' (WL 32), and soon afterwards, even when he is 'pleased with life' (after Jane has belatedly joined in the haymaking), we see him in the doorway of the dining-room, towelling his neck before sitting down to lunch (WL 35). Later in the story, however, the hesitancy of this illegitimate cousin and estranged husband gives way to wrathful indignation, and he comes into his own as the masterful father who will have no truck with the underhand dealings of his youngest daughter when she tries to 'sell' him the love-letters she has taken. Fred becomes the stern Old Testament father Maud has longed for at the very moment when he wrenches the letters from her (though, ever critical, she is ashamed of the spectacle he has made of himself by losing his temper). He also comes into his own as husband, and 'passion [is] still racing through his system' (WL 100) when he brings the letters to his wife.

The following reconciliation scene in the garden between Fred and Lilia is held in a tone of mutual tolerance and understanding vastly different from their former exchanges, and their very speaking together now is an 'act of love' that promises well for the future (WL 105). A door comes in again here, and an archway. Hearing the garden door creak and imagining it to be Guy, Lilia expects to meet him round the corner of the path (as he has in real life, so to speak, been 'leading her up the garden path' all along). It is Fred she has heard, however, and this time he does not hesitate in the doorway but comes straight through, deliberately, twice. The new understanding between husband and wife comes about after they have passed through the garden door together and are sitting on the mounting block under the chestnut tree that forms a canopy over the stone arch (the tree and archway that were mentioned already on the first page of the book). It is tempting to see the arch now as triumphal, confirming Fred's final mastery over the image of Guy that has hitherto cast a blight on his marriage. Through this archway Jane sees her father and mother as if for the first time as man and woman, framed in the same way they had stood in the Montefort doorway after their wedding (WL 18) and anticipating the repetition of that scene in the final chapter:

> Watching the van drive away, bearing the children, the three stood – Antonia outside the fence, Fred and Lilia framed in the doorway. This was an echo, a second time – second time of what? Wedding afternoon. All was repeated almost exactly – summer emptiness darkening along the edges, hypnotic sky. Yes, and today could, if one wished, be counted an anniversary; for the Danby wedding had been, had it not, on much such a day as this was, near the end of a June. Left behind in that doorway the pair had stood, watching Antonia drive away in their wedding taxi, free of them. (WL 139-140)

A theatrically framed setting, at Montefort and elsewhere, is not the prerogative of the main characters in the story: when Antonia fetches her from the Latterly dinner party Jane looks back at the castle, 'to which lighted windows and butler still on the steps gave a farewell theatricality' [WL 71]; the eligible young man who arrives at the very end of the story is also framed in a doorway, albeit that of an airliner; and cattle are seen by Antonia through the open front door at Montefort, in a memorable image of the ongoing natural life on the demesne:

> Antonia, beginning to go downstairs, was met by the arid breath of outdoors – the door, standing as it had stood last night, open, let the afternoon's bright shadows into the hall. One by one, across the view through the doorway, cattle were in a listless file proceeding towards the river woods: this, as the one movement, she stood intently watching from the foot of the stairs, where she had herself come to a stop. (WL 115)

Looking at *A World of Love* as a *rite de passage* in which a young girl comes to maturity (a favourite subject of Bowen's, though only one aspect of this novel), we may expect to find Jane passing through some of the numerous doors and gates at Montefort and the neighbouring castle. True enough, she does so many times: coming home from the Fête she unchains the gates before bicycling up the drive (WL 27); once inside the house she looks into all the rooms and passes through the drawing-room, 'in at one door, out again at the other' (WL 28). After midday dinner the next day she leaves the house through the kitchen door and enters the walled garden (WL 43). At Latterly Castle she glimpses the 'theatrical emptiness' of the drawing-room before being taken up to Lady Latterly's sumptuous bedroom (WL 56); the drawing-room, when she does enter it, is 'black and white at the door end with standing men' (WL 58), and when Lady Latterly comes 'swishing in at the door behind her' (WL 59) everything seems to indicate that Jane is about to lose her innocence. That she does not do so is in large part due to her intelligent awareness of the role as 'young country beauty' (WL 60), 'the lovely nobody' (WL 61) she has been called on to play in this charade 'reek[ing] of expense' (WL 61) where 'everything cost, nothing was for nothing' (WL 61). Her critical attitude also appears in her reaction to the lack of simple good manners on the part of her hostess, who does not bother to introduce her ('If this *were* behaviour, one had yet to learn how to deal with it' [WL 61]) – and in her Alice-like dismissal of the displaced rich who make up the party: '"You're nothing," she thought of the company, "but a pack of cards!"' (WL 61).

Otherworldly Elements
But it is clear that Jane has been enticed into the Otherworld by a malignant, predatory power; the Latterly car has even been sent twice to Montefort, and we recall that it was a memory of Lady Latterly's hat that led the girl to find Guy's letters in the first place. The witchlike appearance of her hostess is evident as soon as Jane arrives for the dinner party, when she 'claw[s] the air in the direction of Jane's hand'

by way of greeting (WL 55). Her throat is like whipcord (WL 60), her nails like talons (WL 68). She may well have a hollow back, like many supernatural beings, for she 'brace[s] herself against the fortification of Jane's body' when they walk across the room together (WL 60), and she and the other woman guest, Mamie, sit one at each end of the sofa, 'each with her spine supporting a stack of cushions' (WL 62). There are several allusions to the extra-sensory: spell, telepathy, banshee, family curse, ghosts who disappear at cock-crow; besides, the reference to the party (other than Jane herself and one old 'native') as 'aliens' (WL 63), which on the face of it means they are not Irish, may also be read as meaning that they are inhabitants of another world. There is little colour in the drawing-room, and Lady Latterly's yellow chiffon, echoed by Jane's 'yellowed' muslin, stands out against Mamie's black diagonal on the white sofa and the black and white of the anonymous, lifeless men. The yellow of Lady Latterly's dress is less akin to the sun than to the fading light Bowen described in the beginning of *The Heat of the Day* as being 'so low, so theatrical, and so yellow' (HD 7), and the colour's connotations of jealousy and infidelity far outweigh those of warmth. Mamie's pomegranate toenails are one of the few other flashes of colour, one that helps to bring out the otherworldly aspect of the location. As Robert Tracy points out (251), 'pomegranate' recalls the ancient myth of Proserpina or Persephone, who had unwittingly placed herself in the power of the Underworld because she had eaten a few pomegranate seeds there; Jane still has a hayseed in her hair from the morning's haymaking, and Antonia speaks of her evening excursion as 'a seedy outing' (WL 72). She herself has refused to enter the castle, which causes some surprise there:

> 'What is it *now*?' she [Lady Latterly] snapped at the butler, who had come in and was waiting by her chair.
> 'If you please, m'lady, the young lady's cousin has come for her.'
> 'Why, when? Who's the young lady's cousin?'
> 'She gave no name.'
> 'Well then, bring her in then, for heaven's sake!'
> 'She'd prefer, she said, to stop at the door.'
> 'How very, very peculiar,' said Lady Latterly. (WL 71)

Peculiar it may seem to the mistress of the castle, but folklore knows better. Antonia has come to rescue Jane, who has been playing dangerously into the hands of the fairies, the *sidhe*, by drinking a 'potion' – in actual fact three martinis – within their confines. Of course

Antonia will not cross their threshold herself. She does not give her name, moreover, for to know a person's name is to have a certain power over that person. This belief is alluded to later when Lilia is less rattled on meeting Harris for the second time than she was when he first turned up: 'The entire ambience of their meeting was different this time – for one thing, she knew his name' (WL 137).

Instead of following Fred and Jane into the kitchen when she has brought the girl home from the castle dinner, Antonia feels drawn towards the door, which has been 'left wide open upon the allaying night'. In this central passage (WL 77; quoted above, p. 154), where Antonia feels Guy's and her own youth rushing towards her out of the dark, the sense of her cousin's presence is so closely bound up with the countryside as to indicate affinities with spirits of the woods and fields and river, and to suggest that he has more than a similarity of name in common with Maud's familiar. It seems very likely, as Robert Tracy suggests (247), that Gay David is himself an indigenous spirit, and that his name may be part translation, part anglicization of the Irish *aerach* (= gay) and *deamhan* (= demon). He can hardly be a benevolent spirit; echoing Edgar's words in *King Lear* (III.iv) Maud refers to him as a 'foul fiend' (WL 143), and she seems to spend a lot of time scuffling with him. The fanatical, authoritarian little girl is part Black Magic and part Old Testament judgment, and she has other witchlike attributes besides a familiar. Her hives may thus be seen as the witch's marks of popular superstition, and her only headwear we hear of is a pixie hood. In the present context it is interesting to note her association with gates: waiting for the school bus, the 'Protestant Van', she sits 'in wet weather rendered still more terrible by a pixie hood, and often perched atop of a cracked gatepost' (WL 109); and Fred wrests the letters from her 'near the gate of the Horse Field' (WL 107).

After Jane's return from the Latterly dinner party, Antonia's exchange with Lilia, while she is still standing in the doorway and still feels her cousin's presence in the night landscape, is so worded as to suggest that she includes Guy among those who have come 'back':

> 'Wait, I – ' she hurriedly said, aloud.
>   Above, Lilia came to her bedroom window. 'What's the matter? Who's that you're talking to?'
>   'Is that *you*, Lilia?' queried Antonia, shaken.
>   'Yes. Why not?'
>   'Can't you sleep?'

> 'Is Jane back – everyone back?'
> 'Everyone's back.'
> 'Who did you say?'
> 'Everyone.'
> 'Who's that down there with you?'
> 'You must be dreaming.'
> 'Your voice sounds funny, Antonia. – You'll lock the door, then?'
> 'Yes. Go back to bed. Good night.' (WL 78-79)

This looks back to the scene at the castle, when Jane feels that Guy is among them and even the 'barbarian nerves' of the other guests (WL 67) realize that 'there *had* been an entrance' (WL 68); and while the men in the party 'helped to compose Guy, they remained tributary to him and less real to Jane – that is, as embodiments – than was he' (WL 68). The very fact that the other men in the party are 'anonymous masks' (WL 58) makes them 'apt conductors' (WL 67) of the electrical current they all feel between Jane and the empty chair opposite her at the dinner-table, where a place has been laid for the Priscilla who does not turn up – unless, it is subtly suggested, it has been laid for some guest from the Otherworld, Guy perhaps? An explanation of sorts is offered by Lady Latterly's current lover: 'I know there's a castle in this country where an extra place is laid every night for dinner. It's in some way connected with the family curse' (WL 66).³ We may take this as a hint that there is also a curse on Montefort – which there surely is: the curse of the past, not to speak of the Old Testament vengeance Maud calls down on her father in Chapter 9 of the book.

Evocative Settings

In the night scene just referred to, where Antonia feels a 'windlike rushing' out of the dark – 'her youth and Guy's' (WL 77) – it is interesting to note that she is standing on the doorstep, as if she were on the threshold of some other world, the world of the past she shared with her cousin; tellingly, the doorstep receives a good deal of prominence:

> [H]ere was the universe filling up – all there had been to be, do, know, dare, live for or die for at the full came flooding to this doorstep. Doom was lifted from her. Moreover all was certain: nothing could have been firmer than this doorstep on which she bodily stood (this stone which though it had cracked and sunk had cracked no wider, sunk no further) except Antonia's certainty of tonight. (WL 77)

---

³ The empty place at the dinner table recalls an actual tradition at Howth Castle associated with Granuaile or Grace O'Malley, a notorious 16th century pirate queen.

Lilia and Jane feel Guy's presence in a similarly evocative atmosphere. Lilia thinks she sees him in the walled garden, where she is sitting on the stone bench when she hears the creaking of a door: 'Somebody had come in and was in this garden. But not again a sound, not a step – there ensued more than a silence of moss, sloth, airlessness and the exhausted river: something more than human was at intensity. In depth, dead-still, branches screened the doorway – of whom was this the ghost in the afternoon?' (WL 97). The day before this, lying in the bracken on the Montefort side of the river, where 'water-mint wet in the dwindling current and meadowsweet creaming frothily the river bank sent up a scented oblivion round her' (WL 47), Jane realizes that she is in the exact spot described in one of Guy's letters; she can see the clown's face in the cliff opposite and the crooked thorn tree he writes of, and to the words in his letter, '*I thought ... if only YOU had been here!*' she protests, 'But here I am. Oh, here I *am*!' (WL 48). The location of the scene is one of the most suggestive in the book – it is possibly even more of a *locus amoenus* than the Mount Morris landscape described in *The Heat of the Day* – and we have already heard that the 'summer-idle water dawdled in shallows, slid on skeins where it had brightly appeared to be least moving, and in a tea-brown clear pool mirrored the cliff above' (WL 47). Under this cliff is Gay David's Hole, a 'small low cave under the cliff's face' (WL 47). It is a private, secluded spot ('*my* place,' says Maud, who has taken the name of the cave for her familiar), and Antonia imagines that the elder-tree where Jane has hidden the letters masks a 'secret gateway' to this haunted part of the river (WL 46). The text makes much of the fact that Jane is on 'the Montefort side' (WL 47), 'this side of the river' (WL 49), and that the turf itself breaks into a small cliff 'this side of the water' (WL 48). Her sister is in Gay David's Hole opposite (and the very first page of the novel has encouraged us to notice that the cliff was on the other side: 'the cliff arose from the water, opposite' [WL 9]); they have to shout to each other, Maud bawling '*Ca-ar* ... Car, car, car', uncannily like the croaking of a raven (WL 47), and then wading purposefully through the shallows to get home – an insistence on the barrier created by the river that brings to mind ancient beliefs in the supernatural power of running water. (Perhaps Maud is not truly a witch, since she can after all cross the river? Or perhaps the water is so sluggish that it hardly counts as 'running'?).

Other Thresholds

Doorways other than those at Montefort help to strengthen the threshold aspect of the story. Even the dismal, dung-spattered main street of Clonmore offers examples: its shops have 'insanely similar doorways' (WL 88), and Maud stands sucking a sweet in the door of Lonergan's, the Clonmore grocer (WL 85). Shannon Airport is entered by a 'succession of glassy doors' (WL 147), and once inside Jane can hear voices blown towards her by 'far-off doors sucking open and shut from time to time' (WL 147). The final vignette, similar to that of the nameless uncle standing in the hotel porch in 'A Day in the Dark', is of Richard Priam, theatrically framed as he gets off the plane:

> An individual trailing a carried overcoat and inexpertly holding a gift parcel, forgotten, gone back to his seat for and recovered, which had prolonged farewells to the air hostess, head-stooped under the door and all but pitched himself down the steps. The descent was made with a look of ease at being at large again. (WL 149)

Richard Priam, it seems, has been as much in a 'cage' as Lady Latterly's present lover, Peregrine (WL 118) – whether the 'cage' has been more than merely the aeroplane, we can only guess at – and he and Jane are now equally free to fall in love.

A Choice of Worlds

It is perhaps an implication of its title that *A World of Love* offers us entrances into many different worlds. Some of them are specious: the ballroom world of romance where Lilia fell in love with Guy, or the 'courts of love' at Latterly Castle (WL 68), or the supernatural world of witches and familiars, or the dreamworld of the past. Some worlds are rejected because they are founded on wealth: the money-grabbing present of the displaced rich and *nouveau-riches* – Latterly Castle here, too – or the gossipy, servile and equally money-grabbing village of Clonmore, which is 'deadly glazed' by the sun into a 'picture postcard such as one might receive from Hell' (WL 88). It would seem that the only world which is not seen to represent negative values is that of Montefort: not the house, but the working farm with its tractor and haymaking, and the cattle that are recalled throughout the book – polishing the obelisk and leaving a 'bald-trodden circle on the grass' (WL 10), fouling what is left of the river, making it necessary to have a fence in front of the house and gates at the entrance to the drive. This is the world we have seen in Antonia's glimpse of the cattle through the open door I have just quoted; Fred's world, in fact.

The old Anglo-Irish Ascendancy does not come out well, and *A World of Love* may arguably be read as a critique of their now-gone world, as I have noted in an earlier chapter. There is not much left of the 'gaiety' of the pre-1914 past. The Hunt Fête, which 'drew the entire country' (WL 28), is a solitary relic, but the flashy brilliance of its marquees and the urns bright with geraniums on the castle terrace cannot hide its fundamental tawdriness. Pointedly the text tells us that one 'paid money' to enter (WL 28), and we even hear from the mercenary Maud the exact sum that was taken in – 'Four hundred and ninety-eight pounds, sixteen and fivepence' (WL 36); and money is a constant consideration throughout the novel, as John Coates points out (98a:187). At the Fête Lilia only buys worthless gewgaws at knock-down prices, and Maud, ever on the look-out for easy money, wants full payment from Antonia for the bottle of whisky she has won in the raffle. The concern with payment links this 'challenging social gathering' (WL 28) to the very different but similarly moneywise – and, to Jane, equally challenging – world of Lady Latterly and her guests, where the girl is well aware that she has been invited because of her commodity value. A personal link between the two worlds is provided by old Terence Fox, apart from Jane the only other 'native' at the dinner-party; he is explicit: 'These days, one goes where the money is – with all due respect to this charming lady. Those days, we went where the people were' (WL 64). The Protestantism underlying that former world is not much in evidence. Maud attends a Protestant school and is taken there in the 'Protestant Van', which she puts to good use as a convenient place in which to bully her school-fellows by kicking and pinching them, pulling their hair, or sticking pins into them; and at church she is, as we are informed parenthetically, 'the solitary, seldom-failing occupier of the family pew' (WL 28). That Antonia reads the Bible – it is on her bedside table – is an aspect of her complex personality that is not explored. To Maud, the Bible is above all a good place to find maledictions when she needs them, as she does when her father has beaten her for trying to sell him the bundle of letters she has taken.

The world of local beliefs and superstition that I looked at a few pages back, which is embodied first and foremost in Maud's familiar, Gay

David, is also represented in the book by Kathie: the little servant girl wonders if she has not seen 'a Vision' (WL 20) when she sees Jane go out to the obelisk wearing the old muslin gown, and she dares not burn Guy's letters because she sees a name in them. Kathie is only a minor figure in the story, but, like the forbidding picture of Maud, her portrait – naive, lazy, vain, slipshod – contributes to the text's effective rejection of that fairy world, despite its haunting beauty in the river valley. On another level, the fact that Guy's dominance lasted long after his death shows that the world of the imagination can be both dangerous and false: his memory has crippled the emotional lives of his contemporaries Fred, Lilia, and Antonia, and he provides no real lover for Jane; it is therefore fitting that, by burning his letters, she finally rejects him.

Jane also rejects Antonia and the presumably glamorous London world she has long inhabited with her, at the cost of staying at Montefort and developing a closer relationship to her parents. The crisis triggered off when she finds the letters is to change her whole future, and she knows she cannot go back to her former way of life, 'to the girls' residential club where Antonia put her when at a loss, to the room-mate who was the sort of bore who was not a virgin' (WL 145); London, it seems, was only glamorous when seen from Montefort, especially by Lilia. Jane also knows that her dependence on Antonia will soon be a thing of the past: 'I *shall* never see Antonia again, Jane thought. Something has happened. Somehow she's gone. – She's old' (WL 130). Jane takes leave of Antonia, as it were, with a 'dwelling kiss, at once comforting and beseeching' on 'the tarnished cheekbone' (WL 130). This poignant moment occurs just after Big Ben, the voice of Time itself, has craved a final reckoning and marked the end of Guy's power to dominate the lives of others. After Jane has kissed Antonia they both look towards Fred's usual place at the head of the table, empty just now because the present master of Montefort is not yet back from his drive with his wife:

> Simultaneously, both looked at the head of the table. As ever, it was after Guy had gone that he most nearly was to be seen. Gone for good, he had never appeared more clearly than he did at this last. (WL 130)

From the cliché-like ending of the book, when Jane sees Richard Priam getting off the airliner and 'they no sooner looked but they loved' (WL 149), it would seem uncertain whether the world of romantic love that she is now entering with a real flesh-and-blood lover will prove any more substantial than her 'falling in love with a love letter' (WL 39). Or, for that matter, than her mother's infatuation with Guy in the 'ballroom blue moonlight of Maidenhead' (WL 15). The reliability of that world of heady love has been called into question not only by the glimpses we have been given of Guy's ability to love several women at the same time, but also by the surprising information that Antonia has once briefly been married – 'So soon over, so long ago had been the try at marriage that it was not a substantial memory' (WL 135). In view of the repeated insistence on the resemblance between her and her cousin Guy, emotional stability in marriage is not to be expected from the Montefort family.

Altogether it would seem that only the ramshackle world of present-day Montefort, and Jane's role there, hold out any hope for the future. 'The tide might turn,' the text tells us fairly early on (WL 31), mentioning in the description of the drawing-room two pink cornucopias that Jane has 'restored' to the chimney-piece and sometimes puts flowers in, and the lovely photograph of her as a child that 'some other hand' (her father's?) has propped up between them. Rather than the 'happy ending' offered by the too-convenient appearance of the transatlantic hero, the new-found harmony between Lilia and Fred towards the end of the book combines with the exorcism of Guy, and with him of the past, to suggest that the tide is indeed turning and that Montefort will in fact survive, now that the place at the head of the table will be taken not by an unreliable revenant from the past but by a true, universally respected master.

Chapter 12

Picnic on the Sands

(*The Little Girls*)

The three protagonists are 'Little Girls' only in the second section of the novel of that name, when the narrative present is the summer of 1914. This part describes the life of the three friends as eleven-year-olds at home and at school in 'Southstone', a fictionalized version of Folkestone on the Kentish coast. The precariously peaceful pre-WWI chapters have been prepared in the first part of the book, which is set in the 1960s; its last lines describe WWII damage to the town, with Shakespearean echoes ironically balanced by modern slang:

> '*At* St. Agatha's hadn't we better meet? Agreed?'
> Sheila said: 'It's not there.... As you may know or not know, we were shelled at Southstone.' A snobbishness, far from unsympathetic, o'erspread her native countenance: anyone could be bombed. 'They lammed away at us, onward from 1940. I don't say every day; it was off and on. One of those fine days, St Agatha's copped it.'
> '*Sheikie* ... not all the girls?'
> 'Gracious, no. Girls? – they'd been long gone. That old place had not been a school for years. When it was hit, it was empty and boarded up.'
> Clare said: '"Into thin air."' (LG 63)

The present discussion will focus on the last chapter in the second section (II,7). The preceding chapter has dealt summarily, in a mere three pages, with the eagerly awaited climax of the project that has held the reader's attention for most of this section: the actual burying of a coffer containing a relic from each of the three girls (in its very brevity more of an anti-climax or non-climax, as so often in Bowen's fiction). The following 15 pages now constitute Chapter 7, which describes in some detail an outing that takes place on the first day of the school holidays in the summer of 1914, on the eve of the First World War. The chapter has seemingly little relevance for the relic-burying plotline that ties the three sections of the book together; its immediate importance lies in marking the sudden end of childhood and of the speciously innocent pre-war world, and in the parting between two of the girls, Dicey and Mumbo. But towards the end of the novel, fifty years or so on, Dinah (Dicey) speaks of her fear that little Trevor Artworth might have died in the drain-pipe she chased him into on the day of the outing and that his 'whitened skeleton' was still stuck up there (LG 222), giving us in a flash a gruesome vision of those many thousands of skeletons that lie buried in the Flanders landscape that is evoked in the location of the scene.

The picnic has been carefully and considerately prepared by the Pococks for their daughter's birthday on a sandy beach some twelve miles from Southstone, at 'Wanchurch' (to all appearances based on the real-life Dymchurch). It begins peacefully enough, with French cricket on the sands and a feast of scones and birthday cake. But after the candles on the cake have been blown out – symbolically, in the light of the context – there is 'an element of scrimmage' (LG 122), which echoes earlier references to the girls' habit of pushing ('shoving') their way through the streets of Southstone. There is some punching and kicking, a little boy is scalded by a carelessly placed tea-cup, and before races can be organized by the adults, the children almost of their own accord set up a lugubrious rendering of 'Way Down Upon the Swanee River' – 'a terrible wolf-like ululation with a spectre of tune in it' (LG 124), well calculated to introduce a dismal atmosphere into the party. The song is quoted on a full page; it is the more noticeable because the children have hitherto been silent, first awed by the sight of the immense sands and then politely waiting for the candles to be lit on the birthday cake.

During this mournful singing we hear of adults talking seriously among themselves. What they say is not reported, but it surfaces in an apparent non sequitur from Dicey's mother: 'But there is not going to be a war, is there?' (LG 125). Three pages later Dicey puts in her own non sequitur: 'I say, Mumbo? ... Who did kill that Australian duke?' (LG 128). Mumbo, being both intelligent and 'Army', knows what is going on:

'Austrian,' she enunciated, 'Archduke. Get that into your head.'
'Oh, all right, Mumbo,' said the willing learner.
'It's not all right!' (LG 129)

Chapter II,7 as a Metaphor for the First World War

Prompted by these references and by the time-setting, July 23rd 1914, the whole chapter is readily seen as a metaphor for the First World War. Though the date would in itself be enough to call forth associations to the coming war, it receives extra prominence by being given in a line drawing of the birthday cake, which is inscribed: 'Very many happy returns of the day. Olive. July 23 1914'; the text tells us that the words are surrounded by 'a sort of victory wreath ... glacé cherries, crystallized green angelica set like jewels into the icing' (LG 122). The picnic takes place a matter of days before the outbreak of hostilities: Archduke Franz Ferdinand was assassinated in Sarajevo on June 28th, and Britain declared war on August 4th. Military imagery points up this historical reality. There is a war-metaphor already in the initial description of the location, with its 'grass-topped sea wall *defending* the Marsh' (LG 119; my italics). The actual site of the picnic among the sand-dunes is repeatedly referred to as an *encampment*, the land *advances* as the tide *retreats* leaving only *dead* foam on the hard sand-ripples; and Clare's *wiry* hair wages *battle* with the wind. The handful of men present are explicitly *civilians*, and when Clare's officer-father joins the party he is in *mufti*. Three-legged races are ruled out by the adults because they make the children *fight*, and egg-and-spoon races are vetoed because they make them *knock each other down*; at one point the only acceptable activity seems to be a *tug-of-war*. In the context of so much warlike imagery, the common sight of the smaller children building *castles* with *battlements* in the sand assumes some of its originally martial force, and the reference to the picnic as a 'great outing' (LG 119) carries overtones of the coming war, which was long called The Great War (and which proved to be 'no picnic'). Two visual images are almost uncannily like war photographs and drawings. One is the children 'cataract[ing]' down off the sea wall onto the sands (LG 120); they have arrived in an open charabanc with a collapsible canvas hood that may bring to mind actual cars with collapsible hoods that figure conspicuously in some of the memorable photographs from the summer and early autumn of 1914 – the open car in which Franz Ferdinand was shot dead in June, the Paris taxis that brought reservists to the Battle of the Marne in September. The other striking image is the silhouette of Mumbo that closes the chapter:

> The rough child, up there against the unkind sky, on the rough grass, glanced at and over the sands once. She threw a hand up into a rough, general wave. Then she leaped down on the land side of the sea wall. She had disappeared. (LG 133)

Other Military Imagery and References
The war-imagery of this chapter is underscored by numerous references to war and the Army dotted about in the rest of the novel. The bleak Flanders landscape pitted with trenches is echoed – or, in terms of reading, anticipated, since the image occurs in the first chapter of the book – in the adult Dinah's garden: the vegetable plots are *trenched* (LG 17), and the lawn is *scarred* where the ornate flower beds have been turfed in (LG 20). Sheikie's mother is known to have a regard for *the military* (LG 81), and the gardening carried out by Mumbo's mother is a model of military precision:

> She was now stepping about purposefully with a watering can.... The can, having been giving warning by growing lighter, of a sudden declared itself all but empty. Tilted at whatever angle, it barely dribbled. Mrs Burkin-Jones shook the final drops, fair-mindedly, over the defaulters – more than they deserved! She then put the can down, looked back at the house, and waited: by clockwork, out came the soldier servant bearing a can of the same size, filled to a nicety. Exchange was effected. (LG 112-113)

Military imagery crops up in the very first page of the book, when Dinah *attacks* a jotting-pad with her pencil. Later, the meeting of Sheila and Clare in the Knightsbridge tea room is compared to a *council of war* (LG 30). It is Clare herself (Mumbo) who brings the most constant reminder of the army into the story. She is the daughter of an ill-matched dreamy officer father and an insensitive mother who lavishes on her garden the attention and affection that she withholds from her family. Being a soldier's daughter Mumbo has led an unsettled, peripatetic life (her father has been stationed in India). Her home, which is described very cursorily in the text, is merely a 'residence let furnished to married officers' (LG 112); it has none of the clutter of Dicey's mother's drawing-room or the pretty-prettiness of Sheikie's bedroom. Mumbo is by far the most intelligent of the three girls, and she provides a commonsensical sounding-board for the vagaries of one friend and the obsessive respectability of the other. In the poetry class at school she makes a hash of reciting Wordsworth's Immortality Ode, which she finds 'silly, in a way' (LG 68); but, soldier's daughter that she is, she launches passionately into Sir Francis Doyle's Kiplingesque ballad 'The Private of the Buffs', which is quoted prominently in the text. In adult life she runs her chain of gift-shops with the efficiency of a military operation. She speaks with a *veteran* lack of concern (LG 45) and has a no-nonsense attitude to her friends which Dinah accuses of being *military* (LG 166, 168). Her style of dress is both mannish and military: dark tailor-mades, hogskin gloves and turbans of varying colours (fashionable enough in the early 1960s, but perhaps also a reminiscence of her early childhood in India).

Military imagery is put to comic uses at the end of the novel with echoes of *Tintin*, when Dinah's Thomson-and-Thompson-like sons arrive expressly (but not immediately) on hearing of their mother's accident, but – defeated by the willpower of Sheila and Dinah's houseboy, and by their own reluctance to take action – postpone actually seeing her for more than an hour:

> Francis got rid of, they had been talking ... a *breakthrough* would have to be made and they were *planning* it. So far, the situation at Applegate made less rather than more sense with every minute, thanks to the bafflingness of Mrs Artworth, the spider's web ambiguities of Francis. The idea (later acted upon) of announcing that they were going to see their mother, then walking upstairs, began to commend itself more and more. Having agreed upon it, they drank to it. (LG 214; my italics)

When they do make a move to go up to their mother, 'the sons, a *phalanx* of two, *wheel[ed]* in the direction of the staircase' (LG 213; my italics); and when Sheila asks them why they did not come earlier and they do not wish to discuss it with her, they '*close[d] ranks*' (LG 233; my italics).

It is in line with this pervasive war imagery that though there are no actual deaths in the narrative (apart from that of Sheila's sister, of whom we are told practicalllly nothing) we hear of many people whose lives have been cut short: Mumbo's father, Dicey's mother and father, Trevor Artworth's first wife and his elder brother. Frank Wilkins never knew his grandmother, who 'died young' (LG 11). Cousin Roland's friend went down on the Titanic. Sheila's lover died just after she left him.

Mumbo had a young brother who died of meningitis in India. And Dinah is early left a widow with two young boys. This formidable list receives additional emphasis from the recurrent use of the words die/death in the novel, and from macabre images like the wings of a dead magpie on a woman's hat. (The novel's death-imagery is treated more fully in Chapter 6).

Violence

Reflecting the violence that was unleashed by the war, the violence that erupts at the picnic is a concentrate, as it were, of the energy hitherto displayed by the children (which persists in their adult lives): they *bolt* their breakfast and *tear* back to school in the mornings, always moving at top *speed* as though they are driving themselves as one would drive a *racing-car* (LG 99). When they *race* one another in swimming, they do so not for the sake of winning, but for the sake of *speed* (LG 87). The local *roller-skating* rink is a favourite outlet for surplus energy, and *biking*, for the fortunate owners of bicycles, means *skimming along*. Even the swallows on the frieze in Sheikie's room are *darting*. Sheikie herself makes a revealing mistake in the poem she recites:[1]

> Up the airy mountain
> Down the rushing glen,
> We daren't go a-hunting
> For fear of little men.

The slip is duly corrected by her teacher: 'And one word wrong in your second line. It should be "rushy", not "rushing". How could a glen rush?' – 'I thought it meant they were all rushing about,' says the girl (LG 71).

Again, partly following from the plot of the novel – burying some memento of oneself and one's contemporaries for later generations to find – there is talk of other wars of destruction, and other possible human races. Thus the first scene in the book, where Dinah is collecting objects to bury in her cave, occasions a good deal of talk about posterity – if there is to be any posterity and we do not all 'go with the same bang', in the words of the doleful Frank Wilkins (LG 16). It appears that he has almost an obsession about future inhabitants of the earth, which

---

[1] William Allingham's 'Up the airy mountain' was a favourite recitation piece.

A pre-WWI photograph of the Old High Street in Folkestone, which gives some idea of the 'steep and extremely cobbled' Old High Street in 'Southstone' in *The Little Girls*. This is the scene of the girls' shopping expedition in search of a large dog-chain to use as 'fetters' for the coffer they intend to bury; it is a noisy, smelly street down which they always rush at top speed: 'Last-moment swerving, at high velocity, was their forte - to bump into anyone meant enormous loss of prestige for the bumper-in. So, no one had anything to complain of. (Shove they did, but that was another matter)' (LG 99). *Reproduced by kind permission of Mr Alan F Taylor, Folkestone.*

is highlighted in the last part of the book. Forgetting that he is 'terrified of children ... terrified that some terrible Hostile Race, which will go on to drive everyone else out, is at any moment going to begin to be born' (LG 196-197), Dinah thoughtlessly lends him John Wyndham's *The Midwich Cuckoos*. This is a work of science-fiction where a quiet English village is almost destroyed by a group of yellow-eyed children unnaturally born there some eight years earlier; their uncanny hold on the peaceful village is reflected in *The Little Girls* in a scene of almost diabolical bell-ringing which is hard to escape from, where Dinah's car becomes 'a thing trapped' (LG 181).

There can be little doubt about the violence, cruelty even, of the children in Bowen's book. Their pursuit of young Trevor Artworth is a graphic example of this, and of adult non-intervention: Mumbo tramples on his spectacles and stuffs sand down his mouth, and Dicey scares him with matches and chases him up an unsavoury drain. Trevor's sand-encrusted mouth and the drain whose 'mouth was slimed on the lower lip' (LG 126) is anticipated by the lemon sherbet powder bought by the girls on an earlier occasion, which 'not only fizzed deliciously on the tongue but enabled one to froth at the mouth ad lib., bright yellow' in a vivid picture of gas warfare (LG 97). The drain incident makes a veritable Lady Macbeth of Dicey, who proudly shows Mumbo her 'rust-reddened hands' (LG 127), and her breakdown at the end of the book, corresponding to Lady Macbeth's madness, is thus foreshadowed in the childhood chapters.

Uncaringness
The girls' hounding of Trevor is seen by Mrs Pocock and Mrs Piggott strolling along the beach, but it is airily dismissed by Mrs Pocock, who merely calls Dicey 'a little over-excited' (LG 126). It is difficult to see the tranquillity of the mothers as other than downright irresponsible: when Mrs Piggott asks Trevor 'pleasantly' whether he won't come out, and the terrified little boy replies 'I like it in here, thank you' (LG 127), she does no more about it – in spite of the fact that the danger of his catching typhoid fever has been voiced. The enchanting Mrs Piggott is quite unfitted to cope with unpleasant realities. Even when, on an earlier occasion, she reproves Mumbo mildly about the girls' attempt to blow up the Beakers' bicycle shed ('so bad-mannered' [LG 80]), she veers away from asking about details: 'Nor had she any intention of knowing

anything, other than how the land lay ... how the gelignite or supposed gelignite had been come by, she would go to her grave rather than know' (LG 81). In point of fact, the girls' teachers at St Agatha's are equally reluctant to intervene, e.g. when Mumbo jerks Dicey's leg away from under her:

> From the cool dark inside an open window, Mademoiselle, Miss Brace (the geography mistress) and Matron, holding their coffee cups, looked on. They had seen much the same thing happen before. The victim was plump and the lawn, though hard-baked, not as hard as the asphalt from which the same child had rebounded the other day. Nevertheless they melted back from the window: Matron, whose afternoon peace could be most imperilled, the first to do so. *Better have witnessed nothing*. (LG 76; my italics)

Deliberate or feigned ignorance like this is a recurring Bowen motif, shading off into the 'vice of uncaringness' (WL 54), the deadly sin of *acedia* or *accidie*.[2] One thinks of Lady Naylor in *The Last September* (1929), who makes a point of not knowing what people say, or Colonel Pole in *The Heat of the Day*, who does not know the whole story of Stella's divorce, and does not want to know. The vicar's wife in *Eva Trout*, Mrs Dancey, is out of the same drawer: in the very first scene she pretends to take a nap in the car rather than be caught looking at Eva. Acedia often appears in *The Little Girls* in the remark, 'I don't care', and it turns up at the end of the book as part of the explanation of Dinah's breakdown; in the words of Frank Wilkins:

> '[S]ee the way this has taken her. She doesn't give a damn. Doesn't care a damn. Any more. Now.... [I]n a woman who cared so much, not caring a damn *is* an illness, isn't it? Yet it's not that she's ceased caring; she's switched her caring. Simply ceased to care for anything since *then*.' (LG 220)

Many years after the scene on the beach, the adult Dinah remarks almost incidentally that she was for years afraid that Trevor had died in the insanitary drain on the beach:

> 'There were hundreds of reasons why I advertised for you, Sheikie, but among them certainly one was, you'd be the first person I had a hope of seeing whom I *could* ask, "Did Trevor come out?" For *how* many years I needn't tell you, because you know, I thought about Trevor and his wedged-

---

[2] The original Greek literally means 'un-caringness'.

in bones. As time went on, I almost imagined I had succeeded in reasoning myself out of that – but no. Because when, in 1940, Mr. Churchill gave us that splendid, rousing talk about probably fighting on the beaches, do you know what my first reaction was? "Now they'll blast open that drain-pipe, and there'll be Trevor."' (LG 222-223)

If this is not more than a flippant remark of Dinah's, like many others, it is merely one more case where she is 'acting up', to borrow a phrase used about Frank Wilkins by both Sheila and Dinah's son William (LG 173, 215). And if she really has lived with this fear for almost a lifetime, it says a good deal about her fundamental irresponsibility; in this respect, as in others, she is like her mother. Everyday standards of morality seem to have been less than clear-cut in her childhood world (though Mumbo as ever provides a stern corrective): burglary is wrong, for instance, but it is quite in order to 'get tick' (habitually and seemingly indefinitely) in buses and shops. Mrs Piggott's irresponsibility is in line with the girls' freewheeling mentality and calls into question the value of an upbringing that puts a premium on the ability to recite poetry, observance of etiquette, and punctilious politeness.

Anticipations

Dicey's mother is never lovelier than when she arrives at the beach:

> Mrs Piggott, wearing the tussore dust-coat and with her hat bound on with a chiffon motor-veil, scrambled up the land side of the sea wall among the children, on the heels of her daughter. When she reached the top, wind caught the transparent mauve ends of the veil, sending them flying against the sky – which was so lightly grey as to itself seem a veil over wide light. There she stood a minute, looking down at the sands, smiling at the beginnings of so much pleasure; a weather-signal. She was the first indication that there was a wind, playful so far. (LG 120)

The wind mentioned in the last line in this quotation soon becomes anything but playful. It makes the methylated flames of the little stoves dance sideways and threatens to blow out the birthday candles before Olive Pocock can do so, it forces Sheikie off the breakwater, it plays havoc with Mrs Piggott's veil, and blows Dicey's hair into rat's tails. It is an active force, soon described as 'masterful', and it seems that only the intelligent loner Mumbo can take it up: her 'shock of hair' wages its 'individual battle' with the wind (LG 133).

An old picture postcard showing Dymchurch Sands in the early twentieth century. This is a landscape very like the beach at 'Wanchurch' which forms the setting of a central scene in *The Little Girls* – the birthday picnic in July 1914, on the eve of the First World War. The actual breakwaters at Dymchurch are now gone, but in the text those at 'Wanchurch' are an integral part of the scene's stage properties, 'sticking out far apart like teeth left in an otherwise broken comb' (LG 125). It is on such a breakwater that Sheikie, 'Southstone's wonder, the child exhibition dancer' (LG 69), does her elegant two-step that contrasts so sharply with the martial imagery in the rest of the chapter. *Reproduced from* Dymchurch in Old Picture Postcards *(1998), European Library, Zaltbommel, The Netherlands, by kind permission of the publisher.*

In the light of the revelation in the last part of the book that Sheikie's much famed dancing came to nothing, a charming vignette where she dances on the breakwater takes on a tone of tragic irony. Mumbo and Dicey are on the same breakwater in equally characteristic attitudes. Mumbo is literally sitting on the fence, self-protectively working a piece of glass out of her thin shoe-sole to prevent it cutting her foot. Dicey heaves herself up on her stomach and balances head down on the breakwater, as she has done on the swing at St Agatha's and the railing on the Southstone promenade, perhaps seeing the world no less clearly for seeing it upside-down. Sheikie is doing a tightrope two-step:

> To and fro, backward and then forward along the woodbone, bone-dry, dry-slippery edge of the topmost board jaunted the airly-balanced dancer – going away, returning, turning each turn into a nonchalant pirouette. She danced her music.
>
> Her hair, in honour of Olive, wore four bows: one behind each ear, one at the end of each plait. *She* wore an American new-style little girl's dress: chequered gingham. Her sandshoes, from whose points she never descended, were not only sandless but snow-white. The clean fine pink line dividing her skull in two was to be seen when she turned her back, as was the line of big black American buttons. She was distinct as a paper doll.
>
> Wind came in a gust at her, bending her over. She wobbled once – once was enough! Off she sprang from the breakwater, of her own volition. Away she strolled. (LG 128)

It seems natural to see the 'lovely dancer', as she is called elsewhere, along with the enchanting Mrs Piggott as a gracious representative of the carefree world of art and beauty before 1914 – a world that is to prove no match for the realities of war, which have all along formed an ominous undercurrent to what should have been, as Mrs Piggott expected, 'so much pleasure'.

Chapter 13

The Gothic of *Eva Trout, or Changing Scenes*[1]

Bowen was fond of anything that smacked of Gothic, and very knowledgeable about it. Several of her own short stories may aptly be called 'Gothic' ('The Demon Lover', for one), and there are Gothic features in many of her novels (Cousin Nettie in *The Heat of the Day*, for example, hidden away in a nursing home like the Mad Wife in the Attic). But *Eva Trout* is the only full-length novel she wrote in the Gothic strain. It has all the makings of a historical Gothic tale – castle, rich orphan, imprisonment and escape, flight and pursuit, wicked guardian, knight in shining armour, etc. – burlesqued and transposed to a contemporary setting, the 1960s. Associations to a historical tradition are prepared already in the title, which harks back to an early convention of supplying a novel (or a play, or a poem) with an alternative title: Thomas Nashe's *The Unfortunate Traveller, or the Life of Jack Wilton* (1594), for instance, or Samuel Richardson's *Pamela, or Virtue Rewarded* (1740). The subtitle Bowen gave her novel looks back more specifically to titles like Henri Murger's *Scènes de la vie de bohême* (1847-49) and George Eliot's *Scenes of Clerical Life* (1858); the latter is openly alluded to in the heading and first line of Chapter I,3 in *Eva Trout*, that entitled 'Clerical Life': 'The vicarage had witnessed various scenes of clerical life' (ET 27). As John Coates points out (98b:61), there is also an allusion to the hymn 'Through all the Changing Scenes of Life'. Descriptive chapter headings were earlier in common use – by Dickens, Thackeray, Trollope, and Le Fanu, among others – and their presence in *Eva Trout* is yet another of its historical affinities: 'Outing', 'A Summer's Day', 'Visits', and so on.

---

[1] A shorter version of this chapter was read in Limerick in 1998 at the Conference of IASIL, the International Association for the Study of Irish Literatures.

Eva Trout is made up of some straight third-person narrative with a good deal of flashback plus letters, telephone conversations, pages from a diary, etc. This is reminiscent of the way that, for example, *Dracula* is told, in letters, diaries, and journals, and there is actually an early reference to Dracula when the young pupils at the experimental school in the lakeside castle amuse themselves by what is called 'doing a Dracula' from balcony to balcony (ET 51). In the same paragraph we hear about another of their pranks: setting an 'Oedipus trap' for one of their teachers by arranging an effigy of his mother in his bed – which may remind us that this is also an Oedipus story, and that, in finally killing Eva, her adopted son is killing both his father and his mother.

Setting
The story is played out in a Gothic setting that is immediately obvious from the use of an isolated castle as mood-setter. The castle appears on the dust cover of the American as well as the English first editions; the English one has, by Bowen's express request, a drawing by the French artist and writer Philippe Jullian, a specialist in Art Nouveau and the author of a book on Oscar Wilde. The castle dominates from the first page of the novel, in a scene that reads almost like a take-off on the heroine's first sight of the castle of Udolpho in one of the most central texts of the Gothic, Mrs Radcliffe's *The Mysteries of Udolpho* (1794) – the fading daylight is there in Bowen's text, too, and the suddenness with which the distant castle is pointed out. This is Mrs Radcliffe: '"There," said Montoni [the villain of the story], speaking for the first time in several hours, "is Udolpho."' (*Udolpho* 226); and here is Bowen, with the very first lines of *Eva Trout*: '"This is where we were to have spent the honeymoon," Eva Trout said, suddenly, pointing across the water.' (ET 11). But the young beholders in Bowen's novel have none of the 'melancholy awe' with which Mrs Radcliffe's Emily gazes at Montoni's castle (*Udolpho* 226), they are thinking only of when they can stop for tea as they scramble over one another on the back seat of Eva's car in order to see better through the window – for, just as its predecessor is first seen from a carriage, Bowen's castle is of course seen from a car. And though it resembles a 'Bavarian fantasy' (ET 11), the nameless castle in *Eva Trout* is pure fake. We are told first that it looks like a cardboard cut-out (ET 13), later that it is like a propped-up canvas (ET 229); the cellars are full of fungus, and one can chip off stucco with a nail file (ET 52). This almost crumbling pile crops up several times in

the book: at one point it houses the mixed school where Eva spends a few months, and in the second half of the book Eva visits the castle again.

There are other castles, too; apparently, Eva has a weakness for castles. The plot takes her twice past the mock-fortress at Kingsgate in Kent; on the first occasion she keeps looking out of the rear window of the car, and the text tells us that 'She could by no means behold it often enough' (ET 88). Moreover, as I have mentioned earlier, there is quite a long section towards the end of the book set in Fontainebleau, where the real castle plays an important thematic part in stressing that Eva's and Jeremy's life together now belongs to history. The house Eva buys for herself is also a kind of castle – the pretentious, isolated, dilapidated villa on the South-East coast which is called by the old romantic name for China, *Cathay*, though there is nothing remotely oriental about it and it calls to mind rather a word rhyming with its name: decay. Constantine Ormeau refers to it mockingly as Eva's 'château' (ET 99), Eric Arble calls it 'baronial' (ET 85); the dining-room furniture is '*manoir*-style' (ET 80), the dense hedge between the house and the road is 'like a fortification' (ET 97). And there is Gothic galore (Gothic Revival in the well-known Victorian form) in many of the houses in the book: Cathay's neighbouring houses have balconies, mansards, gables, and turrets, and the vicarage where Eva's friends the Danceys live is a Victorian monstrosity with peaks and gables (ET 27), and a 'gothic portal' (ET 149).

Characters
Within this Gothic setting the plot is played out by a set of characters that mirror the characters one might meet in a bona fide historical Gothic tale.

There is first of all Eva herself: she is an immensely rich orphan, as befits a heroine, and like the princess in a fairy-tale she cannot cry (until she cries for happiness at the very end, when Henry has revealed his love for her). She is not the scion of a noble family, however, but the daughter of a wealthy financier and a flighty, unstable woman who ran off with another man when Eva was a few months old. Her father has taken her along with him on his business trips, and the text makes one feel he had treated her like a parcel he could just dump with strangers when it suited him:

He took her to Mexico, where they were joined by Constantine; then, business calling him to the Far East, dropped her off with a Baptist missionary family in Hongkong, reclaimed her, left her in San Francisco with some relations of his chiropodist's, caused her to be flown to him in New York, flew her from thence to Hamburg, where he picked her up later and asked her if she would like to become a kennel-maid, decided it might be better for her to go to Paris and was about to arrange things on those lines when she said she would like to go to an English boarding-school: one for girls. (ET 57)

When we first meet her Eva is a very large, blowsy young woman, immensely strong. The text, perhaps echoing Mrs Dancey's thoughts, calls her a 'giantess' (ET 12), and the timid estate-agent, Mr Denge, thinks of her as a 'she-Cossack' (ET 81). Her violent and uncoordinated movements may be seen as examples of the excess inherent in the Gothic tradition: she *strides* rather than walks along, *breathes heavily*, *tugs* on her gloves, *punches* her hat straight, *wrenches* open the door of her car and *hurls* in her bag – 'a mighty crocodile handbag' (ET 29). Eva at 24 has a very loud taste in dress: there is, in addition to the handbag, an ocelot coat and ocelot-backed gloves, and bright red stockings. But like the ugly duckling in the fairy tale she is transformed at the end of the story – in fact, in the second half several characters comment on how handsome she has become – and when she stands in her pale going-away suit at Victoria Station in the final scene, she is absolutely magnificent.

Eva's adopted son Jeremy is probably the most horrible of all Bowen's horrible children and a Gothic figure *par excellence*, a changeling, whose deaf-muteness makes him an outsider even more than Eva herself is. His candid expression and beautiful manners disguise, at first sight, his violent nature. But on the first day he appears on stage, his presence makes the vicarage tea-table feel as if it were 'bugged, if on an astral plane' (ET 158), and there is something 'unearthly' in his eyes; Henry Dancey speaks of his way of communicating with Eva as 'extra-sensory' (ET 158). Exorcism is mentioned, devils, 'possession' (ET 175). Towards the end of *Eva Trout* there are signs that Jeremy is hostile even towards Eva, and she begins to feel, like many Gothic heroines before her, that she is in the power of an alien force: 'Jeremy'll never let me go', she says (ET 187), and she thinks of him as 'manacling' her (ET 190). Though he is not there when Eva is talking to the woman who has been teaching him modelling, his presence is so forceful that he seems to 'flit like a marsh-light' across the room (ET 199). To all intents and purposes

Jeremy is a frightening replica of the destructive extraterrestrial children with yellow eyes in Wyndham's *The Midwich Cuckoos* who underscore, intertextually, the posterity motif of *The Little Girls*.

The wicked guardian of the piece is Constantine Ormeau, who is even called, and calls himself, the 'Wicked Guardian' (ET 100, 153). He holds Eva's money in trust until she is 25. A very bland businessman with an expensive office in London and a private chauffeur, he is a bit of a mystery man, but there is of course nothing very wicked about him – except perhaps that his same-sex philandering apparently occasioned the suicide of Eva's father. His only passion seems to be eating well. His friendship with Willy Trout was obviously homosexual, so was his friendship with the young man who ran the school at the castle, and so is his later friendship with the fashionable East End priest, Clavering-Haight.

For of course there is a clergyman in this mock-Gothic story. There are two, in fact. None of them is the slightest bit villainous, though we are clearly meant to remember the usual kind of priest in a Gothic novel: talking of weddings, Henry Dancey even speaks of a 'bogus ceremony with some villainous unfrocked priest, as in gothic fiction' (ET 239). One of the two in the novel is the myopic Clavering-Haight, a worldly High Church cleric with homoerotic leanings and a taste for antiques and delicacies, who spends a lot of time in Chelsea and Knightsbridge. The other is Henry's father, the Rev. Alaric Dancey, the stern moral touchstone of the novel.

The Tempter is there, too, in the form of[2] the handsome, over-bright, and mercenary Henry Dancey himself, as a child called 'horrid little Henry' by Eva's former teacher. Tempter-like, he pictures to Eva all she could do with her money; he wages battle with his clergyman father and faints when he hears him denounce the sins of unfaithfulness; he has a familiar, his younger sister, who writes a savage incantation in her prayer-book; and his name has a common pet-form that may remind us of a nickname for the Devil: Old Harry. At the same time there are other Gothic overtones to his name, for phonologically 'Henry Dancey' brings to mind Henry Tilney, the hero of Jane Austen's *Northanger*

---

[2] This phrase is suggestively used in the text: 'Henry appeared, in the form of a young man' (ET 149).

Abbey. This classic Gothic burlesque is also recalled in the papers revealing her address that Eva has inadvertently left at the back of a drawer, like the papers, in actual fact laundry bills, which the heroine of that book finds at the back of a cabinet.

For the traditional witch in the story there is Miss Applethwaite, the sculptress whom Jeremy goes to for lessons in modelling and whose negligence is responsible for his brief abduction. The 'monkish' overall she wears, with cowl and 'monastic' belt (ET 197, 200), cannot distract our attention from her witch-like attribute par excellence: a black cat. He is called Lucius ('Lucifer', we read), and is 'brindled so darkly as to be blackish', sleeping on a 'blackish chair' (ET 200). Eva is shocked at the woman's apathetic reaction in the face of Jeremy's disappearance: 'Are *you* human, Miss Applethwaite?... – you must be infernal' (ET 200).

There is also a knight in shining armour, or a knight errant, in *Eva Trout*: Eric Arble, the husband of Eva's once-beloved teacher. He is called 'your knight' by one of the characters, but in actual fact he is rather a sorry figure, a brash failed fruit-farmer turned garage mechanic, who drinks too much, with red-rimmed eyes and a language full of clichés and vulgarisms. He is indeed a far cry from the perfect gentle knight of historical romance; he is 'errant', moreover, in living with an au pair girl after he and Iseult have broken up but are not divorced. In the beginning of the book Eva is a paying guest at the Arbles, but she feels she is being treated like a prisoner and runs off on her own, covering her tracks as best she can; here is the imprisonment and escape of the Gothic plot.

Gothic, too, is the madness motif that first appears off-stage in Eva's conveniently dead mother. Though Constantine speaks of her as having been 'maniacal' (ET 41), we can hardly forget that the narrator herself, some pages earlier, has suggested that there was an element of instability in Eva's father, too:

> He had been popular. An apparent artlessness concealed the acumen, approaching genius, through which he had trebled inherited wealth. Possibly the genius side was the rocky side? It was in him to deviate: that, Constantine had unerringly sensed ... (ET 17; original ellipsis)

Later in the story, Constantine offers some not-so-veiled hints that Eva is perhaps as disturbed as her mother was; he leaves plain speaking to Eva, though:

> 'You should see a doctor.... Or more precisely, be seen by one: a psychiatrist. Mrs Arble's right, I'm afraid: in her view, this should have been years ago. I admit, I've opposed the idea –'
> ' – I should talk to this doctor?'
> ' – I feared the disturbance, feared what it might precipitate. I had reason to – remember, I knew your mother. So I've hesitated; "treatment" can be so drastic. Was I mistaken? Now, I begin to wonder –'
> 'Mad would probably be better,' said Eva promptly. (ET 105).

This is, in other words, the old story of the sins of the parents being visited on the child. Now that the idea that Eva may possibly be 'mad' has been implanted in our minds, we may easily come to think of her when Henry remarks, towards the end of the novel, that his father has been saved from the brutalizing effect of life by being 'in a way mad; that's a preservative' (ET 235), thereby voicing a commonly held view that the insane, the simple-minded, the innocent are immune from the snares of this world. This link between Eva and the most uncorruptible figure in the book, Mr Dancey, goes to confirm the suggestions of her fundamental honesty which I have pointed to earlier – her upright stance, her consideration for other people, her association with the strawberries that in Christian art symbolize perfect righteousness – and her killing by her changeling son becomes the stuff of tragedy: the murder of innocence by forces we cannot control.

Iseult, Eric Arble's wife, is the dark-haired beauty of the story, and quite a bit of a schemer. She is described as both a temptress and a nun: meeting Eva in Dickens's house in Broadstairs, she wears a 'pinkish' dress, 'garb of a votaress with a touch of the ball gown' (ET 113). Her name is that of the famed ill-fated lover of Arthurian legend, but any associations of high romance are undercut by the fact that her husband calls her 'Izzy', and by her unmarried surname, Smith – as Eva's name is undercut by her surname, Trout.

I have discussed earlier the relationship between Eva and Iseult, which has been explored by several feminist critics. The lesbian element and Eva's ambiguous sexuality are important ingredients in the novel, parallelling the homosexuality of several of the male characters, and unconventional sexuality is an integral part of the novel's Gothic ambience. There is nothing hole-and-corner about the young Eva's sexuality, and Bowen calls a spade a spade in *Eva Trout*, as she had done in *The Little Girls*. Eva is openly asked by one of her young schoolfellows, 'Trout, are you a hermaphrodite?' (ET 51), and later she is asked whether she has had a 'sapphic' relationship with Iseult (ET 184 – this latter question characteristically coming from Clavering-Haight, who is fully alive to any such relations).

While on the subject of character it may be appropriate to mention, as one of the stock Gothic features that are undercut in *Eva Trout:* the portrait that comes to life (Wilde's *The Portrait of Dorian Grey* is a prime example). Bowen goes by the book in introducing portraits into the novel – no less than the entire National Portrait Gallery – but they emphatically do not come alive; it is quite the other way round, for Eva discovers that everyone she knows is really just as inscrutable as the portraits in the gallery, and 'there is no hope of keeping a check on people; you cannot know what they do, or why they do it' (ET 196).

Dandies
Oscar Wilde's name has already cropped up, and it will be natural to bring him in again here – or, more precisely, the aura of homosexuality and decadence that his name and his dandyism conjure up.[3]

Eva's adopted son is explicitly associated with dandyism. He is a neat, well-dressed little boy, elegant even: when we first see him he is flying to England with Eva, 'dressed in rather a British manner, cream silk shirt with a blue tie, short grey knickerbockers' (ET 147). Going for a walk with Eva and Constantine, he takes with him his malacca cane, a near-antique with a silver band which has the 'florid initials' of some *dandy* (ET 168).

Constantine himself, the 'wicked guardian', is as good an example of the dandy as any (apart perhaps from the fact that he does do something useful with his life, or at any rate makes a lot of money doing it). He has a luxuriously appointed office with an onyx box of Egyptian cigarettes

---

[3] Declan Kiberd approaches Bowen's use of the dandy from a different point of view in a chapter of *Inventing Ireland* called 'Elizabeth Bowen – The Dandy in Revolt' (364-379).

on his ormolu writing desk, he speaks and writes in an extremely mannered language, is devoted to *haute cuisine* – and is homosexual. His surname Ormeau ('Little Elm') provides a clear dandy-pointer: move one of the letters in 'Ormeau' around and you get 'Moreau', the name of that dandy of dandies, the protagonist of Gustave Flaubert's *L'Education sentimentale*. In case the reader does not immediately see the connection, Bowen has Henry Dancey openly refer to Flaubert's novel: 'Have you read *L'Education Sentimentale?*' he writes in a letter to Eva. 'I suppose hardly. There's a Fontainebleau part' (216). Just as there is 'a Fontainebleau part' in *Eva Trout*, too.

Henry himself may also be included among the book's dandies. In Part II he is a 20-year old undergraduate at Cambridge with an unformed personality, uncertain sexual proclivities and doubts about the future, captured in several vignettes where he stands balancing on one foot. He is a handsome fellow and attractive to both men and women: he has a college friend who moves 'gracefully' and is called Jocelyn, which may be either a boy's or a girl's name; and Constantine Ormeau is eager to pursue his acquaintance. In the final scene of the book, where he is to all intents and purposes the bridegroom, he wears the appropriate buttonhole which, along with the cane, is also part of the Wildean dandy's get-up.

Cultural Anxiety
Whether one calls *Eva Trout* a pastiche or a burlesque, its Gothic pointers are so obvious that we as readers can hardly help looking beyond the text; and one interpretation that almost forces itself on one is to see the novel as a reflection of cultural anxiety and a vehicle of social criticism – criticism of the insincerity and superficiality of the contemporary world: the castle is a sham; Dickens is reduced to a tourist attraction; many of the characters are 'displaced persons', and children are rootless, like the young delinquents Eva is at school with in the castle, and like Eva herself; there are broken marriages, and there are false emotions. One scene haunts Eva for years: when her roommate at the castle school is ill in bed, she hears the girl's mother come into the room saying 'How is my darling?' – words that no-one has ever said to Eva, and which conjure up the kind of love she has always dreamed of. Later she runs into the girl again, however, only to find that she is now an out-and-out neurotic, who cares as little for her mother as her

mother cares for her. But not-caringness, *acedia*, is not the only sin in the novel, and Eva's school-fellows are not the only delinquents. In the last count, few of the characters have a clean slate, and it is a supreme instance of irony that it should be Eva herself who, in adopting Jeremy, commits the greatest illegality in the book. If we add to this universal dishonesty the pervasive sense of how impossible it is for people really to know one another, *Eva Trout* will be seen as a deeply pessimistic picture of a future society of dislocated characters in a dislocated world dominated by greed, violence, and heartlessness.

Comedy

All this may perhaps give the impression that the novel makes serious reading. Nothing could be further from the truth, it is full of hilarious characters and incidents that can vie with any in Bowen's earlier books. There is the mothering, dithering Mrs Dancey, for instance, who is never quite sure what is happening and does not always recognize the person she is talking to. Then there is Mr Denge, the obsequious estate agent who is always ready to raise his hat, and the hypochondriac American professor Portman C Holman, who is quite taken with Eva on the Atlantic flight. And there are grotesque scenes, even an element of slapstick. When Mr Denge shows Eva over the house she has leased, for instance, he infuriates her sense of propriety when he makes sure that the toilet is in order by reaching past her and pulling the chain, with a resultant 'cataclysmic' roar (ET 81); when he has left, she joyously rides figures-of-eight on her new bicycle on the asphalt sweep, trying out the four-speed gear and brakes and bell for so long that 'when and if she took her thumb from the bell, birds, temporarily astounded, began to flute again' (ET 82). In Chicago, in the 'raspberry tinted darkness' of a coffee shop, all the guests look 'decapitated' because of the small red down-turned lamps over the tables (ET 131); and, in what passes for home life in an American family, dust bakes in the overheated Anapoupolis apartment, with its dominant smells of cooking and floral air spray (ET 136-37).

Serious events and themes are seen through a similar veil of comedy. The confrontation between Henry and his father near the end of the book will serve as an example (ET 247-248). Henry has been moping around the house and making himself impossible when he is accosted by his father, intent on 'having things out'; and though no names are mentioned Mr Dancey is well aware, to his great distress, that the intrigue his son admits to having is with Eva. It is a highly charged interview between two hypersensitive characters who will not or cannot recognize the love they feel for each other; yet it takes place in utterly mundane surroundings, 'not far from the hall hat-stand', with an absurdly irrelevant registration of time, 'about two on Saturday afternoon' (ET 247). The atmosphere of mock-heroics has been introduced by inflated imagery when the hay-making that brings Mr Dancey's hay-fever to a peak is described in military terms as 'the enemy', with the 'besieged' household like a 'garrison' within 'beleaguered earthworks'. Sight and sound both contribute to the comic overtones of the emotional dialogue between father and son: Mr Dancey's face is inflamed and streaming as he accurately and deliberately tears a circular into small pieces that flutter unheeded to the floor; then, his voice cracking to a whisper, he begins aimlessly to pull at an overcoat hanging on the hat-stand. The scene is brusquely cut off by Henry's sister who comes 'thundering' down the stairs on her way to play cricket, 'bashing' her canvas bag about; the slangy verbs point up by contrast the ponderous military imagery one or two pages back. Comedy like this runs all through *Eva Trout*, making it Gothic writing with a difference and earning it the predicate of Bowen's contribution to the Black Comedy of the 1960s.

'Gone Away'

It is tempting to bring in here a short story which has certain affinities with this last novel of Bowen's – negative affinities, largely, for it is set in the future and there is nothing of the historical Gothic about it: 'Gone Away', from 1946. This is more of a vignette than a story proper. It has a story-book vicar complete with pipe and crested tobacco-jar like a clergyman in an advertisement; he receives a visit from an old friend called Van Winkle, as in Washington Irving's story, who has been asleep for several years. It turns out that the vicar is merely surviving as a showpiece in a sham village:

> Van Winkle was struck ... by the almost hallucinatory old-worldness of the scene. He might have been stepping into a picture postcard. A pub with a Lion sign, a row of creeper-draped cottages, two plum-red late Victorian villas, a stucco gentleman's residence, a smithy, a gabled post office showing bottles of sweets, a once new-art village hall and a general shop all stared at him with the two-dimensional brightness of a cinema set-up. (CS 759)

Most of the houses are mere facades supported by struts, the ducks on the village pond are stuffed, the surrounding town is a ghost-town empty of people. 'Brighterville', as it is called, is a model city with well laid-out avenues and parterres and fountains, factories and cinemas and a culture-centre; the machinery keeps working but the people have gone, and in the gymnasium the riding machines jog away, clattering their empty steel stirrups. It is a Brave New World kind of vision, expressing in no uncertain terms Bowen's misgivings about the future of the civilization she is part of – as *Eva Trout* does.

Short Story and Gothic Novel

In conclusion it may be appropriate to quote something Bowen herself wrote in 1959, almost ten years before *Eva Trout*, about the relations between the novel and the short story. This was in the preface to a collection of her own short stories. Remarking on the large percentage of fantasy-stories in the book, she says:

> More than half of my life is under the steadying influence of the novel, with its calmer, stricter, more orthodox demands: into the novel goes such taste as I have for rational behaviour and social portraiture. The short story, as I see it to be, allows for what is crazy about humanity: obstinacies, inordinate heroisms, 'immortal longings'.[4]

What Bowen says here seems to apply particularly to the traditional 'classical' kind of novel she had been writing most of her life, but it hardly holds true of *Eva Trout*. Perhaps one might suggest that in the mock-Gothic mode she found a way of reconciling the demands of the short story and the novel as she saw it; or that, because the Gothic mode has no 'calmer, stricter demands', it can in fact do what the short story does: allow for 'what is crazy about humanity'.

---

[4] 'Stories by Elizabeth Bowen'. Preface to Vintage Books edition, 1959; reprinted in *The Mulberry Tree*, 130.

APPENDIX

Time Structures

Insisting on the need to incorporate time into a novel, Bowen stressed the importance of the 'spacing-out of events along time'.[1] The following time-charts and surveys will suggest some of this 'spacing-out' in the novels under consideration. In the surveys, double slashes indicate extra spacing within chapters (double-line spacing in the Penguin edition). Bowen used this typographical device in short as well as longer fiction; the three sequences in 'A Day in the Dark' are thus separated by extra spacing. The first chapter of *A World of Love* is divided into six scenes, and the final chapters of *The Little Girls* and *Eva Trout* are even more subdivided. It is tempting to see this as an act of defiance against the traditional division of a novel into 'chapters', and to link it up with Bowen's use of time gaps referred to earlier. In point of fact the novels are more episodic than the spacing suggests. In *The Heat of the Day*, for instance, Chapter 17 goes straight from Stella's evidence at the inquest to an analysis of Louie's thoughts and finally shows us Roderick at Mount Morris; not until after this do we meet extra spacing. As the texts stand the episodic chapters, whether marked or unmarked typographically, enhance by contrast the all-of-a-piece effect of undivided chapters such as Robert's confession to Stella (HD Ch. 15) and Clare's and Sheila's tea-room conference in *The Little Girls* (LG Ch. I,3).

Of the short stories I have glanced at, both 'Ivy Gripped the Steps' (1945) and 'A Day in the Dark' (1955) show the kind of tripartite structure – present-past-present or past-present-past – that Bowen was to use again in *The Little Girls* (1964) (and had used much earlier in *The House in Paris* [1935]). Thus 'Ivy Gripped the Steps' opens in September 1944 with the forty-ish protagonist looking at an overgrown house where he had spent some time as a child before the First World War, then takes us back to those days to show how he was emotionally exploited by the callous mistress of the house, and ends up again in 1944 showing us the habitual womaniser he has become.

---

[1] 'Notes on Writing a Novel'. *Orion 2* (Autumn 1945); quoted from *The Mulberry Tree*, 45.

SURVEY 1: The Heat of the Day

Chapter	Story	Time
1	Harrison, Louie in Regent's Park // Louie's history; Louie, airman in park // Louie, Harrison leave park	September 1942: first Sunday
2	Stella at home; her history; Harrison to Stella	Same evening
3	Roderick to Stella; his history; Roderick, Stella coffee	Same evening: later
4	Cousin Francis' funeral; history of Nettie and Francis; hotel buffet; Stella, Harrison in train; Stella, Roderick in tea-shop	2 days in May 1942
5	Stella and Robert's affair; its beginnings in London, autumn 1940 // Stella moves; Robert to Stella	One day, some days after Ch. 3
6	Robert, Stella visit Holm Dene	Early October: Saturday
7	Harrison to Stella	Same evening
8	Louie, Connie; Louie in Chilcombe St; Connie at ARP post	October 1942
9	Robert, Stella // Stella to Mount Morris	4 consecutive days in October-November 1942
10	Stella back to London; taxi with Robert and Ernestine // Stella, Robert dinner	An evening in early November 1942
11	Letter Roderick to Stella; Roderick, Cousin Nettie at Wistaria Lodge	Another day in early November 1942
12	Roderick phones Stella; Stella, Harrison dinner, to them Louie	Same evening
13	Connie, Louie, pillow-talk	Same evening
14	Stella alone // Robert at Holme Dene	Same evening
15	Robert confesses to Stella	Next night
16	Bells for El Alamein heard by Louie // Stella to Roderick's camp	15 November 1942
17	Stella at inquest; Louie; progress of war 1942-44; Roderick to Mount Morris // Harrison to Stella // Louie pregnant; Connie's letter to Tom; news of Tom's death // D-Day; Louie to Seale with baby.	Late November 1942 to September 1944

CHART I: The Heat of the Day

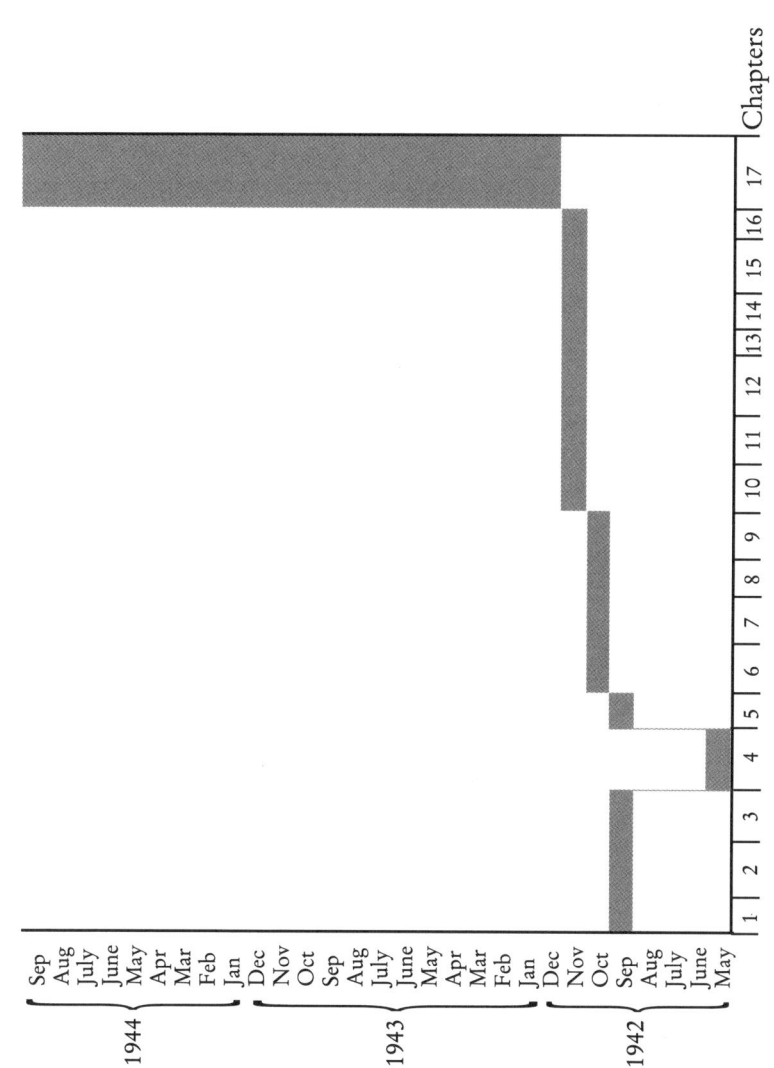

Historical time figures prominently in *The Heat of the Day*, which follows naturally from the documentary aspects of the book's storyline. For this is a novel about the London of the Second World War, and the elements that make up the plot are precisely dated by the actual events they parallel. Most conspicuously, the centrally placed turning point of the plot, when Stella's suspicions about her lover's treason are confirmed and she resolves to have it out with him, coincides with Montgomery's victory at El Alamein (4 November 1942), which proved to be a turning point in the war. The main events of the novel take place in the autumn of 1942, with a brief flashback to the May of that year and a coda telescoping almost two years (November 1942 – September 1944) into one single chapter.

SURVEY 2: A World of Love

Chapter	Story	Time
1	Montefort in landscape // Jane with letters at obelisk // Antonia in bed, to her Lilia // history of Antonia, Guy, Lilia, Fred // Fred, Lilia, Maud, Kathie in kitchen // Jane to Antonia	Day 2: June, early morning + flashback 21 years
2	Jane back from Fête, finds letters // Fête, others home // Jane reads letters in bed	Day 1
3	Lunch; Jane hides letters	Day 2: midday
4	Antonia meditates on death and on Guy; Maud, Jane by river; Lilia, Maud at tea; Daimler with invitation	Day 2: afternoon
5	Dinner at Lady Latterly's // Jane looks across table	Day 2: evening
6	Antonia brings Jane home; Antonia, Jane, Fred in hall, then kitchen	Day 2: night
7	Jane, Antonia, Lilia in garden // Lilia, Jane, Maud in Clonmore shop // Jane, Lilia at hairdresser's // Lilia's earlier flight to London // hairdresser	Day 3: midday + flashback 7 years
8	Lilia sewing in garden recalls parting from Guy; to her Fred with letters found by Maud; Lilia, Fred by mounting-block	Day 3: afternoon
9	Maud calls down vengeance; to Antonia's room; Antonia finds letters in hall	Day 3: late afternoon
10	Jane driven to castle // Antonia attempts to burn letters, seen by Kathie in kitchen // Lilia, Antonia in Lilia's room // Maud, Antonia at supper, to them Jane; Big Ben; to them Lilia, Fred from drive	Day 3: evening
11	Jane discards dress, puts on blazer; Antonia writes to ex-husband // departure for Shannon; Jane reveals burning of letters // Jane, Maud to Shannon; arrival of Richard Priam	Day 4

CHART II: A World of Love

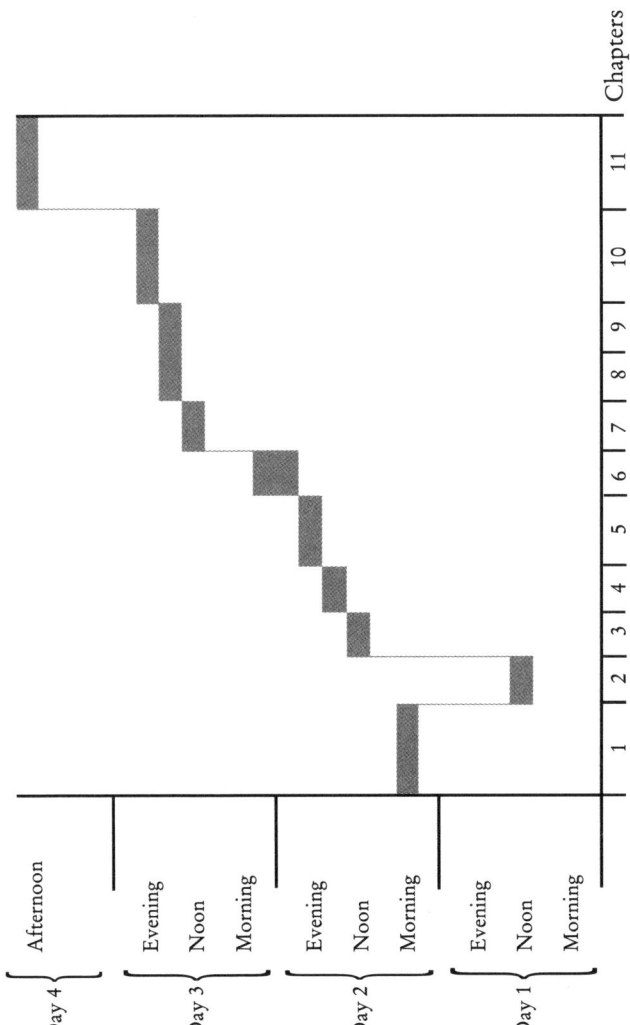

Compared with the close dependence on contemporary events in *The Heat of the Day*, Bowen's next novel, *A World of Love*, is almost a-historical in the sense that the story is not time-set to any particular year (though some time shortly after the Second World War is clearly indicated). The 'timeless' four days covered by the story are set against a wider historical frame of reference, however – the First World War and the decline of the Anglo-Irish Ascendancy – that has reverberations throughout. Like *The Heat of the Day* the novel structurally builds up to a turning-point in the centre of the book, in this case an evening and night where the presence of Guy is felt intensely in the surrounding landscape. The many time markers make it possible to plot in the storyline almost hour by hour.

215

SURVEY 3: The Little Girls

Ch.	Story	Time
I,1	Dinah, Frank at cave; to them Mrs Coral	September, early 1960s
I,2	Francis' history; Dinah, Francis	A day later
I,3	Sheila, Clare in tea-room	A later day
I,4	Dinah, Clare at cross-roads // to Applegate, where Sheila, Frank // Frank glimpses Clare // lunch // garden	Early October
II,1	Poetry class // St Agatha's; girls in school garden	A Tuesday, June 1914
II,2	Feverel Cottage; Clare to Mrs Piggott; to them her father	Same day
II,3	Swimming // Dinah meets suffragette aunt	Next day
II,4	Conference in bathroom // Southstone; home	Following Saturday
II,5	3 girls to Sheila's home for coffer // Dinah and Clare's secret relics // quiet days; Clare, mother in garden	Same day + next days
II,6	Burial of coffer; Clare's language	Early July 1914
II,7	Picnic on the sands // Dinah, mother, Clare's father	July 23 1914
III,1	Dinah to Clare in shop; Dinah phones Sheila	Early 1960s: one week after I,4
III,2	Letter Dinah to Clare requesting butterknife	Same evening
III,3	Dinah, Clare in Southstone; met by Sheila // coffer found empty // drinks at Sheila's	Thursday, ca. one week after III,2
III,4	Clare, Sheila walk dog; Sheila reveals past life	Same evening
III,5	Frank, Francis see knife; to them Dinah	Some days later
III,6	Letter Dinah to Clare; they buy masks; Frank's cottage // Dinah, Clare to Applegate // Frank at Applegate // supper in kitchen // Dinah, Clare in drawing-room	A Sunday in November
III,7	Dinah in bed, Sheila nurse // Dinah's sons in drawing-room // Francis, Dinah's sons // granddaughter Emma pours bath // Dinah, Sheila about Macbeth; to them Mrs Coral // sons, Mrs Coral, Sheila // flashback 1 hour to sons' half-seeing Frank // children cutting out // Clare, Dinah's granddaughter Pamela try to untie knot of cave // Frank, Clare in garden; Clare asleep in car // Dinah tells Sheila about Trevor in drain // Frank to Dinah // Clare, children; Clare, Sheila // Sheila, Dinah's sons at dinner; Sheila reveals secret object // Clare to Dinah	November: next Wednesday

CHART III: The Little Girls

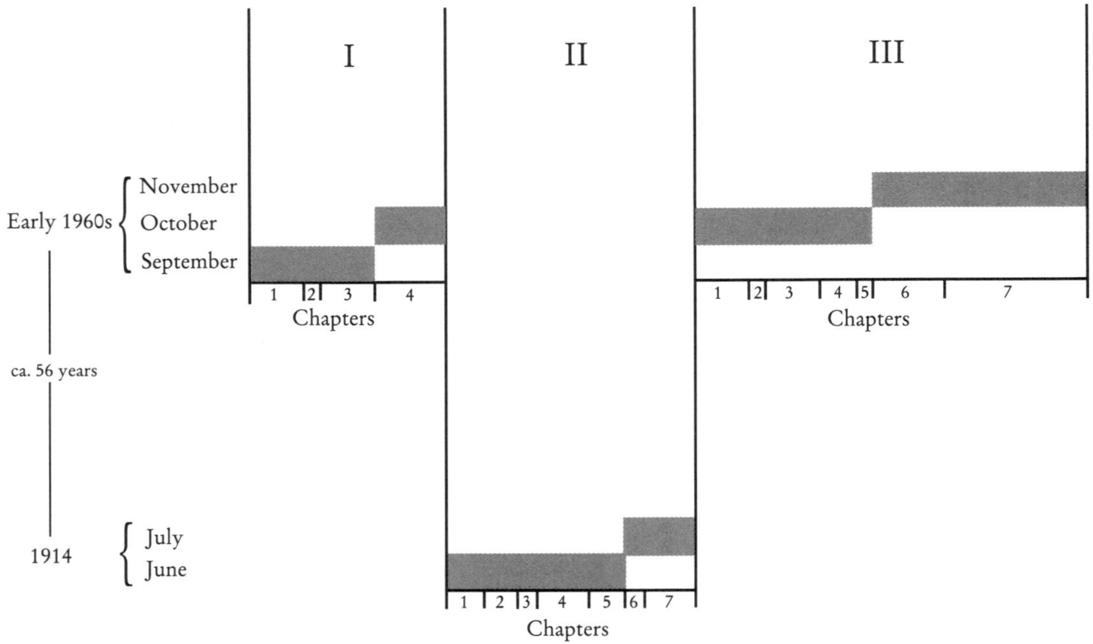

A broken time-sequence is a notable feature of *The Little Girls*. In Part I, four chapters cover September-October of an unspecified year in the early 1960s; Part II consists of seven chapters set in the summer of 1914; and the seven chapters of Part III, following on from Part I, take the plot through to November of the same year in the 60s. Many cross-references reflect the close intertwining of past and present in the minds of the adult characters of parts I and III, much as the long-dead Guy is ever present in the minds of the characters in *A World of Love*. In contrast to the other three novels discussed in these studies the pace is slowed down in the last chapter of *The Little Girls*, which is more than twice as long as the other chapters yet covers a single day. It is sub-divided into 15 scenes separated by extra line spacing.

217

SURVEY 4: Eva Trout

Chapter	Story	Time
I,1	Eva shows Danceys castle	January 1959
I,2	Eva and Arbles; Eric home to nervous Iseult	Same day
I,3	Rev Dancey's hay-fever; Catrina meets Eva off to London	Next day
I,4	Letter Constantine to Iseult // their lunch	Some days later
I,5	Eva feverish at Arbles // Castle and Lumleigh schools; Iseult, Eva // Iseult back from London	Same day + flashbacks 10 + 8 years
I,6	Eva, Henry, to them Mrs Dancey, Louise	February 1959
I,7	Eva met by Denge // letter from Henry; Eric turns up: drive, driftwood, dinner	Tuesday + Friday, March 1959
I,8	Iseult types diary	March; same Friday as I,7
I,9	Eric takes nap at Cathay // Constantine arrives; he, Eric leave	March; evening of same Friday
I,10	Iseult, Eva in Broadstairs, then at Cathay	A day in June 1959
I,11	Professor's letter to Eva describes flight to USA	October 30
I,12	Eva meets Elsinore in Chicago; to friend's home	A day in late November
II,1	Eva & Jeremy to Larkins, then vicarage where Henry & father	A day in mid-April 1967
II,2	Letter Eric to Eva; she and Jeremy have visited Cathay; to Richmond, then to them Constantine at Paley's Hotel	24 April; some days earlier and later
II,3	Eva, Jeremy at Cambridge // Eva's house-hunting; Eva, Clavering-Haight; memory of American years; phone call from Iseult; Eva to Nat. Portrait Gallery; Jeremy abducted	Several days in April 1967
II,4	Eva, Jeremy to Paris // letters; Iseult to vicarage where Mrs Dancey; letter Henry to Eva; Eva, Jeremy to Fontainebleau // letters // Eric to Constantine's office // Bonnard, Eva in Fontainebleau // Constantine, Iseult in Soho // Eva, Henry at castle // Iseult, Clavering-Haight // Henry, father; sermon // Eva at Paley's, to her Jeremy // Victoria Station	May to late June 1967

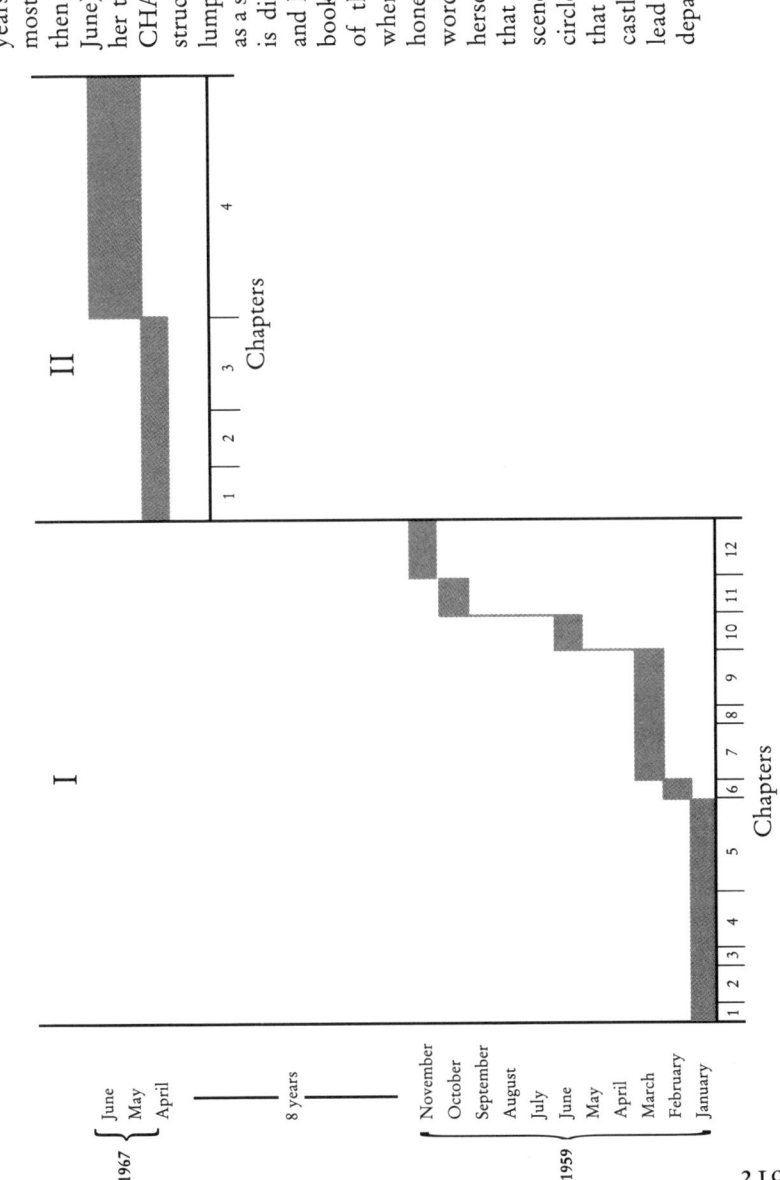

Eva Trout falls into two distinct halves separated by a gap of eight years. The actual narrative covers most of 1959, when Eva is 24, and then three months (April – May – June) early in 1967, when she has with her the little boy she has adopted. As CHART IV suggests, one remarkable structural aspect of the novel is the lumping together of the last 64 pages as a single 'chapter' (May – June). This is divided by spacing into 18 scenes and letters, a hotchpotch recalling the book's Gothic affinities. The long title of this long final chapter, 'This is where we were to have spent the honeymoon', is identical with the first words in the novel, spoken by Eva herself on the shore of the wintry lake that forms the location of the first scene. The wheel has thus come full circle: it is Eva's own sexual fantasies that originally made her invent a castle honeymoon which ultimately lead her to stage the wedding-departure that brings about her death.

Select Bibliography

Works by Elizabeth Bowen discussed or cited

The Heat of the Day (1949). Penguin ed. 1962.   Abbr. HD
A World of Love (1955). Penguin ed. 1983.   Abbr. WL
The Little Girls (1964). Penguin ed. 1982.   Abbr. LG
Eva Trout (1968). Penguin ed. 1982.   Abbr. ET
Collected Stories (1980). Penguin ed. 1983.   Abbr. CS

The Last September. London: Constable & Co, 1929.
To the North. London: Victor Gollanz, 1932.
The House in Paris. London: Victor Gollanz, 1935.
The Death of the Heart. London: Victor Gollanz, 1938.
Bowen's Court. London, New York, Toronto: Longmans, Green & Co., 1942.
'English Novelists'. *Impressions of English Literature*. London: Collins, 1944.
The Shelbourne Hotel. New York: Alfred A. Knopf, 1951.
A Time in Rome. London: Longmans, Green & Co, 1960.
Pictures and Conversations. Ed. Spencer Curtis Brown. New York: Alfred A. Knopf, 1975.
The Mulberry Tree. Writings of Elizabeth Bowen. Ed. Hermione Lee. London: Virago Press Ltd, 1986.
Notes From Eire. Espionage Reports to Winston Churchill, 1940-42, with a review of Irish neutrality. Aubane Historical Society, 1999.

Other works

Atkins, John. *Six Novelists Look at Society*. London: John Calder, 1977.
Auden, W H. *Collected Shorter Poems 1927-1957*. London: Faber (1966), 1969.
Austin, Allan E. *Elizabeth Bowen*. New York: Twayne Publishers, 1971.
Bacon, Francis. *The Works of Francis Bacon, vol. IX = The Letters and the Life, vol. II*. London, 1862; reprinted Stuttgart – Bad Cannstatt, 1961.
Bennett, Andrew and Nicholas Royle. *Elizabeth Bowen and the Dissolution of the Novel*. Houndmills and London: Macmillan Press, 1995 and New York: St. Martin's Press, 1995.
Chessman, Harriet. 'Women and Language in the Fiction of Elizabeth Bowen.' *Twentieth Century Literature* 29 (1983), 69-85.
Christensen, Lis. 'A Reading of Elizabeth Bowen's "A Day in the Dark"'. *Irish University Review* 27, 2 (1997), 299-309.

Coates, John. *Social Discontinuity in the Novels of Elizabeth Bowen*. Lewiston, Queenston, Lampeter: The Edwin Mellen Press, 1998. Cited as Coates 98a.

Coates, John. 'The Misfortunes of Eva Trout.' *Essays in Criticism* XLVIII, 1 (January 1998), 59-79. Cited as Coates 98b.

Coughlan, Patricia. 'Women and Desire in the Work of Elizabeth Bowen', in *Sex, Nation and Dissent*. Ed. Éibhear Walshe. Cork: Cork University Press, 1997.

Craig, Patricia. *Elizabeth Bowen*. Harmondsworth: Penguin Books, 1986.

Dorenkamp, Angela G. '"Fall or Leap:" Bowen's *The Heat of the Day*'. *Critique. Studies in Modern Fiction* X, 3 (1968), 13-21.

Eliot, T S. *Four Quartets*. London: Faber and Faber, 1944.

Ferguson, George. *Signs and Symbols in Christian Art* (1954). New York: Oxford University Press, 1961.

Flaubert, Gustave. *L'Education sentimentale*. 1869.

Foster, R F. *Paddy and Mr Punch*. Harmondsworth: Allen Lane. The Penguin Press, 1993.

Glendinning, Victoria. *Elizabeth Bowen. Portrait of a Writer*. London: Weidenfeld and Nicolson, 1977. Phoenix Paperback, 1993.

Glendinning, Victoria. 'Gardens and Gardening in the Writings of Elizabeth Bowen'. *Elizabeth Bowen Remembered. The Farahy Addresses*. Ed. Eibhear Walshe. Dublin: Four Courts Press, 1998.

Greene, Graham. 'The Dark Backward: A Footnote'. *London Mercury* 32 (1935); *Collected Essays*. London: The Bodley Head, 1969.

Heath, William. *Elizabeth Bowen. An Introduction to Her Novels*. Madison: University of Wisconsin Press, 1961.

Herbert, George. *The Works of George Herbert*. Ed. F E Hutchinson (1941). Oxford: The Clarendon Press, 1972.

Hoogland, Renée C. *Elizabeth Bowen. A Reputation in Writing*. New York: New York University Press, 1994.

Johnson, Toni O'Brien. 'Light and Enlightenment in Elizabeth Bowen's Irish Novels.' *Ariel. A Review of English Literature* 18, 2 (April 1987), 47-62.

Jordan, Heather Bryant. *How Will the Heart Endure. Elizabeth Bowen and the Landscape of War*. Ann Arbor: University of Michigan Press, 1992.

Joyce, James. *Dubliners*. 1914.

Kenny, Edwin J. *Elizabeth Bowen*. Lewisburg, Pennsylvania: Bucknell University Press, 1964.

Kiberd, Declan. *Inventing Ireland*. London: Jonathan Cape, 1995.

Lassner, Phyllis. 'Reimagining the Arts of War: Language and History in Elizabeth Bowen's *The Heat of the Day* and Rose Macaulay's *The World My Wilderness*.' *Perspectives on Contemporary Literature* 14 (1988).

Lassner, Phyllis. *Elizabeth Bowen*. Houndmills & London: Macmillan Education, 1990.

Lassner, Phyllis. *Elizabeth Bowen. A Study of the Short Fiction*. New York: Twayne Publishers, 1991.

Lee, Hermione. *Elizabeth Bowen. An Estimation.* London & Totowa, NJ: Vision and Barnes & Noble, 1981. Revised edition: Vintage, 1999.

Leech, Geoffrey N and Michael H Short. *Style in Fiction* (1981). London & New York: Longman, 1991.

McCormack, William. *Dissolute Characters. Irish Literary History through Balzac, Sheridan Le Fanu, Yeats and Bowen.* Manchester & New York: Manchester University Press, 1993.

McDowell, Alfred. 'Identity and the Past. Major Themes in the Fiction of Elizabeth Bowen'. Unpublished dissertation: Bowling Green University, 1971.

McGowan, Martha. 'The Enclosed Garden in Elizabeth Bowen's *A World of Love.*' *Éire-Ireland* XVI, I (1981), 55-70.

Meredith, George. *Selected Poetical Works of George Meredith.* Ed. G M Trevelyan. London: Longmans, Green & Co, 1912.

O'Toole, Bridget. 'Three Writers of the Big House: Elizabeth Bowen, Molly Keane and Jennifer Johnston' in *Across the Roaring Hill. The Protestant imagination in modern Ireland.* Ed. Gerald Dawe and Edna Longley. Belfast and Dover, New Hampshire: The Blackstaff Press, 1985.

Radcliffe, Mrs Ann. *The Mysteries of Udolpho* (1794). London: Oxford University Press, 1966.

Rule, Jane. *Lesbian Images.* Garden City, New York: Doubleday & Co, 1975.

Sellery, J'nan and William O. Harris. *Elizabeth Bowen. A Bibliography.* Austin: Humanities Research Center, University of Texas, 1981.

Smith, Patricia Juliana. *Lesbian Panic. Homoeroticism in Modern British Women's Fiction.* New York: Columbia University Press, 1997.

Spark, Muriel. *The Prime of Miss Jean Brodie.* 1961.

Stanzel, Franz K. *Theorie des Erzählens* (1979). Göttingen: Vandenhoeck & Ruprecht, 1989.

Tacitus. *Agricola*, trans. M Hutton, rev. R M Ogilvie, in vol. I of *Tacitus in Five Volumes.* Loeb Classical Library. London: Heinemann (1914), 1970. *De Vita Agricolae*, ed. R M Ogilvie and Sir Ian Richmond. Oxford: The Clarendon Press, 1967.

Tracy, Robert. *The Unappeasable Host. Studies in Irish Identities.* Dublin: University College Dublin Press, 1998.

Walshe, Eibhar, ed. *Elizabeth Bowen Remembered. The Farahy Addresses.* Dublin: Four Courts Press, 1998.

Wessels, Andreis. 'Elizabeth Bowen's *A World of Love*: A "Cultural Analysis" of the Anglo-Irish Ascendancy in the Twentieth Century.' *The Canadian Journal of Irish Studies* 21, 1 (1995), 88-95.

Weston, Ruth D. *Gothic Traditions and Narrative Techniques in the Fiction of Eudora Welty.* Baton Rouge & London: Louisiana State University Press, 1994.

Woolf, Virginia. *Night and Day.* 1919.

Woolf, Virginia. *Mrs Dalloway.* 1925.

Yeats, W B. *Collected Poems* (1950). London: Macmillan & Co, 1961.

Index

Among the works of Elizabeth Bowen, the four post-war novels that form the basis of the present studies are not listed here: *The Heat of the Day* (1949), *A World of Love* (1955), *The Little Girls* (1964), and *Eva Trout* (1968).

Alaric 47
Alice in Wonderland 172
Allingham, William 96, 191
Aristotle 63
Asquith, Cynthia 24
Asterix 45
Auden, W H 170-71
Austen, Jane 63, 202-03

Bacon, Francis 166
Bennett, Andrew 34, 105
Berlin, Isaiah 17
The Bible 172, 175, 179, 180, 183
Boucher, François 77
Bowen, Elizabeth, works by
  A Day in the Dark and Other Stories 19, 28, 35
  'A Day in the Dark' 25, 35, 38, 63, 122, 128, 130, 182, 211
  Afterthought: Pieces about Writing 26
  A Time in Rome 26
  Bowen's Court 16, 23, 35, 156, 165
  Collected Impressions 22
  Early Stories 22
  Encounters 16, 49
  'English Novelists' 63
  'Gone Away' 20, 35, 124, 130, 208-09
  'Hand in Glove' 24, 35, 130
  'I Hear You Say So' 19, 35, 125
  Ivy Gripped the Steps and Other Stories 18, 20
  'Ivy Gripped the Steps' 19, 35, 46, 63, 125, 130, 211
  Look at All Those Roses 20
  'Mysterious Kôr' 34, 173
  Notes From Eire 18
  'Notes on Writing a Novel' 36, 107, 110, 124, 149, 211
  Pictures and Conversations 30, 36, 113, 124-5
  Seven Winters 26
  Seven Winters and Afterthoughts 26
  'Sunday Evening' 49
  'The Bend Back' 158
  'The Demon Lover' 34, 198
  The Demon Lover and Other Stories 18, 20
  'The Dolt's Tale' 19, 35, 122, 198
  The Good Tiger 28
  'The Happy Autumn Fields' 18
  The House in Paris 12, 33
  The Last September 12, 16, 24, 38, 92, 149, 174, 194
  'The Move In' 30
  The Mulberry Tree. Writings of Elizabeth Bowen 13, 18, 22, 34, 36, 38, 107, 110, 124, 125, 149, 158, 209, 211
  The Shelbourne 23, 156
  The Shelbourne Hotel 23, 156
  To the North 12
Bowra, C M 17
Brown, Spencer Curtis 36, 113
Brueg(h)el 170-71

Calder, Angus 13
Cameron, Alan 17, 22, 24
Carroll, Lewis 172
Cecil, Lord David 17
Coates, John 146, 183, 198
Connolly, Cyril 18
Coughlan, Patricia 55, 57, 62

Dante 133, 172
Dickens, Charles 51, 59, 60, 125, 138, 172
Doyle, Sir Francis 190

Dracula 199
Eliot, George 198
Eliot, T S 154
Essex, Earl of 166-7

Ferguson, George 143
Flaubert, Gustave 36, 206
Foster, Roy 16
Fougasse 70

Glendinning, Victoria 15, 17, 23, 24, 108, 113, 127, 132, 166, 174
George, Daniel 82
Granuaile 180
Grattan, Henry 156
Green, Henry 20
Greene, Graham 18, 33

Haggard, H Rider 34, 173
Harris, W O 15, 19, 35
Harrison, G B 167
Hassall, Joan 136
Herbert, George 59, 76
Hoogland, Renée C 152

Icarus 39, 165 sqq.
Irving, Washington 208

Jordan, Heather Bryant 15, 35, 126
Joyce, James 32, 80, 133, 173
Jullian, Philippe 199

Keats, John 19
Kiberd, Declan 16, 205
Knopf, Blanche 23

Lawrence, D H 47
Lee, Hermione 33
Leech, Geoffrey N 101, 108
Le Fanu, Sheridan 22, 28

McBean, Angus 14
McCormack, William 32, 81
McGowan, Martha 134
MacNeice, Louis 17
Meredith, George 28, 96, 115, 138
Millais, Sir John 32, 62
Milne, A A 172
Murger, Henri 198

Napoleon 144
Nashe, Thomas 198

Oedipus 199
O'Malley, Grace 180
Orwell, George 74
Ovid 170

Piggott, Stuart 48
Plomer, William 126
Potter, Beatrix 43

Radcliffe, Mrs Ann 199
Richardson, Samuel 198
Ritchie, Charles 15, 17, 166
Rodney, Admiral Lord George 48
Royle, Nicholas 34, 105
Rule, Jane 54, 56, 119

Sarton, May 24, 174
Sellery, J M 15, 19, 35
Shakespeare 172
   As You Like It 36
   Hamlet 172
   King Lear 179
   Macbeth 28, 116, 117, 140, 172, 193
Short, Michael H 101, 108
Sidney, Sir Philip 167
Sir Gawain and the Green Knight 46
Smith, Patricia Juliana 55, 56, 57, 60, 76, 115
Spark, Muriel 75
Stanzel, Franz K 101

Tacitus 74
Tennyson, Alfred Lord 140
Thomson and Thompson (Tintin) 190
Tracy, Robert 93, 156, 178, 179
Traherne, Thomas 24, 112

Waugh, Evelyn 113
Welty, Eudora 22, 23
Wilde, Oscar 199, 205
Winnie the Pooh 172
Woolf, Virginia 17, 48, 149
Wordsworth, William 28, 172
Wyndham, John 140, 162, 193, 202

Yeats, W B 50